LOVE LOCKED DOWN

LOVE LOCKED DOWN:

A GUIDE TO FINDING A LASTING LOVE RELATIONSHIP

By Okyeame Kwame and Annica Nsiah-Apau
with Kyei Amoako

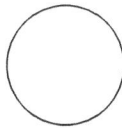

Spotlight Publishing

Columbus, Ohio | Accra, Ghana

The book is available for sale at various online and offline retail outlets. For special discounts on bulk purchases by corporations, associations and other groups, please write to the publisher at Books@Spotlightcg.com.

Content Editing by Adelaide Aba Ansah, Annica Nsiah-Apau
Proofreading by Elsie Gifty Lamptey, Annica Nsiah-Apau
Cover Photos by Sarfo Boateng (Sarboat Photography)
Cover Design by Vincent Samuel Darko Ntow
Worksheet Designs by Adam Hayman
Layout by Ryan Magada

Love Locked Down/ Okyeame Kwame and Annica Nsiah-Apau with Kyei Amoako
ISBN 978-0-9998312-6-7 (Ebook)
ISBN 978-0-9998312-5-0 (Paperback)

DEDICATION

We dedicate this book to you, our dearly loved children, S. Kwame Bota Nsiah-Apau and Sante Abena Antwiwaa Nsiah-Apau.

We have unbridled discussions about a lot of subjects, so we pray that you never lead a monotonous lifestyle, cave in to some meaningless pressures of society, and be forced into any relationship you deem NOT WORTHY. Even though you are not old enough for the romantic love we discuss in this book, we pray that someday, when you get there, you find our experiences a guiding beacon. No matter when you find out that your partner is not meant for you, may this book guide you to have the willpower to make the best decision that will not leave you to succumb to a depressing 'ideal' in suppression of a lifetime of happiness. Love is beautiful, marriage is a whole hearty meal but do not take the plunge because it will make someone else happy. By all means, do not be afraid to make mistakes, but learn the key lessons from them and forge forward.

We wish total love liberation for you, and no matter when, where and why you pick this book, may you always be encouraged to find true love that locks you down!

Love, Mum and Dad

Special Acknowledgement:

Otumfour Osei Tutu II and Lady Julia Osei Tutu for their dedication to education and literacy, and for the love they show to our family.

Special thanks to the shining examples of couples working together and staying together, no matter what:

Albert and Comfort Ocran
Iyiola and Theresa Ayoade
James Ebo Whyte and Florence Whyte
Wilson Arthur and Adwoa Amofah.

TABLE OF CONTENTS (BOOK 1)

PART I: FINDING SOMEONE TO LOVE

PART II: BEFORE YOU SAY "I DO"

FOREWORD

by Uncle James Ebo Whyte
Playwright, Author and Motivational Speaker

C elebrity marriages make the headlines and send social media into a frenzy. Unfortunately, the reality is that most celebrity marriages do not last. But then there is Kwame and Annica, a celebrity couple who have found a way of keeping their marriage fresh and exciting and their home functional.

Take a young man and a young woman who are both strong personalities and very assertive; let them have different views about a number of things; let one be private and reserved, and the other outgoing and loving the limelight; now, get these two to marry. Under normal circumstances, this is a recipe for disaster unless the couple stumble upon the keys for making a relationship work. I believe Kwame and Annica have found the keys.

If all Kwame and Annica accomplished was to make their celebrity marriage work, that would have been incredible but this is not your usual couple. This is an extraordinary couple and they do extraordinary things. They have gone beyond just making their relationship succeed, to taking on the challenge of helping others make a success of theirs by the writing this wonderful book, Love Locked Down.

There are two kinds of people who write books on marriage. There is the person writes to portray their dream of an ideal marriage that has alluded them and for whom writing is their therapy. Such books are, of course, easy to spot because they are not practical.

And then there are those who discover a secret formula for making their marriage work and devote themselves to sharing the secret with the world. Kwame and Annica fall into this category. I have always appreciated the openness and transparency of Kwame and Annica.

With them, what you see is what you get. They have nothing to hide and they chose to remain as open a book as possible. They bring this level of integrity to their book. They are not perfect as human beings but they seek to do the best they can in every aspect of their lives, including building and sustaining a great marriage.

In the pages of Love Locked Down, you are not going to read theories; you are going to be invited into the world of Kwame and Annica; you are going to have a VIP seat to the feast of their love and you are going to learn and be challenged to be a better lover, a better spouse and definitely, a better human being.

I count my wealth in people and by that standard, I think I am a very wealthy man. And when I count my treasures, I count among them, the friendship and association with Kwame and Annica. And in the pages of this book, you will understand why I celebrate Kwame and Annica and value my association with them so highly.

Enjoy the read and encourage your friends to also own a copy.

WHY THIS BOOK
AND
WHO SHOULD READ IT

Thank you for picking up this book and for your interest in what we have to say. Thank you for your time and for giving us an opportunity to share our ideas and experiences with you. My name is Sir Kwame Nsiah Apau, known by most people as Okyeame Kwame, the musician, the husband, and the father. My wife, Annica Nsiah-Apau, and I are the parents of two delightful children, S. Kwame Bota Nsiah-Apau and Sante Antwiwaa Nsiah-Apau. We have been together since 2005 and have been married since 2009, a relationship journey on which we have both grown tremendously as individuals and as a couple.

We are thankful for the experiences, the advice and observations that have shaped our lives. We have learned from our experiences and those of others, have benefited from the wise counsel of others, and we believe those lessons are not meant for us to keep to ourselves.

Humbly, we offer our thoughts on romantic relationships, love and family life as a contribution to the many fantastic resources that exist within our communities and in the world at large. We trust that our points of view, which are unique to us, will bring fresh perspectives to these topics and help others find clarity about the kind of relationship they seek. We also hope to provide individuals with tips and ideas to help them navigate this important area of life that many of us seldom learn about properly as we grow into adulthood.

Some of us have had parents or mentors or other adults who have modelled for us how to thoughtfully approach matters of love, romantic relationships and family life. Some have had to figure things out through trial and error. Some of us sometimes have clues about what we are doing and some of us are often in over our heads when it comes to relationships. Some of us have been so disappointed by previous relationships that we have built up walls to prevent ourselves from ever getting hurt; and some of us have benefited so much from relationships that we swear that they were the best thing to have ever happened to us.

Wherever you find yourself in your relationship experience, we hope you will learn something new that may challenge your own thinking about how you approach and manage love relationships. Above all, we hope you will be inspired about the possibility of finding and maintaining the lasting love relationship you seek.

Of course, we are safely assuming that anyone reading this book wants a lasting love relationship – or at least, is curious about the subject. However, if you are not interested in a lasting love relationship and just want to find out what my wife and I have to say, that one is also fine. We appreciate your time and attention.

Annica has always been a private person – and I have never been. However, the decision to candidly share our experiences and ideas about love, romantic relationships and family life was a unanimous one. Our private interactions with one another, our private conversations with friends, acquaintances and strangers, and our observation of relationships around us led to conversations that gave birth to the idea for this book.

While the decision to write this book was a shared one, our perspectives and ideas are not always the same on every topic. There are some important topics on which we don't share same views. However, we have benefited tremendously from the diversity of thought as we have travelled our relationship journey. Therefore, we will share this diversity with you.

There are ideas and opinions that you will read about here that are exclusively from Annica; there are also ideas and opinions you will read about here that are exclusively from me. In fact, you will read about accounts of the same events that Annica recalls differently from the way I vividly recall them. The beautiful thing, however, is that we share a common goal to thoughtfully share our stories and ideas in a fun, candid and inspiring manner to help you on your journey.

Each of us is on a journey in this life and especially in our respective relationships. There's an Akan proverb: *Obisafoɔ nyera kwan*, which translates into English as, 'The one who asks for the way will not go astray'. So, consider us strangers you met along the way who are pointing you in the direction you may like to go.

Wherever you are on your journey, whether you are a university student excitedly thinking about your first serious relationship, a young professional anxiously making plans for the future, a hopeful single adult who has never married, a divorced adult who is sceptical about love, a married person who is thriving in your relationship, an almost-divorced person in a dysfunctional relationship, or any other relationship situation you find yourself in, it is our hope that the time you are investing in reading this book and the actions you take afterwards will be worthwhile.

Someday, we hope to hear the stories of personal transformation that came about as a result of something you read here. Much more than that, we hope that you pass on the lessons and your experiences to others to help them on their journey as well. If you don't want to do too much talking, simply get them a copy of this book. We will do the talking for you.

Years ago, as we came closer to planning to get married, Annica clearly expressed that she wanted a modest civil marriage ceremony with only a handful of close family members. I wanted to make a major event of our marriage so that I could get all the media and public attention I could out of it. We struck a compromise; we were going to get married in a modest civil ceremony at the court. On our tenth marriage anniversary, we were going to have a major grown-and-sexy beach party with all the guests dressed in white tops and jeans under the cover of moonlight.

At the time, Annica made me believe that she had agreed to the idea, but I found out later that she only pretended to have agreed and hoped that I would move on from that idea eventually. She tries to avoid events that put her at the centre of attention. She was evasive every time I asked for her thoughts on our tenth anniversary celebration.

As we reached the seventh year of our marriage, I revisited the idea. While it was obvious that Annica was not too excited about a party of any kind, my friend and colleague Kwame Farkye thought it was a brilliant idea. He was convinced that the party would serve a dual purpose – celebrating a milestone in our marriage and also providing a means to relaunch my brand as an evolved artist who had successfully combined being an entertainer with being a devoted family man for a decade. It was going to be called "Love Locked Down". As he described the concept, we would have made it through ten years of marriage, which would be enough basis to declare the marriage rooted and firmly established. That milestone would certainly be worth a major celebration. I loved the idea and Kwame Farkye's enthusiasm about the event, which was fuelled by the potential sponsorship opportunities. He got me really energised.

In 2008, Kanye West released an amazing song called *Love Lockdown,* which was one of our favorites that year. That song became an added inspiration for the celebration.

Annica never warmed up to the idea of the beach party because she said she dreaded being the centre of attention. Needless to say, our ten-year anniversary has passed and the "Love Locked Down" party has not happened yet. I have not given up hope on that event. When I envision the "Love Locked Down" party and let my imagination loose, I am able to hear the waves of the Atlantic Ocean crashing onto the shores of Labadi Beach, as Annica and I walk along the beach and under the moonlit night towards the crowd welcoming us with smiles, and Kidi performing an acoustic version of Kanye's song.

The idea of a romantic beach party that is reminiscent of a scene from a romantic movie appeals greatly to Annica. The time will come for that – I am quite sure.

"Love Locked Down" emerged at the top of the list of options of titles for this book partly because of the concept but mainly because of how clearly those words articulate the purpose of this book. We believe that most people desire to fall in love with each other, get married, start a family and remain firmly established. We believe that most people would like to find love, lock it down and thrive in it. Therefore, we share our experiences and ideas with that singular objective – that you will become firmly established in your love relationship, continue to thrive and enjoy all the benefits of that relationship.

Each adult has the power to make decisions that will impact their love relationships. No one can fix or improve anyone's relationship without that person's participation. Therefore, we hope that you will use our suggestions and take the necessary actions to find and/or maintain the love relationship that you desire. There are no shortcuts. You have to do some work on you and on your mind, and don't try to manipulate the other person to fit them into your idea of what your dream partner should be. In fact, you will be better off in the long run when you focus on developing yourself before, during and after you find the one with whom you choose to be in a relationship.

Our wish for you is that if you are looking to settle down with someone, you find that person. And if you are in a relationship already, we pray that relationship blossoms. We wish that all people in relationships become rooted and firmly established in love; and that whenever you think of three words to describe your love relationship, you will come up with "Love Locked Down" followed by a broad smile.

So, get in a comfortable sitting or leaning position – or in your favourite reading position – and let's get going. We promise to keep it fun, enlightening and real.

HOW WE MET
AND
OUR JOURNEY SO FAR

In 2005, Annica had graduated from university and was job-hunting in Kumasi. She had visited a law firm to enquire if they had an opening so she could request to be posted there for her National Service. She was heading towards the Amakom roundabout to get into a taxi and go home.

I was leaving an interview at Luv FM, a Kumasi-based radio station that shared a compound with the law firm Annica had visited. She looked very decently and nicely dressed. Her extra dark complexion, her big forehead and bulging hips caught my attention. I walked up to her with a calm confidence and told her that I thought she was "oozing class"! She smiled at me, and then we both laughed calmly. As I came to learn later, her silent response was, *Ei, akoa yi te brɔfo* – translation: "This guy is pretty eloquent in the English language".

Even though she knew who I was as a musician, that was when we met for the first time. I asked if I could become a friend to her, and she gently responded, "Yes, why not?" I then asked if she knew who I was, and she nodded. She was excited to meet me and didn't hide how excited she was. My first impression of Annica was very positive largely because she did not unnecessarily play hard-to-get like some women do when a man approaches them – even when they are interested in the man.

Playing hard-to-get – when you like the person approaching you but pretend you're not interested, to make the person work extra hard to win your affection – is from an old and unproductive playbook. I'm glad Annica was confident and reasonable enough to acknowledge that she liked that I had approached her, and did not hide her attraction towards me.

Annica knew I was Okyeame Kwame the musician; she liked my music and she thought of me as a really cool guy even before meeting me in person. I offered to give her a ride home in my car. She mentioned that if she accepted the ride, I would have to come into the house to say hello to her father when we got there.

For a guy who is up to no good, meeting the parents of a girl you're interested in often feels like walking into a minefield. Your nefarious agenda could be blown apart by the discerning father in a single meeting. I, in this case, had good intentions towards Annica and therefore did not think twice about going with her to say a quick hello to her parents. Moreover, it is a very Ghanaian cultural practice to purposefully say hello to others; saying hello to the parents in the home where I was dropping off my new female friend seemed like a sensible thing to do. So, I did.

Annica's father was sitting on the balcony of the top floor of their home. With his bulging eyes, he looked like a pensioner with a double-barrelled gun under his bed, who would not hesitate to use the gun if he felt the need to do so. He exuded gentlemanliness and certainly looked like a man who had lived a full life. I said, "Hello, good afternoon, sir" and we had a brief exchange of pleasantries. He was insistent that I correctly observe the Asante protocol of greeting, stating the purpose of my visit and allowing the host to respond. So, I accepted a drink of water from him, followed that by announcing my purpose for the visit (my *amaneε*), and then he responded by acknowledging my purpose. What was supposed to be a brief hello and goodbye had turned into a sit-down conversation.

When I announced that his daughter was my friend and I had given her a ride home, he sought clarification about whether I would continue to visit his house. I responded with a yes. At the time, I had small locks in my hair. I was a stylish musician and I thought I looked really cool in that hairstyle. Annica's father thought otherwise. He asked that I cut "those things" on my head.

I wanted to continue seeing Annica, so I needed to do something about her father's request. The next time I went to Annica's house, I had combed out my hair into an afro. Her father laughed out loud when he saw me enter the house in my afro and reminded me that he had asked me to cut my hair and not to simply comb it out. That day, he lectured me on becoming a dandy. I had never heard that word, which he explained meant an exquisite gentleman with class.

I liked his recommendation, not only because that would make it easier for my future father-in-law to welcome me into his home. I liked his recommendation also because it sounded like a clever way to set myself apart in the music industry. At the time, most of my peer musicians dressed in baggy clothes and all looked the same. I could stand out not only as the fresh boy who was going to be dating a pretty and classy girl but also as a musician with a unique sense of style. That was the beginning of my embrace of suits and fine shoes as part of my extensive fashion repertoire.

Annica's father was friendly and intimidating at the same time. He made it clear to me that Annica was dear to his heart, and that he would smoke me out of any hole and deal very harshly with me if I treated his daughter recklessly. He reminded me that he was very aware of many musicians, policemen, contractors and cocoa merchants who often had girlfriends and children all over the place, and he was not going to have any of that as far as I was concerned. I laughed off his comments and assured him that he would have nothing to worry about regarding my behaviour.

We did not introduce ourselves as getting to know each other for the purpose of dating. I did not think her father knew that I was interested in her romantically. He probably thought we knew each other already just as friends. As an elderly person, I'm sure he had his own suspicions about what I was up to, but I did not give him any cause to interfere.

As I continued going to the house, Annica's father remained nice to me. He succeeded in becoming a constant presence in my mind whenever I thought of Annica. For a while, I jokingly referred to my relationship with Annica as a tri-partite relationship involving her, me and her father. It was certainly a unique situation that sometimes felt intimidating (because her father asked a lot of questions) but always pleasant (because her father seemed to trust and like me).

I should also add that her whole household – her mother, who often didn't say much, her sisters, and her brothers remained warm towards me. I was well-liked in their home and they all welcomed me gladly any time I visited. I felt at home and I liked that. Those initial experiences gave me a good impression of the kind of family Annica belonged to, and contributed to my imagination of the future Annica and I were likely to have together.

I had listened to many of Kwame's songs and liked his creativity, didacticism and the lyrics in his songs. His public persona was that of a gentle and considerate person. At the time of our first meeting, I found the locks in his hair very attractive. I love unconventional people and he came across as unconventional, which was exciting to me.

Kwame likes to tell a story he heard from my mother about me telling her (when I was 16 years old) that I would marry Okyeame Kwame someday. I will neither admit nor deny that story. I'll plead the fifth on that one. However, Kwame was certainly the kind of guy that appealed to me and I totally liked him, even before meeting him in person.

Before meeting Kwame in person, I had taken his phone number from someone who knew him personally. My sister was getting married at the time and I was helping to coordinate the ceremony. I planned on booking Okyeame Kwame to perform at the event as a special treat to my sister. I ended up not calling him because plans changed for the ceremony. So, when I met him that day, I was pretty thrilled – but I kept my cool. I think it is normal to crush on a guy you are attracted to but it's never a good idea to swoon over him the first time you meet him.

Within minutes of meeting me for the first time, Kwame asked if I had a boyfriend. I told him I did not. He followed up with, "I am vacant"! I thought that statement was hilarious, especially since I was job-hunting that day. I broke out in laughter. He smiled along, asked where I was headed, and then offered me the ride home.

We talked for hours each day from then on. Free SMS text messaging and free night calls facilitated our constant communication. We talked throughout the day and also through the night. Free night calls, at the time, were from 9 pm 'til 5 am daily, and we would stay on the phone from 9 pm 'til 2 am on most days. Sometimes, we kept talking 'til one of us fell asleep in the middle of the conversation.

On the 15th October 2005, five days after we first met and also the date that marks when I was born, we drove together from Kumasi to Accra. I lived in Accra at the time; Kwame lived in Kumasi but was travelling to Accra for work. It was a happy coincidence that we were both travelling to Accra around the same time, and therefore, I accepted his invitation to ride with him. We spent the four-hour journey talking about our respective life goals and the future each of us had in mind. Kwame made a strong impression on me with his intelligence, his expansive worldview and his eloquent description of where he imagined himself in the future. It was clear that he was a man with plans for his future, and I liked that. His constant broad smile was also very charming, and I liked that too.

Within days of getting to know him, I was quite sure that he was a genuine person with whom I could spend my life. He didn't operate under false pretences and he acknowledged it when he didn't know something or when he had limited means. His candour and honesty reminded me of my father. The more time we spent together, the more confident I grew about the two of us getting married in the future. For most of my young adult life, the guys in my social circles did not excite me enough for me to imagine a future with any of them. Also, I thought most Ghanaian men were not as romantic as I expected them to be towards the women they liked. Kwame was a pleasant surprise in the manner he treated me and made me feel. I found in him the qualities of a life partner and totally embraced him.

At the time, Annica was 22 years old and I was 29. Up until that point, I had not imagined myself as a husband or father. But when I met Annica, the urge to settle down as a family man started to bubble inside of me. I had been in various relationships – both the short-term and the long-term kinds – and had grown tired of how unproductive many of those relationships had been. Six months prior to meeting Annica, I had been celibate and had shut out romantic relationships from my mind. From our many conversations, it did not take me long to realise that Annica was the right girl for me to settle down with.

Her humble confidence, self-awareness, her physical appearance, and her sound relationship with her family were the key things that won my heart. It was evident from very early on that her moral values were above average, and that she was a good girl. I was serious about my plans for life and preferred a smart, beautiful, good girl (or woman) for my life partner. I found all those attributes in Annica.

In the four years that we dated, we both enrolled at Kwame Nkrumah University of Science and Technology (KNUST) – Annica for her master's degree and I for my bachelor's. We spent a great deal of time together, got to know each other better, and grew comfortable and confident in our relationship. We eventually got married in a modest civil ceremony and began life as a couple.

Before getting married, we had many conversations about the type of future we wanted. We used Kwame's family and mine as case studies. We talked about what we liked about his parents' marriage and how they managed their household, and discussed my parents' marriage and their management of our household. We realised that we were both very grounded largely because our respective parents paid close attention and raised us with dedication. We wanted to do something similar for our children. For example, we both wanted to raise our children ourselves and not hand over the raising of our children to their grandparents or a nanny. While that is an option that works for some people, we were adamant about being hands-on parents.

We also discussed how many children we would have. Kwame wanted to have three and I didn't want children at all. I saw children then as a lot of responsibility and felt they would disrupt the cosmopolitan life that I had imagined for myself. I didn't want to take on a task that significant and not do it well. He had decided on three because he considered that to be the number of children that he could comfortably support as a responsible parent. Kwame thought my not wanting to have children was understandable but unusual. He seemed certain that I would eventually come around to realising how much better our lives would be if we had and raised children together. After months of long negotiations, I agreed on having one child – or maybe two.

We moved to Accra shortly after Kwame graduated from KNUST. Kwame preferred living in Kumasi but the nature of his work demanded that he visited Accra about three days out of each week. Travelling back and forth that many times didn't feel safe to me. Besides, not being in Accra permanently made him lose out on career opportunities. As the nation's capital and where most national and international decisions were made, Accra was where the key players in the music industry were based. On many occasions, we heard about opportunities only after the opportunity had passed due to the out-of-sight-out-of-mind nature of the music industry. Even though I had been nursing the idea of returning to live in Accra, where I had lived most of my years before meeting Kwame, we relocated mainly for his career to thrive. I found a job in Accra not long after our relocation. Our respective careers thrived, and we carried on with life as a happily married couple.

Our son had been born in Kumasi shortly after I completed my master's degree programme and our daughter was born after we moved to Accra.

Through many long, honest and thoughtful conversations and quality time spent together, we established a strong foundation during our four-year courtship period and also during the early years of our marriage. That strong foundation set the tone for our relationship and has continued to inform how we relate to one another. We have navigated many of the same issues that confront most married people. For the most part, our relationship has turned out exactly the way we imagined.

Typically, musicians have not been known to have the kind of family life that most people would want for themselves. The reports of rampant infidelity and the gross recklessness displayed by some musicians towards their spouses have contributed to a public perception that, statistically, gave our relationship a very low likelihood of survival. However, the type of family life Kwame and I have does not fit the stereotype.

I was very deliberate about choosing a partner whom I believed shared my moral values and vision for life. For his part, Kwame was clear about having a stable family life and committed to putting in the work required to make that happen. Over the years, some people have reached out to ask if our relationship is as functional as it looks from the outside. It is. It is functional not simply because we don't have disagreements but functional because we have a system that allows each of us to thrive and be our very best selves.

I am a very private person and I always knew some of our family life would be in the public eye. Being married to the outgoing and public personality that Kwame has always been, we had to figure out a way to meet each other in the middle. It has taken a significant amount of effort to nurture our relationship to where it is now. We have the kind of family life we have because we have been intentional about how we relate to each other.

Being in the public eye, we are conscious that we are surrounded by a great cloud of witnesses all of whom may not have the best of intentions towards us. There are people looking for opportunities to score cheap media points for financial gain. There are also others – young and old – who draw inspiration from how we live our lives. For those who are inspired by the way we live our family life, we hope to continue to be a positive example.

Over the years, Kwame and I have publicly and privately shared our ideas about relationships. I frequently receive direct messages on Instagram from people around the world with questions regarding how to handle issues in their relationships. I always share my perspectives thoughtfully and candidly. As an extension of those private conversations, I hope what we share in this book helps answer some questions for you and gives you more clarity about your own situation.

Annica is the planner in our relationship. She likes to define goals, plan the necessary actions, and then execute the plan. I am more of a live-and-learn type of person. I operate with a guiding compass that requires me to assess whether what I'm doing at any point in time is the right thing and if I'm giving it my best effort. If it is the right thing, I put in all the energy I can and give it my best shot. That is how I approach my craft as an artist; that is how I approach business opportunities; and that is how I approach my relationship with Annica. When I started a family and knew it was the right thing to do, I committed to giving it my best shot.

By virtue of the industry I work in, I am often in the company of guys with an assortment of personal values. I frequently encounter girls with all kinds of motives. I am often confronted with the choice of compromising my moral values and making decisions that could have devastating personal consequences. Often, the short-term pleasure that would come from indulging in the fringe "benefits" of being a celebrity do not match the satisfaction of having the devotion and love of a beautiful wife and two amazing children.

So, while it was never my goal to become a great father and a great husband in order to use it in positioning my brand, it has turned out that way because I intentionally made certain daily choices. My choices have always been driven by my sincere answer to the question of whether my chosen action would be the right thing to do at any given moment, and then giving it my best shot.

Two decisions that I'm most proud of – the decision to become a rapper and the decision to marry Annica. At the time, I sincerely believed that each of those decisions were right. I have so far given each my best shot and I have had no regrets. I have given my relationship with Annica my best effort, and it has met and exceeded my expectations.

Annica's father often tells us that the way our marriage has turned out is like we have won the lottery. He acknowledges that at the time we were getting married, he saw our marriage as a recipe for disaster. With me not being a Jehovah's Witness, Annica being as strong-headed as she can be, me being an Asante man raised to view the world in a patriarchal or male-dominated way, and me being a musician, he worried that the odds were significantly stacked against us.

As it turned out, we have come a long way and continue to enjoy a blissful and productive relationship. Getting to this point has taken a tremendous effort to be devoted and considerate towards each other, and has very little to do with luck.

Together, we are thankful for the opportunity to share our experiences and ideas with you. There are more stories about our life together and we will share them in the chapters that follow.

PART I:
FINDING SOMEONE
TO LOVE

Adinkra Symbol Name:

Akoma (Heart)

Significance:

Patience and Tolerance

· 1 ·

FALLING IN LOVE

One of the best feelings in the world is the feeling of euphoria that comes from thinking about another person and feeling warm and fuzzy on the inside. Thoughts of that person flood your mind and you smile effortlessly at the idea of being at the centre of their universe. Your heart beats faster when their text pops up on your phone; you read the text over and over and cherish every word. You feel slightly nervous around them but look forward giddily to being in their company.

When you meet, you cannot keep your eyes off them and soon as you part ways, you miss them. You remember how they smell, and you take in slow deep breaths to relive being in their presence. You relish the attention they give you and hang on to every word they say. You comb through their social media pages and smile at photos of them staring your way.

When your favourite love song plays, every word truly feels like something you wrote. You feel your protective walls coming down and you want to let them into your world. You feel special and you feel good; you want that feeling to go on forever. Your imagination carries you along into a happy place where nothing else matters and everything is about just the two of you.

That is what it feels like to fall in love.

The phrase "falling in love" suggests an act where the person falling in love is not fully in control. No person will let themselves fall without an urge to stop the fall. Instinctively, we catch ourselves from falling, and only fall when we are not in full control. When a person falls in love, it involves losing control of their feelings about the object of their affection; the person with whom they are falling in love.

Falling in love is a beautiful sensation. That sensation carries the one falling in love into developing stronger feelings for the other person. That sensation also prompts the one falling in love to care more about the other person, and makes them desire to get closer to the other person. Whoever came up with the expression "falling in love" did a great job by giving us words to aptly describe this very human experience.

As human beings, we are designed to fall in love. We fall in love with genres of music; we fall in love with specific sports; we fall in love with certain brands; and we fall in love with individuals. We fall in love with these objects, activities, and people because our bodies and minds want to continue to experience that beautiful sensation that comes with falling in love.

We may *like* a lot of things, but we fall in *love* with a few things. We may like many people, but we fall in love with very few people. In most cases people fall in love with one person at a time. The things people see, read, and hear from their environment about falling in love contribute to their mindset about what it means to fall in love. Those things also inform how falling in love happens for them. For most women, as an example, we fall in love with the alpha male, a man with poise and charisma, and with a compassionate presence about him. There are other alpha males out there who are domineering and who impose their will on others, and I don't know that many women who are attracted to that kind of alpha male. The alpha male for me is a man whose mind works well – someone who can reason and also be reasonable.

As a young adult, the books I read contributed to my ideas about what it would feel like to fall in love. Most young people I knew growing up read Mills and Boon's romantic novels, but I was not interested in those books. They felt overly mushy and placed too much emphasis on the women characters being sexually dominated by their male counterparts.

On the other hand, I found crime fiction and stories with detectives solving crimes exciting. They drew me in and fully engaged my body and my mind. Books by James Hadley Chase, Mary Higgins Clark and those by John Grisham were some of my favourites. In small sections of those thrillers, the villain or hero fell in love. Through the descriptions of what the characters were thinking and feeling leading up to their falling in love or how they thought and behaved, those characters modelled for me what falling in love was supposed to feel like.

At the time, I didn't think a Ghanaian man was capable of being as romantic as I had imagined based on the novels that I had read. Even though my father had always affectionately called my mother "darling", I had never witnessed my father kiss her, or act overly affectionately towards her. He was certainly devoted to making sure she was well taken care of, especially when she was ill. To the best of my knowledge, there was very little public display of affection in their relationship. The way my parents expressed love to each other seemed to work for them, but it was nowhere near what I was reading about and imagining. I looked forward to experiencing some of what I had read about whenever I got married.

In my early days of meeting Kwame, I felt attracted to him. Even though his physical looks and personality appealed to me, it was our conversations that drew me closer to him. His way of speaking was quite different from the conservative nature in which most of the males I knew expressed themselves. He appeared confident and candid, and that was a turn-on for me. Even though he was self-censoring and polite, he still came across as edgy compared to the types of males that existed in my social circles. He fit my preferences in a male companion, and that was wonderful.

Kwame's passion for his career and his vision for the future stimulated my mind. He did not fit the stereotype that musicians often get tagged with as individuals who are not forward-thinking and who are also not serious about life. By the way, I have always been drawn to the uniqueness of musicians even though I was well aware of the stereotypes some associate with them. Thus, when Kwame did not fit the negative stereotypes, that was a big plus for the possibility of developing a long-term relationship with him.

Kwame had significant life experiences including developing a career in a then-unknown music genre. He had travelled the world and had experiences that were not always rosy; he spoke optimistically about his dreams for the future; he didn't harbour resentment towards people he had fallen out with; he backed up his dreaming with actions; and came across as a well-grounded human being. He swept me off my feet with his positive attributes, his thoughtfulness, and with the care he showed me. I remember constantly thinking about him, reading his text messages with glee, enjoying listening to him speak, and looking forward to seeing or talking to him again soon after we parted ways or ended a phone conversation. I had fallen in love with someone I really liked and was very proud of – and it felt really good.

The closest I had come to falling in love before I met Kwame was the way I felt about Bill Clinton. I had never met Bill Clinton. I had only seen him on TV. I was a student in junior high school, and he was president of the United States of America. The intelligence he demonstrated during interviews and the classy confidence he projected when he interacted with people prompted a strong and unforced affection from me towards him. For me, Bill Clinton embodied the attributes I wanted in a man and that became the standard requirement I sought. That was certainly far out of reach for most of the boys in my social circles.

Obviously, Kwame was not Bill Clinton, but he stimulated my mind in a way that no one had ever done. His charm and charisma, his intelligence, and the way he spoke made me feel like a teenager watching Bill Clinton on TV. I found myself falling in love with Kwame and I couldn't help it. Even if I could have stopped myself from falling in love with him, I wouldn't have stopped it. It was a beautiful sensation, and I was experiencing it with someone I thought very highly of. I had fallen in love with Kwame, and I knew clearly why I had fallen in love with him.

Most love relationships are unique. Just as the individuals who enter a relationship are unique. The kind of attraction that happens between them is bound to be unique. However, human beings have similar characteristics and therefore share some similar experiences, such as falling in love. The reasons for which people fall in love vary, and the reasons for which many people fall in love are informed by their definition of love.

In my 2012 song *Woara*, about two disappointed lovers reminding each other of the elaborate promises they made (to each other) and then failed to honour, I asked:

What is love?
Is it nature's trick to ensure continuity?
What is love?
Is it a hidden trick that will build my insanity?
What is love?
Is it an actor's skill that evokes little reality?

What is love?

Is it a sudden thrill which is not meant for eternity?

Love is a promise from a devoted person to uplift the other to blossom – no matter what. When you devote your time and effort to make sure another person or object is seen in the right light, you love that person or that thing. In a relationship, love requires devotion, and that devotion should not be because the one you love is devoted to you in return. In other words, you should love not because the person deserves to be loved but because you want to be devoted to seeing that person blossom.

I started out in life as a young adult with a warped definition of love. That warped definition was informed by popular ideas I had heard about love being a commodity to be traded for the things we needed from the opposite sex. As a younger man, I fell in love many times partly because of the affection I wanted to give and the affection I wanted to receive in return. As my definition of love evolved, so did my understanding of what it meant to fall in love.

While the emotional aspect of love can come over anyone and cause such a person to declare their love to another person, there is more to love than merely expressing a feeling. I needed to grow up in order to realise that.

With my increased understanding of what love is in its complete sense, I added "no matter what" to my definition of the concept of love. I realised that my devotion to the one I love should not be contingent on whether or not the person is devoted to me in return. If your "love" for another person is because they can or will love you in return, then you're not talking about love – you're talking about a transaction.

That kind of transactional love is on one end of the spectrum. On the other end of the spectrum is the "no matter what" kind of love that I'm talking about. The love many people share exists somewhere along that spectrum, and the objective for each of us should be to love the other person, no matter what. I have promised to love Annica, no matter what. So, even if Annica becomes a crackhead, I will still love her. It will be challenging but I will still love her. The concept of love teaches me to increase my level of devotion when she's at her lowest point. If she hits her lowest point, I will not be loving her because I want something in return from her; I will be loving her because I am devoted to her.

No one should love because of what they will get in return but rather because of what they have to give. If a person loves another person because he or she has love to give, giving that love is a reward in itself. Loving another person is an act of selfless generosity.

With this deepened understanding of love, love will never feel like an obligation or a transaction. A couple's relationship, without a doubt, will flourish when the devotion is two-way, and each of them is devoted to uplifting the other to blossom – no matter what.

Falling in love is not a one-time event. I fell in love with Annica years ago, and I have fallen in love with her many times during the course of our years together. I look forward to falling in love with her over and over again. Whenever I fall in love with her, I renew my devotion to her.

Falling in love is the beginning of an unending journey. When you fall in love, you continue in love. Continuing in love is a process of inclusion where you deliberately include your partner in your thoughts and decisions to the point where you will not knowingly do anything that hurts your partner or lover. Rather, you devote yourself to thoughts and actions that help the other person to blossom – no matter what.

For Annica and I, falling in love started with a physical attraction. I was drawn to her looks, her hips and the way she carried herself. She liked my hairstyle, my personality and the way I related to her. By spending time with her and having many extensive conversations, I got to know her more. The connection we shared deepened and I became convinced that she was like no other girl I had been in a relationship with previously. With that conviction about how I felt about her, my likeness for her evolved into something deeper. I didn't just feel attracted to her – my body and mind were in alignment in my desire to focus on sharing my life experiences with her.

Although I had been in love in the past, with Annica it was different. Her stunning physical attributes were what I preferred. I found her intelligence and how much of a lady she was to be intellectually stimulating. She had a clear way of thinking. She was a disciplined young woman and moral values were important to her. There was much more to her than met the eye, and I desired to have her in my life.

Annica and I went out to eat one afternoon after we had been hanging out for a few weeks and talking frequently. She knew I liked her, and I knew she liked me too. I told her that I thought if we continued hanging out and talking as much as we did, I might fall in love with her. She responded with, "It will not be out of the ordinary if you fell in love with me"!

When I told her how I felt and thought about her, she told me how she felt and thought about me. She felt and thought about me in a similar way as I felt and thought about her. The feeling was mutual. Our conversations about how we felt and thought about each other flowed naturally. I didn't have to rehearse what I was going to say before I said it. I didn't worry whether she was going to think I liked her too much – I wanted her to know that I liked her a lot.

Unlike in previous situations with other women where I felt the need to be guarded and not open up fully to them, I felt a sense of connection with Annica that made me feel comfortable about sharing my thoughts and feelings without reservation. I had fallen madly, deeply in love with her – and that felt OK.

Differentiating Between "I Like You" and "I Love You"!

A friend told me a story about how he incorrectly used "I love you" when he intended "I like you". At the time he was trying to woo a girl he had known for about two weeks. He liked her and wanted her to know how he felt about her. The girl gently corrected him saying, "You like me – you don't love me. You don't know enough about me to love me".

In Twi, we say *"Me pɛ wo"* when we mean "I like (or want) you" and *"Me dɔ wo"* when we mean "I love you". There is a big difference between *"Me pɛ wo"* and *"Me dɔ wo"*. *"Me pɛ wo"* or *"Me pɛ w'asɛm"* are expressions of superficial affection based on the physical. On the other hand, *"Me dɔ wo"* expresses something deeper. The word *"dɔ"* means depth. When something is deep, we say *"emu dɔ"*, meaning that thing is deep. That's where the Twi word for love, *"ɔdɔ"*, comes from.

Liking someone and loving someone are two very distinct ideas. You can like someone and not love the person, and you can also love someone without liking the person.

For many people, the intensely good feeling they feel whenever they think about the other person is only that – a good feeling they derive from being around that person. That is what it means to "like" another person. That feeling can be so intense that it can overtake a person's ability to make rational decisions. The urge to sustain that feeling is what will make a man take a woman he barely knows to an expensive restaurant to wine and dine her with the goal of impressing her. For a woman, the urge to sustain that intensely good feeling is what will make her constantly look for ways to stimulate the man's senses and keep his attention on her.

In each scenario, the person leading the action is solely motivated by the desire to sustain the good feeling that comes from the response they get from the other person. The desire could be one-way or mutual. The two people could mutually enjoy that experience, which over time could transform into something deeper. However, the experience could remain at that level and never go beyond. That is why a woman can tell a man pursuing her that she likes him but does not love him. That also is why a philandering man could say he likes his concubine but loves his wife.

Most romantic relationships start with liking. Through spending time together and thoughtfully getting to know the other person, you may develop a genuine vested interest in that person. A genuine vested interest is that selfless devotion to see the other person blossom. It is important to note that we are not talking about a vested interest that comes about because you have spent a lot of money on her and think she owes you love, or that you helped him find a job so you think he owes you affection. The genuine vested interest that comes about when you genuinely love someone is not motivated by an expectation of a reward.

At the point your liking for a person evolves into loving them, you would know enough about that person to know their intentions or motivations for being around you. You will know if that person offers a fertile enough ground for you to invest your emotions and dreams. That knowledge helps you determine whether or not the person you like shares your vision of where the two of you are headed relationship-wise.

Sometimes, people who like each other agree to start a relationship and to explore whether the liking will develop into something deeper. At other times, people like each other without entering into a relationship. Many times, the mutual liking eventually develops into a deeper connection. With time, their devotion towards each other deepens and their mutual desire for each other grows as well.

When you tell someone "I love you", you are saying "I am willing to make significant sacrifices for you" or "I will be with you no matter what". That is how the mind interprets the words "I love you". The mind connects those words to a devotee who is promising to see him or her blossom, no matter what.

So, before you tell someone you love him or her, please understand what you're saying. When you see a girl and you like her, say that. When you are with a guy who makes you feel good and you want to spend more time with him, say that. And when you intend to be devoted to your lover and see him or her blossom no matter what, say that with the words "I love you"! Remember to examine and weigh your emotions critically before you utter those words.

F alling in love is a natural phenomenon. Most people, if not everyone, fall in love. While falling in love is often an involuntary action, there are reasons or factors that make a person fall in love. These factors include desirable features or qualities of the other person; shared personality traits and ways of thinking; the other person meeting an important need in your life; the pleasant emotions that the other person arouses; and a sense of compatibility.

Most people fall in love in response to the human desire to bond with another person. In most societies, the norm is to bond romantically with one person at a time. Therefore, many look for or discover that special person, fall in love if they find enough reasons that sweep them off their feet, and then continue to take actions that sustain the connection.

Falling in love often makes the two people want to create something together, such as creating shared experiences or building a future together. Please note that while falling in love often makes the two people involved want to create something together, falling in love is not the only reason for carrying on with a relationship. In most cases, you will need more than falling in love to build a relationship. In fact, you will need more than love to sustain a fulfilling relationship. Therefore, don't be surprised when the person you love (and who even loves you too) explains to you that you two are not compatible for a relationship.

Some people develop a liking for each other, fall in love, and then start a relationship. Some people develop a liking for each other, start a relationship, and then fall in love. It is also possible for some people to start relationships (for a variety of reasons), and never fall in love. People are unique and so are their relationships. Regardless of the reasons or circumstances under which a person falls in love, that special feeling associated with falling in love often makes the object of your affection "the special one".

When that special someone means the world to you and your world revolves around that person, you have fallen in love. The excitement you feel, the deep concern for the other person's wellbeing, and the closeness you feel towards the other person are all signs that you have fallen in love.

2

HOW PEOPLE MEET

Growing up in the Jehovah's Witnesses faith, my social circles during my young adult years comprised mainly of the people in my religious community. Generally, Jehovah's Witnesses encourage members to keep our social interactions within the social circles of other Witnesses. To be a Witness often involves adhering to certain biblical moral values and abstaining from many secular activities. As such, Witnesses tend to socialise mainly with other Witnesses so as to thrive in the faith.

We refer to our male Witnesses as *"onua"* (the Twi word for sibling, referring to a male in this context) and our female Witnesses and *"onuawaa"* (the female equivalent of *onua*). As an *onuawaa*, I grew up learning I would have to marry an *onua* in order to comply with my faith. Many of my friends and acquaintances were from the Jehovah's Witnesses community.

Most of the young men in my congregation did not pique my interest romantically. Most of them were polite, morally-upright young men but many did not have what I sought in a potential boyfriend. During conventions, where various Jehovah's Witness congregations from across the city or region came together in one venue, the pool of eligible young men expanded. At such events, I came across very fine and sophisticated *ɛnuanom* (that's plural for Witnesses), but I never nurtured the thought of finding my future boyfriend there.

For me, it was more important to marry a morally-upright person, whether or not the person was a Witness. He had to be of good moral character; he had to be good-looking, well-groomed and presentable. We had to share a mutual connection; and he had to be someone I could confidently acknowledge as my man. He also had to be someone I could envision as the responsible father of my future children, if and when I decided to have children.

At KNUST, we had a thriving community of Witnesses and we got together often for Bible studies and other social activities. Apart from the fact that I wasn't attracted to any of the young men in my social circle, I had not been particularly interested in coupling up. I was friendly towards the males in my group, but I never really entertained their interest in starting a relationship with me. I revelled in my singleness and didn't feel any urge to get into a relationship.

Several years later, I explored the possibility of a romantic relationship with an *onua*. It was my final year and we had been good friends for a few years. He was extremely helpful when I was working on my final-year thesis. Even though he was interested in me, he never directly said that. However, his actions revealed his expectation of a relationship.

I did not have a raging desire to start a relationship with him, but I decided to keep an open mind about the possibility of that happening. When he finally mustered the courage to ask me if the two of us could give a relationship a try, a part of me felt that I owed him a shot at a relationship considering how kind and helpful he had been towards me. I agreed to his suggestion that we see if we could take our friendship to the next level.

Over the following months, we talked regularly and saw each other often. I did not feel any romantic spark with him. There was nothing sensational that developed between the two of us, and I did not see the use in pretending that a viable relationship was possible. I liked him but I didn't love him. I told him how I felt about the situation, and the relationship ended with that conversation.

Even though that brief relationship was my only experience at the time, it helped me to clearly know what I wanted to feel when I met someone that I liked and could fall in love with. I had to feel an inner sensation that made my heart thump, my blood levels rise, and my eyes googly.

I had always been clear-minded about what I wanted from life in general, and do not like to drag on with situations if I do not see the prospect of a desired outcome. My observations of other people's relationships also informed my opinion of what I wanted and what I did not want.

When it comes to meeting and dating women, I have been more fortunate than the average guy. I used to be a popular young rapper named Wizkid, and I've been a popular person since I was about

15 years old. In Form 5 of secondary school when I started paying attention to my interest in girls, most of the girls in my school and in neighbouring schools knew who I was. Some of them sent me letters and messages to express their admiration for me. My popularity continued when my rap group, Akyeame, scored a big international hit with *M'asan Aba*. With that early professional success, I had the kinds of things most women wanted – fame, cars, money and security – and getting the attention of a girl was a breeze for me. For a girl who was not as drawn by my flashy material possessions, I had enough vocabulary to entice her. Since I have always been well-known and admired by many people, I didn't have to do much talking to get a girl's attention. For most men, that is not typical.

If my circumstances had been otherwise – not famous, having only as much money as the average young adult, and with limited confidence and vocabulary to sweep a girl off her feet – I would have gone to places like the library, university campuses, religious organisations, and venues where daytime social functions were held. There, I would have hoped to have run into someone nice with whom I could engage in a conversation and hope to explore the possibility of a relationship.

I know of four general ways by which two people meet and take steps towards a romantic relationship: (a) **the pursuit**, where one person identifies a potential lover and then pursues him or her; (b) **serendipity**, where a random or unplanned circumstance piques two strangers' interest in each other; (c) **the discovery**, where a person develops a romantic interest in someone they already know; and

(d) **the recommendation**, where a third party introduces one person to another for the sole purpose of initiating a romantic connection.

a) The Pursuit

The pursuit is the most common way by which romantic partners meet. Typically, a man pursues a woman, as it is the norm in most cultures, including those of Ghanaians and many Africans. However, a woman can pursue a man if the situation calls for that.

Whether it's a man pursuing a woman or a woman pursuing a man, tact is essential. Tact is having a keen sense of what is appropriate in a particular situation. Since people are different and all situations are not created equal, what you say or do in one situation may not necessarily work in another situation. It takes tact to know that, and to act in a manner that is mindful and tasteful. That way, you avoid any awkward reactions to your pursuit.

Sometimes, the person being pursued may say they need some time think about the pursuer's proposal before making a decision about a relationship. That may not be because they are not interested. Often, that is a tactic some people adopt to make sure they don't come across as being too available. If the person you are pursuing employs that tactic, do not be discouraged. Stay focused.

In a pursuit, you identify a person you are interested in and then focus on winning their affection. The the local parlance, we would say "chasing" or "going after" that person. If you like someone, you need to be SMART about your mission in order not to waste time and other resources.

SMART stands for Specific, Measurable, Achievable, Relevant, and Time-bound.

Be **specific** about what you want. While it may be tempting to assume that the person you are pursuing will figure out what you want, assumptions can lead to disappointments. Clearly communicating the type of relationship you are seeking is as important as asking to know the person's name. If your goal is to spend time with the person and get to know him or her for the purpose of a long-term relationship, clearly state that at the early stages of coming together. That could be part of your opening lines after you introduce yourself. Any serious person will likely appreciate a potential partner who is specific about their goal and intentions. Likewise, if your goal is to pursue a short-term relationship to satisfy your lust, you should say that, too. The person you are pursuing will likely appreciate that honesty and go along with your plans if that is what they are interested in as well.

The pursuer's goal must be **measurable** – it must have specific criteria that measure progress towards accomplishing the goal. To make your goal measurable, you must **answer the question of how you would know when you've reached your goal**, or how you would know if you're making progress. For example, if your goal is to spend time with the person and get to know him or her for the purpose of a long-term relationship, specify how much resource (including time) you are willing to spend before deciding to continue the pursuit or not.

Ask yourself questions that involve "how much", including how much money you are willing to spend or how much inconvenience you are willing to endure before deciding to suspend or terminate the pursuit. Also, ask yourself questions that involve "how far", including how far you are willing to drive or travel to meet a person for a date. You may decide on a total amount of money as your maximum expense limit for deciding to abandon the pursuit. You could also decide that if you do not receive a return phone call after two unanswered phone calls, you will wait a week and then call off the pursuit.

The pursuer's goal must be **achievable** – it must be within reach for you. Be ambitious, by all means. But in your ambition, set attainable goals. To set an achievable goal, **ask yourself whether you have the skills or resources required to accomplish that goal**. If you don't have the skills or resources at the moment, could you obtain them in order to continue with the pursuit? Does the required effort match the reward? If your goal is to spend time with the person and get to know him or her for the purpose of a long-term relationship, honestly answer the question of whether you meet that person's minimum requirements.

For example, if she's a university graduate who works at a bank and you are an unemployed mason, consider the effort it would take to get her to realise that you are good man with immense potential. If you are a working professional in your thirties and looking to get married within a year of meeting someone, assess whether a married man who told you he's divorcing his wife is a potential husband worth pursuing. It is a human tendency to exaggerate our ability to achieve our goals or limit our capacity to attain them. In either situation, an honest assessment of the situation will be key to your chances of success.

The pursuer's goal must be **relevant** – it must answer the question of the goal's importance at the time you hope to accomplish it. Your motivation for doing anything is the most important reason for doing that thing. To set a relevant goal, **answer the question of why you are setting this goal at this time**. Thinking through that question carefully could help clarify your motivation, and help you realise that you may be about to go on a fool's errand. Alternatively, that exercise could help you realise that you're on track to experience the best relationship ever. If your goal is to spend time with the person and get to know him or her for the purpose of starting a long-term relationship, ask yourself whether you are doing so out of the fear that you are getting older and everyone but you seems to be getting married. If you exited a toxic relationship last week, honestly answer why you are on Instagram sending direct messages to a girl telling her you are ready to settle down. Ask yourself whether your goal is aligned with the kind of life you want for yourself. Doing the right thing at the right time is the only thing worth doing.

The pursuer's goal must be **time-bound** – because a goal without a deadline is only a wish. To set a time-bound goal, **create a timeline for accomplishing that goal**. With a timeline, you will spell out what milestones are necessary along the way. You will also decide on a specific time in the future when you will determine whether the goal has been accomplished or not. As an example, I had a two-week time limit for pursuing a girl I liked after I attained success in the

1990s with Akyeame. At the time, I was young and famous with various options in the women I wanted to date. Two weeks was a long enough time for me to decide that a girl who was playing hard-to-get was not worth my time and energy.

Understandably, some people have more patience than others, and some goals may require a longer timeline than others. Therefore, if your goal is to spend time with the person and get to know him or her for the purpose of a long-term relationship, you might set a six-month timeline with specific milestones at the one-month and three-month marks. A time-bound goal has a sense of importance that could serve as motivation for achieving that goal.

At the end of the pursuit, you may accomplish your goal and proceed with a relationship. If the pursuit is unsuccessful, you will have to start over with another person and apply any lessons learned in improving your odds for future success.

b) Serendipity

Imagine you're at a wedding, and you accidentally drop your phone, which falls at the feet of a gorgeous lady seated next to you. She spontaneously reaches for the phone, and trips over in the act. But you catch her from falling. She looks up, smiles shyly at you as she hands you your phone, and says, "Thank you". You calmly respond with, "Thank you, too"! During the reception, you catch glimpses of each other, but you think it would be too opportunistic to ask her for her number, so you don't. At the end of the evening, your best friend, whose wedding it is, asks you for a ride for a good friend. It turns out it is the same lady from earlier. You smile broadly and calmly respond, "Absolutely!"

Serendipity is a favourable occurrence that **happens by chance**. For some people, the person they are to fall in love with will come to them through serendipity. The way Annica and I met was serendipitous. It was by chance that our paths crossed in a large city of several hundreds of thousands of people. Serendipity created a perfect opportunity.

Serendipity will happen without much help from you. You are likely to stumble into that special person at a library, a bookstore, a professional networking event, an intimate concert venue, a wedding, a workshop, a conference or at a religious gathering. You are also likely to stumble into that special person on an airplane, on a train, at the mall, in a classroom, in a bank lobby, or at a restaurant. You are even likely to stumble into that special person online on a social media platform. The most important thing to keep in mind is that serendipity will bring a potential love interest your way when you carry on with your life as normally as possible. Serendipity doesn't like it when you are overly consumed by the expectation of meeting someone. So, just be yourself and live your life normally.

When you are overly consumed by the idea of finding someone to like you, you are likely to come across as desperate. Desperate people are often not attractive. Rather, live your life with a positive attitude and an open mind. Be kind to the people around you and treat people fairly. Invest in developing yourself. Strive to be an emotionally healthy person and think positive thoughts.

While such actions don't guarantee you will attract a potential lover, they'll make you a more pleasant person. The more pleasant you are, the more attractive you become. The more pleasant you are, the more likely you are to attract the partner you desire.

c) The Discovery

There may be someone you have known for years but may have never seriously considered as a love interest. It could be a neighbour, a co-worker, an usher at religious organisation, or one of your friends, who you think wouldn't be interested in you. However, that situation changes after **you realise that you feel differently towards that person**. That change of heart could be because that person improved themselves dramatically and caught your attention with their new look or personal accomplishment. That change of heart could be because you found out that the person likes you; or because your priorities in life changed; or because you started spending more time with the person and noticed desirable qualities that you did not previously see. Whatever the reason for that shift in how you view that person, that discovery opens a door for a pursuit. In some situations, the discovery is mutual – the two people discover their interest in each other around the same time – and they carry on with exploring a relationship.

When the discovery is not mutual, exploring your newly-discovered interest will mean gathering information, developing a strategy, and then proceeding tactfully. It is always advisable not to draw conclusions based on assumptions. Do not mistaken compassion for passion.

That person may have permanently placed you in the "friend zone" and there may be nothing you could do to change that.

Research the situation, gather as much intel as possible, and then proceed boldly. Each situation is likely to be unique, and your strategy for exploring the possibility of a relationship will depend on your unique circumstances.

The familiarity you share with someone you already know could be an advantage – or a disadvantage. On one hand, that familiarity could eliminate the barrier of awkwardness that is often associated with approaching a stranger. On the other hand, that familiarity could introduce a certain level of anxiety based on the fear of the awkwardness that could arise if the pursuit does not go well. No matter the level of comfort or anxiety that is produced by the familiarity, you owe it to yourself to proceed boldly and tactfully. You will never know what could become of what you've discovered unless you explore that discovery.

d) The Recommendation

Some well-meaning people and some self-appointed matchmakers are fond of coupling people up. It could be an uncle, a co-worker, an elder at a religious organisation, or a best friend who deliberately introduces you to another person for the sole purpose of initiating a romantic connection. That may be because the person knows both of you and considers you a good match for the other. It may be that one or both of you have expressed an interest in being introduced to someone who is looking to meet another person. It could also be that people around you simply take it upon themselves to pair you up with another person just because they think you need a partner.

When considering a recommendation, approach the situation with an open mind and give it your best effort. Many successful relationships have been initiated through recommendations. Annica's mother was recommended to her father. According to her father, who at the time was a dedicated member in his organisation, he was not looking for a wife when an elder in their congregation approached him with a recommendation. The elder told him that he knew of a young lady who had the ideal temperament and who would make a good life partner for him. He welcomed that recommendation, took the appropriate steps, and developed a very fruitful relationship from then on. They have been married for more than 55 years.

For some people, a recommendation is the realistic way for them to meet their potential love interest. A person with a specific set of requirements, for example, may find it difficult to meet someone who is a good match. That person may need the help of others. A successful person who wants to avoid the trial and error of dating random people may need help from others. A successful woman who has waited unsuccessfully for the right guy to approach may need the help of others. A guy who lacks the self-confidence necessary for approaching women may need help from others. A Ghanaian who lives in another part of the world where there are few Ghanaians may need the help of others if he or she is interested in meeting and exploring a relationship with another Ghanaian. Sometimes you cannot do it all by yourself – it's OK to ask for help.

When seeking a recommendation or evaluating one, keep in mind that the decision to accept or decline a recommendation rests with you. You are not obliged to accept a recommendation simply because of what the person making the recommendation thinks.

As a fully-grown adult, you should proceed with a relationship because you believe the potential lover will be good for you. Don't accept a recommendation simply because your overly zealous uncle, pastor or friend keeps exerting pressure on you. In the long run, you will be solely responsible for the consequence of your decision.

Good, thoughtful friends are often your extra set of eyes, and may notice things about you that you may not notice about yourself. Such friends may notice signs of compatibility that you share with another person. You may not see those compatibility signs for yourselves. When those friends respectfully decide to set you up with that potential good match, awesome things can come out of that situation. Annica is not fond of the "betweener" concept of someone going between two people to try to hook them up. However, she is very pleased that friends of Meghan Markle, Duchess of Sussex, and her husband Prince Harry hooked them up. Meghan and Harry have publicly acknowledged that their relationship may have never come about without their friends setting them up.

With a recommendation, remember to establish clear boundaries for the person making the recommendation. Some people have a tendency to view themselves as stakeholders in a relationship they helped to initiate. It is important not to allow any undue involvement in the budding relationship from the recommender. It may be reasonable to keep the person apprised – at a very high level – of how things are going between the two of you. However, providing too much information could encourage third-parties to insert themselves deeper into your relationship. Such people may be very difficult to get rid of later if you need to.

Of the ways above – the Pursuit, Serendipity, the Discovery and the Recommendation – none is superior to the other. In the final analysis, where and how you meet a person is not as important as what becomes of that meeting.

Nana Kwame Ampadu sang in one of his songs that, *"Obiara ne baabi a obɛhyia ne dɔ"* – translation: "There are many different places where a person can meet a prospective lover". However, spending time in physical locations where people gather will provide more opportunities for meeting like-minded people. These days, the places people gather transcend physical locations. People also meet online.

Connecting Online

The world has become a much more connected place than it was about two decades ago, thanks to the internet. The number of internet users around the world increased from only 413 million in 2000, to over 3.4 billion in 2016, according to the World Bank's World Development Indicators. In Ghana, the share of the population using the internet rose from 0.15% in 2000 to 35% in 2016. That number is expected to continue to rise.

Decades ago, the technology for connecting regular people around the world was either non-existent or very hard to come by for most people. The only way people met was in physical locations. When the internet became widely available around the world, the physical limitations on meeting people started to crumble. Someone could sit in his living room in Accra, Ghana and establish a friendship with someone in Perth, Australia. Also, people who lived in relative proximity but did not know each other could establish connections as a result of an encounter they had over the internet.

People who meet online and start relationships carry on as legitimately as others who met in person. However, meeting people online for romantic purposes comes with its unique characteristics that require wisdom and discernment.

The options for meeting people online include joining an online dating site where people set up profiles showcasing who they are and the type of person they would like to meet. Another way people meet online is by identifying a person on a social networking site and then sending the person a direct message to introduce themself. A virtual introduction could lead to an in-person meeting and eventually a relationship.

Meeting people online is today's equivalent of pen pals. In the 1990s, people would look in the newspapers for addresses of people across the country and around the world who had expressed interest in meeting strangers for the purpose of writing letters to each other. People wrote letters with pens and paper, and travelled to the post office to mail their letters, which took weeks to reach the other person. Miraculously, many people maintained strong friendships and some people even hooked up with their pen pals. With easier access to the internet beginning in the mid-1990s, many people explored online chat rooms and the early social networking platforms. In the 2000s and 2010s, Facebook, Instagram, LinkedIn, and many more platforms made it very easy for people to connect online.

One of the fascinating features about online social platforms is the instant feedback, where you can see pictures of a person and almost immediately learn a lot about them. Based on what you see on the person's profile, you can carefully vet the person before deciding to reach out to them. You can send a message and receive a response within seconds. You can get a glimpse of the person's personality, the person's intelligence, and the things that are important to that person – all from the pictures and comments that person posts on a social media platform. Such capabilities make social media platforms amazing screening tools for evaluating potential love interests. Even for people who meet in person, some go on social media to research the other.

For people who have intentions of dating people who do not live within the same country as they do, social media offers a convenient means for doing so. The platforms also offer very determined persons the means to target specific types of men or women they seek, and then go for what they want. That is called targeting, and it is very prevalent on social media.

Someone I know was fascinated by meeting women from other African countries. Using Facebook's platform, he could read what people said about themselves, see their pictures, and then reach out to begin a conversation. Through Facebook, he met a girl from Lesotho, developed a long-distance relationship, and travelled from Ghana to Lesotho to meet the girl. Unfortunately, that relationship did not work out.

Eventually, he met a girl from another African country, also through Facebook. They got married and are still together raising children. I know of so many other stories where the couple first met on Facebook or Instagram. Many local and cross-continental relationships owe a debt of gratitude to social media.

The bad news is that many of the stories people share about online connections are the ones concerning deception and the ones that end badly. As a result, when a person announces that he or she has met someone online, the next likely comment the person would hear would be a sceptical question: *"Ei, na wo nim no?"* – translation: "Ei, do you know this person?" Such a question often implies that there is something inherently dangerous or reckless about meeting someone online, simply because you did not see or meet the person through typical channels. Compared to a person you met at a club or even at a religious gathering, a person you met online could be more real and forthcoming with information you will need to clearly assess their suitability for a relationship.

I concede the point that people you meet online could be very deceptive. Online dating sites and social media platforms can make it easier for people to present an alternate version of themselves, and deceive people into falling in love with them.

One of my memorable experiences with online dating sites was with FriendFinder years ago. I set up an account under the guise of being my sister. I was trying to find her a boyfriend and possibly a husband. That dating site seemed like an interesting hub to find an eligible bachelor for my dear sister. She had no knowledge of her profile being on the site; neither did she know that I had been impersonating her. A handsome gentleman named Vijay, from India, messaged my sister (me) and made his case for a relationship. From Vijay's written messages, he seemed like a nice guy; however, his picture was only one of his handsome face. I told my sister what I had been doing on her behalf.

Like me, she became curious about finding out more about Vijay. I asked Vijay to send a full picture of himself in real-life settings, but he never did. He coyly changed the topic every time I asked for the full picture. That went on for days until I gave him an ultimatum – I was going to cut him off if he didn't send a full-body picture of himself. He finally announced that he had sent me the picture – in the snail mail. His elusive behaviour was enough proof that he wasn't who he said he was. In jest, my sisters and I coined the term "snail mail" to refer to delayed events.

The FriendFinder experience made me sceptical about dating sites. A dating site, where anyone can set up a profile and tell you whatever they want, leaves room for too many fraudsters to defraud people. However, if there were a site that screened individuals before they registered, I would be willing to give such a site the benefit of the doubt.

Modern-day matchmakers who are good at what they do intrigue me. Such individuals put their credibility on the line to find credible people for their clients. That is perfect.

When a serious person is putting their credibility on the line, screening people, weeding out the dubious characters, and presenting those serious men and women to their clients, that is a fair path for meeting people for a relationship. Obviously, that is a service that will cost a decent amount of money but the quality of people you meet and the peace of mind you will experience will be well worth the expense. Working with a credible matchmaker significantly minimises the possibility of meeting a serial killer or a gold digger.

For some people, a matchmaker may be the surest way they will find a husband or wife. Just like a person may find a job by themselves or through the services of professional recruiter, using the services of a credible matchmaker to find a life partner could be a worthwhile investment. Combing through dating sites could lead to finding a life partner; engaging the services of a matchmaker could make the process more efficient.

Social media also presents an expanded world of possibilities for relationships. Different social media platforms provide their users unique tools that facilitate connecting with one another. Facebook, Instagram, Twitter and LinkedIn are the largest social media platforms with active monthly users of 2.5 billion, 1 billion, 330 million, and 310 million respectively in 2020.

Social media has its distinctive culture that enables interactions that may not be possible otherwise. Facebook gives its users the tools to share and interact with their friends' personal photos, videos, and blogs, and the users select whose friend requests to accept. Instagram, with its visual storytelling nature, brings to life the saying that a picture is worth a thousand words. Instagram users showcase their personality mainly with pictures and videos and their "followers" interact with that content. Twitter is a microblog site where users share and react to news, opinions and commentary with a few words or an image. LinkedIn is a networking platform that allows people to connect based on professional interests and work-related activities.

On Facebook, Instagram, Twitter and LinkedIn, users can share, like or comment on content with the touch of a virtual button on their digital screen. Users can directly send messages to other users, and they can use privacy settings to restrict who can access their content or who can contact them.

If meeting a person online is an option for you, by all means, explore that. Do keep in mind that you will need to apply wisdom and discernment – just like you would when you are meeting someone for a relationship in real life. On social media, the way people present their looks or material possessions can allow them to project a perception that suits their agenda. That agenda could be noble or a sinister.

There are many successful online relationships. Due to the stigma that some people ignorantly attach to people meeting online, many people stay quiet about the fact that they met online, even if they nurtured a successful relationship that ended up in a thriving marriage. Just like the people who meet each other in real life, the success of a relationship does not rely solely on where the two people met. To dismiss social media as a legitimate means for meeting credible, responsible people is an unfair position to take.

It is worth adding that if you're planning on using an online platform to meet a prospective lover, you should ensure that your brand positioning on that platform is well managed. You will need to pay attention to the photos you post, the comments you post on your page or on other people's pages, and the kind of content you share. Make sure it reflects who you truly are and how you want to be perceived.

Different platforms have their own etiquette, and you should familiarise yourself with them so that you present yourself well. Be mindful of what you share online if privacy is important to you. You could use the privacy options on your account to restrict who sees your content or who connects with you.

Your presence online – on today's social media or whatever is to come in the future – is an important representation of your life on the internet. Being attentive to what you're doing online can add positively to your experience of meeting new people.

No matter where you meet people – for whatever reason – it is important to relate to them in the same way you want others to treat you. Be kind and considerate, and don't base your decisions on assumptions.

Do your best to extend common courtesies to them – say "hello", "please", and "thank you" as appropriate. Also, remember to present yourself well in public and continue to focus on being the best version of yourself. Eventually, you will meet that special someone or someone will see the spark in your eyes, and good things can happen from there on.

When two people meet and one person has an interest in the other, or they share a mutual interest in each other, one of two things are likely to happen if they have honest and candid conversations. The relationship may not start at all, and each person can move on in peace. Alternatively, a relationship could start, and the two of them would have a clear compass for where they are headed.

• 3 •

DATING WITH
PURPOSE

eople go on dates to share conversation and social activities, and learn more about each other with the hope of developing a shared attraction that will lead to the start of a relationship. If they stay in touch and continue to explore the possibility of a romantic relationship, they are dating. Dating is only one stage of the interactions that occurs between two people who share a romantic interest.

Some people incorrectly use the term dating to mean more than it really is. From a recent informal survey to assess the meaning various people attribute to the term dating, it became clear that dating is confused with related ideas such as courtship, being in a relationship, and seeing each other. I asked a pastor, a young adult, a middle-aged woman and her husband, a researcher, a lawyer, and a doctor what dating means to each of them. Each of them gave a different description of what it meant to be dating.

Dating is the unofficial entryway into a romantic relationship. It can span a few days to several months. It could be unrestricted or exclusive. It could be a straightforward process of two people sincerely getting to know each other or it could be a complicated game of mischief where one or both people try to outwit the other for their selfish interests. Generally, the purpose of dating is to gather information about the other person in order to make a decision on whether to pursue a relationship or not. The purpose of dating is not to date perpetually. Dating is actually supposed to be a brief activity.

Dating is like the interview process an employer offers to prospective employees. An employer always has a purpose for interviewing candidates, which is to hire a person for an open position. The employer, therefore, eventually hires the candidate who is the best fit for the job and moves on from the interview process. Likewise, a man or woman dates a person, makes a selection of the best fit for their respective relationship goals, and then transitions from the dating stage to another stage of the relationship.

The manner in which dating fits with the other stages of a romantic relationship can be explained with the **relationship spectrum**. The relationship spectrum is a range of varied-but-related ideas that describe various stages of a typical relationship between two people who share a liking for one another.

The relationship spectrum include (i) liking, (ii) dating, (iii) dating exclusively, (iv) in a relationship, (v) courtship, (vi) engaged, and (vii) married. Transitioning from one stage to another may or may not be marked by a specific event or ceremony.

The Relationship Spectrum

Liking	Dating	Dating Exclusively	In a Relationship	Courting	Engaged	Married

A Date

"Knocking" or Man Asks Woman to Marry Him

Customary Marriage or Wedding

Friends with Benefits

Cheating, Entanglements, Extramarital Affairs

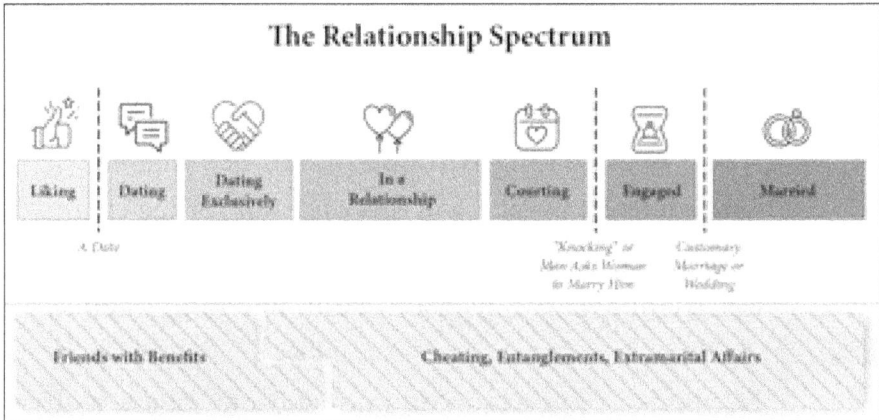

© Adelaide Aba Ansah

i. **Liking:** This is the stage of initial interest in the other person. The two people like each other enough to agree to spend time together, either alone or in a group, with the intention of finding out more about each other. When the two people go on at least one date, they have transitioned to the next stage.

ii. **Dating:** This is when two people are getting to know each other in order to figure out if they can move forward to the next stage. Dating requires more than just hanging out with another person. The two people could meet in public places for social activities, engage in phone conversations, and exchange information about themselves. During the dating period, each party could date other people. During this period, there would have been no exchange of commitment and each party is free to explore their options. If Kwasi goes on a date with Sarah on Friday, and then goes to see a movie with Abigail on Sunday, that is completely OK. Kwasi should not feel like he has to hide that fact from either date; and neither should Sarah nor Abigail be upset about the fact that Kwasi is evaluating two options. In like manner, if Sarah tells Kwasi she will be going out for ice cream with Joe on Tuesday and cannot come with him to his friend's party, Kwasi should not take offence.

Dating is a "knowing-you knowing-me" phase with no strings attached. When people are dating, no one has any obligation to the other and people are free to do as they please. If, after a number of dates, the two people decide that they want to focus on each other and continue to explore the possibility of a long-term relationship, they then transition to dating exclusively.

iii. **Dating Exclusively:** During this stage, the two people have not agreed to be in a relationship but have agreed to not date other people in order to focus on each other. Here, you have selected one person out of the lot, and you share a mild form of commitment with each other. The chosen person has certain privileges that the other people you used to date do not have. When exclusive dating continues and the two people agree to become a couple, the two people then transition to being in a relationship.

iv. **In a Relationship:** Admittedly, each stage is a form of a relationship. However, being in a romantic relationship refers to a specific stage where the two people invest resources such as time, money, gifts, services, ideas, and emotions into the relationship for each other's benefit. Each party reciprocates by appreciating the investments. It is important for each to hedge their level of commitment against the other person's level of commitment. In other words, you should match the speed at which your partner is investing in the relationship and don't move too quickly too soon. When in doubt, ask your partner if the relationship is moving at a good enough pace.

At this stage, it is important to maintain an open and honest conversation with each other; develop confidence in each other; find out about each other's likes and dislikes; find out about the other person's strengths and weaknesses; and discuss what moral values are important to each other. Share your admiration of each other and express how you feel about each other. Celebrate each other's successes and help lighten each other's load; learn about each other's background and each other's life goals; strike a balance between giving up some of your personal freedoms and maintaining your individuality.

People in a relationship often call each other pet names like "bae", "babe", "baby", "honey", "sweetie", and other terms of endearment. They also talk and text often, and spend most of their leisure time together.

It is important for people in a relationship to

directly and indirectly ask questions that help them clarify their partner's goals for the relationship. Some people avoid asking clarifying questions simply because they are afraid of the things they may find out. However, asking clarifying questions is an important part of the learning process. It is also important to be observant and discerning.

If marriage is your ultimate objective, this is the stage to clarify that goal and align with your partner on that goal. It is also during this stage that most people introduce each other to their family and friends as the person with whom they are in a romantic relationship. When the two people begin to seriously consider marriage as the next step in their relationship, they transition to the courtship stage.

v. **Courting:** During the courting phase, the two people have marriage in sight. In certain religious communities, any form of pre-marriage relationship is considered courtship because they view marriage as the only reason for starting the relationship. However, when making the distinction between courtship and being in a relationship it is important to acknowledge that people sometimes remain in a relationship without any immediate intention to get married.

During the courtship period, many of the conversations between the two people begin to focus on plans for marriage. During this period, the couple may privately disclose their intention to get married to important people in their lives, such as their parents and religious leaders. The courtship period ends when the couple publicly announce their intention to get married. In some circumstances, the man would ask the woman to marry him. If she agrees to his proposal and accepts his ring, they're engaged. In other circumstances, especially in traditional Akan homes across Ghana, the man's family will send a delegation to the woman's family to officially express their son's intent to marry their daughter. After the woman's family agrees to proceed with the necessary marriage rites, the two people are engaged.

vi. **Engaged:** When two people are engaged, they're officially unavailable to other suitors. They have made it known to all that a marriage ceremony is imminent. They plan a marriage ceremony, and also prepare for their post-ceremony life together. At a set day and time, the necessary rites are performed to usher the couple into the next relationship stage – marriage.

vii. **Married:** When two people complete the necessary marriage rites, they are considered married. They share their lives together, enjoy the legal protections of jurisdictions that recognise their marriage, and are expected to live happily ever after, in most cases.

There are non-traditional relationships that sometimes develop between two people. Friends-with-benefits, understandings, entanglements, cheating, and extramarital affairs are all examples of non-traditional relationships. Practitioners of such unorthodox relationships often carry out the relationships covertly and often share a bond that is primarily sexual in nature with other parties not their spouse.

Relationships develop over time and the length of time for transitioning from one stage to the next varies from couple to couple, and from situation to situation. Generally, a relationship should last about a year from the dating to the courtship period before transitioning into a marriage. However, there can be exceptions to that unofficial rule. Depending on levels of maturity and discernment of the people involved, a couple may gather sufficient information within less than a year and proceed to having a successful marriage. For example, two intelligent people who engage in frequent, meaningful conversations may know more in six months about each other than another couple who spend that same six months only fantasising about their future together.

It is also worth mentioning that the subject of sex comes up in relationships. While Annica and I have divergent views on whether or not the couple should have sex together before they are married, we both agree that the two people delaying the gratification of sex until later in the relationship benefits the relationship. With the introduction of sex, the two people often impair their ability to objectively assess each other. Sex may be a simple act to some people, but it could have significant implications for the future of the relationship. Along those lines, it is important to limit physical contact to a minimum in the earlier stages along the relationship spectrum.

During the dating period, for example, physical contact should be limited to handshakes and light hugs. During the exclusive dating period, physical contact could be expanded to include holding of hands, depending on how comfortable each person is with such actions. When the two individuals transition to being in a relationship, the two may then define the boundaries of physical contact depending on their shared value system and the goals of the relationship.

When you realise that the status of your relationship is changing or might have changed, ask your partner if they have realised the same. That way, you are both on the same page, and you don't get ahead of yourself expecting benefits you have not earned. Remember to state your enquiry as a specific question. That way, if the answer does not meet your expectation, you are able to let yourself down gently.

Some people date simply because it is fun going out on dates at another person's expense. Other people date because they are interested in meeting new people. Most people date because they're interested in finding the right person with whom to have a long-term relationship. When used properly, the dating period can help a couple identify how compatible they are for a relationship. That period could also help the two people improve the likelihood of selecting the best eligible partner for a serious life-long relationship.

· 4 ·

SOMETIMES, PEOPLE BREAK UP

W hen most people start relationships, they expect to be together forever. For various reasons, relationships sometimes come to an end sooner than both parties thought the relationship would last. They break up and go their separate ways. Depending on the state of a relationship prior to its demise, a break-up could be anticipated by one or both partners, or it may come as a surprise to one or both of them.

While some people may never experience a break-up, others may experience break-ups more than once. The end of the relationship could leave one or both parties disappointed or devastated. It could also be a welcomed relief or liberating for one or both partners. There is life after a break-up and we hope that our thoughts offer an uplifting perspective to help individuals recover if they ever experience such.

Annica and I have never broken up nor contemplated a break-up. I, however, have experienced many break-ups in previous relationships. Some of those I initiated, and others were initiated by the other person in the relationship. I didn't feel any pain or loss when a relationship with a girl I didn't care about ended. On the contrary, the pain and the sense of loss was immense any time a girl I cared about broke up with me.

Following a break-up with someone I cared about, my mind would go crazy and my heart would feel like it had been ripped out of my chest. During such moments, I was unable to think clearly, I lost my appetite for food, and I became depressed.

My first real relationship was in 1995 in Fante New Town, a suburb of Kumasi, and that was also where I experienced my first ever break-up. Even though I was older than my girlfriend, she looked bigger and taller than me. There were rumours in the neighbourhood that an older guy, an air conditioning salesman who owned a pickup truck, was sharing my girlfriend with me. Whenever I went to visit my girlfriend and she was not home, the guys in the neighbourhood informed me that the air conditioning salesman had come to pick her up.

My girlfriend was not very good at concealing her relationship with the other guy, and I was unhappy with her unfaithfulness. I did not walk away from that relationship, even though I knew I had been relegated to being her boyfriend only in name. I became depressed thinking that I may eventually lose her to the other guy. It took about four months before I was able to end the relationship by cutting her off. When I stopped going to her house, she never followed up to find out why I had stopped coming to her house, and the relationship ended.

Over the course of the four months that I contemplated the end of the relationship, it had become very clear to me that she was no good for me, and that the relationship would need to end. As time went on, I cared less about her and the relationship. I didn't feel any pain when the relationship eventually ended.

About four and a half years later, I was living in the Bronx, in New York. At the time, I was a famous, award-winning musician from Ghana, and I had fallen in love with a young Ghanaian lady. I moved in with her, and we carried on with our relationship. Everything was going well. We had planned to visit Ghana together that December but I unfortunately had to visit Ghana earlier (in October) to bury my father. I did not see the need to make another trip home just about two months later, so she travelled alone to Ghana that December. Immediately after she arrived in Ghana, she stopped taking my calls. She would send periodic text messages after my many attempts at reaching her, and blame her behaviour on the bad network and being busy.

One of her friends blew her cover about what was really going on. The friend set up a three-way call with me quietly on the other line while the two of them carried on with their conversation. It turned out that my girlfriend had a boyfriend in Ghana and had been spending most of her time with him. She bragged about how much fun she was having with various men, and I stayed quietly on the phone with my heart thumping inside my chest. I was confused and heartbroken. I walked away leaving the two of them on the phone. I had heard enough to know that our relationship had no future.

The days that followed were excruciatingly painful. I had long-term plans with this girlfriend and all those plans were crumbling. We had come to the end of our road and I had to accept the fact that a break-up was inevitable.

We parted ways when she returned from her trip, and I moved on with my life. How the relationship ended and the fact that the relationship had ended kept me depressed for weeks. I tried to distract myself with other activities, but my mind kept wandering back to her. I knew time was going to heal my pain, but time moved slower than I anticipated. Eventually, I got over her and got over the pain of that break-up.

That break-up hurt me immensely because I cared about that girl. The extent of my break-up pain seemed to correlate with how devoted I was to the relationship before it ended – the more I cared, the more the break-up hurt. If I did not care about her, I would have moved on without blinking. She broke up with me, and I was left to pick up the pieces of my broken heart.

There was another relationship where we broke up because of the complexity of the long distance between us. We lived on two different continents and it was difficult to sustain the relationship. She was a good girl and breaking up with her broke my heart.

After each of my break-ups, I quickly got into a rebound relationship – a short-term relationship with the sole intent of distracting myself from the pain of the break-up. Such relationships tended to be with girls that I did not care for but who offered an outlet for drowning my sorrows. That seemed to work until a girl caused me to rethink my approach to moving on after a break-up.

The girl was pretty but not intelligent. I left my phone with her when I travelled briefly out of the country, and she couldn't help but get entangled with other men. On my return, other men were calling my phone asking to speak to "my sister". She had told those men that I was her brother. She was obviously promiscuous and also unsophisticated about it. So, I ended my relationship with her. However, she was available for sex with me and I conveniently carried on with her.

By drowning my sorrows in casual sex, I was taking the easiest but most short-sighted route to dealing with the loss. I was avoiding the grieving process. I knew I needed something to fill the emotional void created by the end of the relationship, and sex with "anyone" seemed like the fix I needed. I was using sex to pacify myself.

In the course of the act one afternoon, she told me that the next time I had sex with her she would deliberately become pregnant. The thought of fathering a child with a promiscuous and unsophisticated girl whom I was obviously using to satisfy my lust scared the hell out of me. Her statement shut down the little bit of interest I had in her, and I promptly cut her off. It dawned on me in that moment that my short-term fix could have long-term implications.

That realisation shook me to the core and changed my outlook on casual sex. As a result, I suspended myself indefinitely from having sexual relations with anyone. I remained celibate and carried on with my life for months. By realising the detrimental effects of a rebound relationship, I regained control over my emotions and set myself on a path to healing. Staying away from sex kept me focused on refreshing my mind and developing myself.

During that period of celibacy, I experienced significant personal growth. My sense of judgement improved. My vision of my personal and professional future came into sharper focus. Even though several girls offered themselves to me, I was not interested in hooking up with them just for the sake of sex. I had come to realise that rebound sex was not a sustainable way to recover from a break-up; instead, I needed to allow myself time to heal from the end of the relationship. With the healing, which came about over the course of about seven months, came clarity in my thinking. From that point forward, I was better prepared for new experiences with new, high-quality people.

Why Break-ups are Painful

All relationships eventually break up, except in rare situations where both partners die in the same moment. The couple may separate, or one person may be taken away in death. When a meaningful romantic relationship comes to an end, one or both parties experience a degree of pain. Even when a break-up is handled with extreme tact, caution and kindness, it is possible for at least one person to experience some pain. Sleepless nights, loss of appetite, crying, and embarrassment are some of the common symptoms reported by people who have experienced painful break-ups. The reasons for these painful experiences comprise external factors (actions and reactions of other people) and internal factors (psychological and physiological).

When you become **attached** to any aspect of your relationship – the social status, the pleasure you derive from your partner, your investment, and any need the relationship meets – a break-up is bound to cause some pain. With that attachment, you identify yourself with the elements of the relationship, and a break-up tends to take something away from your identity. That can be painful.

It is fine to identify yourself with elements of the relationship. It is, however, an unhealthy attachment when the relationship becomes all-or-nothing for your identity and self worth. Love is about oneness and inclusion. Attachment is an extreme form of inclusion that creates an anxious and fearful bond, sometimes characterised by a person declaring, "If you leave me I will die", or "If you leave me I will kill you".

Since most romantic relationships are public, known at least to friends and family, there is some form of public reaction when the relationship ends. The more public the relationship, the more widespread the reactions are likely to be. What people will say – things that are true, truths that are exaggerated, rumours that may be spread as facts – can cause feelings of worry and stress. For those who broadcast information about their relationship on social media, the end of a relationship can add an extra layer of complexity when they have to purge from social media sites pictures that reflect the now-ended relationship.

For people who are dependent on the now ex-partner for emotional, physical, financial or other forms of support, that support that may no longer be available once the person leaves the relationship could be a source of distress. There could be expensive items borrowed from the ex that may have to be returned. There could be secrets that an ex may not protect from becoming public. All these could be major sources of worry.

While it is normal for one partner to miss the other after a break-up, one or both partners experiencing an apocalyptic sense of void after a break-up may be a reflection of how much that person's identity and self-worth was tied to the ended relationship. People who subscribe to the idea that their partners complete them are often left feeling no longer complete when the relationship ends.

The excessive brain activity from thinking about the ended relationship could make it difficult for the dumped lover to sleep; the sadness from the loss may make the person cry; the anger from the disappointment may make the person's body ache and shake; the feeling of guilt may leave the person with a headache; and the emotional toll of the new reality may leave the person with a loss of appetite.

These natural responses could make a break-up hurt not only emotionally but also physically.

Knowing how painful a break-up can be for one or both parties involved, it is important that people who decide to break up approach the process with empathy.

How to Break Up

Relationships sometimes get to a point when one or both parties have no interest in continuing with the relationship. That may be because the two people have discovered that they have very different life goals; or something happened that caused an irreparable damage to the faith that one or both partners have in the relationship; or the relationship ceased to meet the needs of one or both partners.

When a relationship needs to end, the ideal and mature way is for both partners to sit across from each other and formally terminate the relationship. However, depending on the reasons for the break-up or the circumstances under which the break-up occurs, the ideal and mature way may not be feasible. Instead, one party may walk away from the relationship by ceasing all communications, sometimes with a "break-up text" and/or refusing to answer any calls. Sometimes both parties simultaneously cease all communications with each other.

A relationship could end through arbitration, where a third party such as an elderly family member declares the relationship over and forbids the two people from continuing to be romantically involved. At other times, one party or both parties deliberately get romantically involved with other people and make a bigger mess of the failing relationship. The uniqueness of a relationship may require a unique approach to its break-up. In extreme cases, one party may have to petition a court for a restraining order to keep the unrelenting partner away.

If you are the one initiating the break-up, **make sure you want the relationship to end** and be clear to yourself about why you want the relationship to end. Being clear to yourself about your reasons will help you **clearly communicate your intention** to end the relationship. Clear communication will help prevent ambiguity and allow each party to know what is happening. If you have reasons, and the other party would like to know them, share them respectfully. If you would like to keep your reasons to yourself or the other party doesn't want to hear your reasons, do so with clarity, honesty and respect.

If you are on the receiving end of the break-up announcement, your soon-to-be ex is not likely to tell the whole truth about their reasons for the break-up. They may consciously or subconsciously tell a partial truth or a lie so as not to hurt your feelings. They may not have a reason they deem legitimate enough, and will therefore lie about the reason. Whatever the case, a break-up is likely going to hurt even if your partner gives you the best reason ever. It will not hurt any less even if your soon-to-be ex gives you the classic "it's not you; it's me" reason. You are going to have to put on your big boy or big girl pants and embrace the break-up like an adult.

When a romantic relationship needs to end, there are several things each party can do to make sure there is minimal collateral damage. Whether you are the one leaving or the one being ditched, it is important to do the following:

- **Gain control of your emotions.** The end of a romantic relationship can spark a strong emotional reaction that may include anger, disappointment, confusion, fear, and sadness. If you experience any of these emotions, you are not crazy – you are human. However, as a fully-grown adult, you have the capacity to control your emotions instead of allowing your emotions to control you. It's OK to grieve and even dabble in the confusion and emotion for a while. But by all means, cease control of your emotions.

To gather control of your emotions, identify the emotion you are feeling and acknowledge that you are feeling that emotion. Find a healthy outlet for the emotion you are feeling, such as taking several deep breaths or excusing yourself from that physical location. If you are a person of faith, you can take a moment to say a prayer. Above all, don't react right away. Give yourself time to process the information before you act. You can also confide in a trusted friend, family member or a counsellor for emotional support.

Under no circumstance should you record a video or create an audio recording and send it to your ex hoping to convince them to take you back. That video or audio might end up being shared and you might embarassingly find yourself on social media.

- **Make it a clean break.** Equally important to announcing your intention to break up is your commitment to seeing your decision through. Be empathetic and respectful but do not send mixed signals that could lead your soon-to-be ex to think that there is a chance you will change your mind. Even if you love them, proclaiming your love in the middle of a break-up is a very bad idea – **don't do it**. Don't promise the other person that you will be there for him or her, or that the two of you will continue to be friends. An Akan proverb says, *"W'asum abrewa a, baabi a ɔbɛtɔ nfa wo ho"* – translation: "If you've already shoved an old lady, it is too late to worry about where she will fall". Allow the other person to process the break-up on their own and map out their own healing path.

If you are the one being left, you will need to ensure a clean break as well. Don't drag the break-up out. It's OK to beg for another chance and to seek reconciliation. However, if the person is resolute about their decision, don't keep begging. If the person has decided and has clearly communicated the decision, dragging out the end only delays the beginning of your healing. Do not negotiate the possibility of a future relationship with your new ex. Please don't say things like they will never find anyone like you. Let them find that out on their own. In such a desperate situation, rational decision-making may be difficult but necessary. Do everything you can to remain calm and act thoughtfully.

If you have each other's belongings that need to be returned, schedule an appropriate time and place in the future for such an exchange. It may be wise to have a third party accompany each of you during the property exchange. Alternatively, you could leave each other's property with a reliable third party. A clean break means limiting those interactions that may mislead either of you into thinking the relationship has not really ended. Consider disconnecting from your ex on social media platforms by unfollowing them on Instagram, Twitter, TikTok, Triller and unfriending them on Facebook. Such actions may seem extreme, but they are necessary for ensuring a clean break. When you break up, make it a clean break.

- **Take an honest look at yourself.** You may have done all the right things, but the relationship came to an end anyway. You may not have done all the right things and may have contributed to the end of the relationship. Either way, an honest review of your mindset and your actions during the relationship could help you recognise where you were wrong. That self-assessment could also help you find opportunities to do better in your next relationship. Even if your ex was the toxic one, and you were an angel in the relationship, some of the toxicity of that relationship may have rubbed off on you. You may have learned behaviours that were necessary to survive your previous relationship. Such behaviours may not be needed for a future healthy relationship. Those are behaviours that you may need to unlearn.

Taking an honest look at yourself may involve making a list of things you did well during the relationship and a list of things you did not do well. Pat yourself on the back for the things you did well and identify specific actions you are going to take to avoid repeating your mistakes in a future relationship. How beneficial the self-assessment exercise will be for you will depend on how honestly you assess your thinking and your actions. You may have to do that self-assessment exercise more than once, and that's OK.

- **Create closure for yourself.** Whether you are the one leaving the relationship or the one being left, you will need to close the book on the relationship. In addition to the physical break-up, which will involve terminating all forms of contact and interaction there could be emotional and psychological loose ends that need to be tied. You may have lingering feelings for them, your ex may not have given you an opportunity to have your say, or you may be feeling deceived or treated unfairly. **Closure** is the process of healing that comes with becoming at peace with the fact that the relationship has ended. It may not be easy and will not happen overnight, but it is possible.

Closure does not come simply because time passes. Time is one of the factors that will influence your closure. Your willingness to move on matters. Your discipline to stay the course and not look back will also be key.

You cannot rely on your ex for closure. You will have to create closure for yourself. You create closure for yourself by creating peace within yourself. Forgiving yourself and forgiving your ex is an important step in attaining closure. Ask yourself if there is something for which you need to forgive yourself. Ask yourself if there is something for which you need to forgive your ex.

To forgive means to stop feeling angry or resentful towards someone for an offence, flaw, or mistake. When you forgive, you make a conscious decision to release feelings of resentment or vengeance you may be holding towards the person whom you believe has wronged you. Take it one step further and wish your ex well. That final hurdle – wishing your ex well – will free you up to embrace the good things that are ahead of you. Closure is helpful for healing and you owe it to yourself to create closure – for yourself.

- **Take a break from social media.** If you participate in social media, a purge is highly recommended. When you are healing from break-up, the stream of content from your social media feed could become noise for your soul. Being constantly reminded of how "perfect" other people's lives are could create a sense of inadequacy in you, which could delay your complete healing.

  Also, combing through past pictures and posts on your social media account could stir up memories you shared with your ex. Until you are in a healthy place in your healing process, you may inflict unnecessary pain on yourself by spending time on social media sites.

If you believe deleting your social media pictures and posts will be helpful to your healing, do that. When the time comes and you feel you are in an emotionally healthy place to engage with others on social media, engage thoughtfully. Avoid sarcastic posts that speak indirectly to or about your ex. Block people who drag you into the drama in their lives. Above all, consciously limit your use of social media. Social media is an excellent tool for engaging with others but could become a trap for seeking validation from others. Guard against that.

- **Improve yourself and look forward with hopefulness.** Self-improvement is one sure way to up your confidence and self-esteem. Topping up your confidence is necessary when you are bouncing back from a break-up. The end of a relationship could leave the hurt partner feeling inadequate or dull. However, investing in yourself could provide a boost in confidence that sets you up for future pleasant experiences.

  Improve yourself physically through exercising and eating properly; improve yourself intellectually by reading books and other materials that refresh your mind; improve yourself emotionally by eliminating unhealthy behaviours and unhealthy people; and improve yourself spiritually by devoting yourself to activities such as personal prayer and meditation.

  The end of a relationship is an opportunity to focus your attention on yourself and do some of the things you've always wanted to do but didn't make time to do. You may have wanted to learn how to play a musical instrument – the time after a break-up is a good time to do that. You may have wanted to travel to a dream destination – pack your bags and hit the road. You may also learn a new trade, go back to school, or pick up a new hobby.

It is helpful to know that when you are healing from the end of a relationship, you go through a process. That process is similar to the process of grief following the loss of a loved one. Psychiatrist Elisabeth Kubler-Ross describes five stages of grief in the Grief Cycle – Denial, Anger, Bargaining, Depression, and Acceptance.

The **Denial** stage is where you experience shock and confusion. The **Anger** stage is marked by frustration and anxiety. The **Bargaining** stage is where you struggle to find meaning in everything that happened. The **Depression** stage is where you feel overwhelmed and helpless. At the **Acceptance** stage, you come to terms with what has happened, put a plan in place for moving on, and then move on.

Closure happens at the Acceptance stage. At that stage, you are not accepting that it's OK that the relationship ended but rather you are accepting the fact that it has, and you cannot change that. You are also accepting the fact that even though the relationship has ended, you have your life to live and good things can happen in your future. You are shifting your focus away from what you don't have to what you do have. Your shift in focus keeps you moving forward.

That momentum or energy will allow you to look forward with hopefulness. That hopefulness will help you establish and maintain peace within you.

Closure happens when you become fully detached from the pleasures, the pain and the desires that are associated with the ended relationship; your identity would no longer be tied to that relationship. When you have created closure for yourself, you will not be in denial that the relationship has ended; you will not be angry towards your ex; you will not experience depression from the relationship's demise; and you will be past searching for answers to why the relationship ended. The past will remain in the past.

The fact that your relationship failed doesn't necessarily mean you failed. A break-up may be the saviour that didn't let you take the plunge into life-long misery. If your partner was unhappy with you or with the relationship, you would eventually have become unhappy in the relationship too. A relationship takes two people and you cannot do it all by yourself, no matter how hard you try.

Whether the end of the relationship was due to the lack of good intentions and the lack of effort on the part of one or both parties, or it was despite both parties' good intentions and effort, do your very best to not lose your self-respect or your mind when a break-up happens. There is life after a break-up.

Starting Over After a Break-up

Everyone deserves to be in a relationship that makes them feel fulfilled. The decision to start another relationship after experiencing a break-up is entirely an individual one. However, allowing enough time for healing will be extremely helpful to your mental health and to the health of your future relationships.

While time heals, the length of time needed to recover from a break-up varies from person to person and from circumstance to circumstance. Generally, six months to a year after a break-up is about how long most people need to fully heal. Some people may take less time and others may take longer.

The length of time is not as important as the conscious effort you put into healing after the break-up. If your thoughts and feelings are flooded with emotional and psychological remnants from your past relationship, you are certainly not ready to start a new healthy relationship. The romantic relationship you get into before you heal from your break-up may become a rebound relationship, at best. A rebound relationship is not a viable way to bounce back from a break-up. Healing is.

Sometimes, break-ups are necessary. As painful as a break-up can be, a break-up can be the door through which you walk into a brighter future as a new and improved version of yourself. So, be kind to yourself if you ever have to deal with a break-up. You will get through it.

As Roxette sings, *"It must have been love, but it's over now"*. Having loved and lost, your vision of what you want in a future partner may now be refined.

You may now have more reasonable expectations and be better equipped to prudently handle future relationships.

5

CRUCIAL CONVERSATIONS: FINDING SOMEONE TO LOVE

The overwhelming majority of people couple up with the goal of having successful and fulfilling long-term relationships. Those who do not come with good intentions or the goal of a long-term relationship may disguise their true intentions. Before getting started with a relationship, it is wise to assess a potential lover's capacity to develop and sustain a long-term relationship with you.

Starting a relationship is like putting up a building – you start with the foundation. Generally, the depth of the building's foundation is determined by how tall the building is intended to be. The foundation for a one-floor, two-bedroom house might need to be dug a few feet into the ground whereas the foundation for a skyscraper will need to go as deep as a hundred feet. Not only does the skyscraper's foundation have to be deep, it might need to be reinforced with a significant amount of steel and concrete. That much material, effort and time put into building the foundation is necessary to ensure structural soundness.

Like the depth of a building's foundation, a relationship's foundation will need to correspond with the goals for the relationship – in order to ensure the relationship's structural soundness. That is very important.

It is important to assess the potential partner's physical, emotional, intellectual and spiritual capacity to develop and sustain a successful relationship with you. Therefore, the process requires significant information gathering, a careful evaluation, and informed decision-making.

As part of your information gathering and assessment, ask meaningful questions and listen attentively to the answers. Keep in mind that the best way to keep a conversation going is to ask open-ended questions.

Use the following resources to manage your process.

a) Topics for Crucial Conversations: Finding Someone to Love

Below are some crucial conversation topics to help **both of you** gather useful information, evaluate each other and make an informed decision for the purpose of pursuing a long-term relationship. Weave the following topics into your conversations:

- Their relationship status
- Their intention for dating you
- A brief overview of what each of you does for work
- What each of you likes the most (and the least) about your co-workers
- Their personal goals
- Their relationship with siblings and parents
- Most memorable experiences from their past
- Their likes and dislikes
- Fun activities they like to participate in
- What makes them angry
- What they need when angry
- What makes them sad
- What they need when sad
- How their best friend would describe them to a stranger
- Three personality traits that are most important to them in a friend
- Their views on what factors contribute to the success of a relationship
- Their views on what factors contribute to the failure of a relationship
- What their thoughts are on pre-marital sex

- Their views on polygyny, polygamy, polyandry and faithfulness
- One important lesson they learned from a previous relationship
- Whether they want to get married and have children someday
- How important to them their faith/religion is
- Their relationship deal breakers
- How they prefer to celebrate occasions like birthdays and anniversaries
- Three most exciting places they would like to visit, and why
- What drives their passion

b) The Dating Goal Worksheet

The Dating Goal worksheet is useful for determining what you would like to accomplish by dating the person you are dating. Whether you are the one doing the pursuit or you are the one being pursued, it is helpful to have a goal for dating the person you are dating.

Use the following worksheet to get the most out of the dating process:

Name of Goal: _____

What exactly do you want to achieve?

S
Specific

How can you know when you are making progress or have successfully achieved this goal?

M
Measurable

What skills and/or resources are required for achieving this goal?

A
Achievable

Why you are setting this goal at this time?

R
Relevant

When must this goal be accomplished?

T
Time-bound

c) The Dating Assessment

After one to three dates, assess your date's capacity for a long-term relationship by indicating how they meet your expectations. Use the attributes included below and add your own in the blank spaces provided.

	Exceeds (3)	Meets (2)	Does Not Meet (1)
1. Clear communication (speaking)			
2. Clear communication (listening)			
3. Respect for self and others			
4. Physical attractiveness			
5. Personality			
6. Emotional health			
7. Capacity for empathy			
8. Capacity for commitment			
9. Capacity for financial independence			
10. Commitment to personal growth			
11.			
12.			
13.			
14.			
15.			

i. *For each row, write the number that reflects how your date meets that attribute (3 if they exceed that attribute; 2 if they meet that attribute; 1 if they do not meet that attribute).*

ii. *Calculate an average (add all the numbers you wrote down and divide by the number of attributes used in the assessment).*

iii. *With an average score of 3, your date exceeds your expectations; with an average score of between 2 and 3, your date meets your expectations; with an average score of less than 2, your date does not meet your expectations.*

iv. *Use the final scores to determine your next steps.*

d) The SPISS Assessment

The SPISS (Spiritual, Physical, Intellectual, Sexual and Social) Assessment is intended to help couples identify areas in their relationship that need to be celebrated and those that need work. For single people seeking mates, this worksheet is useful for assessing compatibility.

i. *Honestly assess your mate on the scale below by assigning a number (based on the corresponding facial expression) that matches the way you feel about them:*

	☺ = 1	☺ = 2	☺ = 3	☹ = 4	☹ = 5	☹ = 6	Totals
Spiritually							
Physically							
Intellectually							
Sexually*							
Socially							

*This may not apply in all situations

ii. *Add up totals for all rows.*

iii. *Using the chart below, determine the state of your relationship and what next step is recommended.*

Your Total Score:	**Less than 14** = Your relationship seems to be going very well. Keep doing what you are doing. **Between 14 and 20** = Your relationship could use a tune up. Consider consulting a counselor or therapist. **Greater than 20** = Your relationship is in trouble. Please consult a counselor or therapist.

e) The Relationship Spectrum Questionnaire

The relationship spectrum describes the stages of a typical romantic relationship: liking, dating, dating exclusively, in a relationship, courting, engaged, and married.

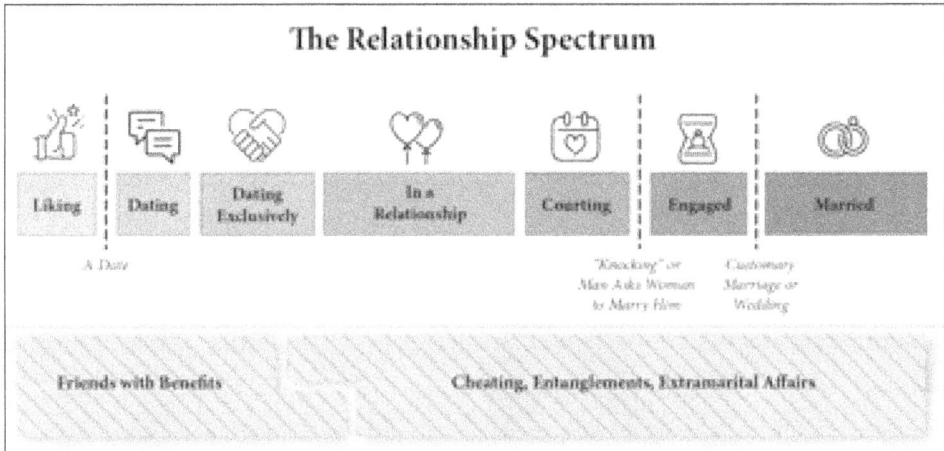

The Relationship Spectrum

Liking	Dating	Dating Exclusively	In a Relationship	Courting	Engaged	Married
A Date				"Knocking" or Man Asks Woman to Marry Him	Customary Marriage or Wedding	

Friends with Benefits

Cheating, Entanglements, Extramarital Affairs

Individually complete the questions below and discuss your responses.

1. Where on the relationship spectrum is your relationship at the moment?

Liking   Dating   Dating Exclusively   In a Relationship   Courtship   Engaged   Married   Other

2. Where do you intend for your relationship to be in _____ months?

Liking   Dating   Dating Exclusively   In a Relationship   Courtship   Engaged   Married   Other

3. What is the likelihood that your relationship will transition during your specified timeframe?

Very Likely   Likely   Not Likely   N/A

4. What important question will you like to ask your partner about the stage of your relationship?

© Adelaide Aba Ansah

PART II:
BEFORE YOU SAY "I DO"

Adinkra Symbol Name:
Mɛ Ware Wo (I Shall Marry You)

Significance:
Commitment and Perseverance

· 6 ·

FINDING "THE ONE"

Sometime during the development of a long-term relationship, the two people decide to officially confer the title of couple on each other. In many cases, that change in status comes about because they have found each other to be a good fit. One or both partners may even describe the other as "The One".

Depending on the circumstances, "The One" may mean the chosen one (as in the one chosen from among many options), or the one they have been waiting for, or even the one that was ordained for them before the beginning of time. Many people use such phrases as "The One" or "better half" or "soul mate" to represent the idea of a partner with whom they are in sync regarding the things that matter the most to them.

The idea of "The One" may have its origin in the Adam and Eve story from the Bible, where Eve is said to have been created from Adam's rib. Based on that story, some people believe a man needs to find his "missing rib" when looking for a wife. That same idea has led many people to believe that there is one person created specifically to be another person's wife or husband. Many religious leaders and their followers have promoted that idea for centuries, and continue to do so. Romantic songs and movies have also helped to popularise this idea.

The story of Eve having been created from Adam's rib is a metaphor for a partner who balances the other so much that it feels naturally like they were made specifically for each other. For some people, it is that person whom they feel so comfortable around that it feels like they have known each other from a previous life. For others, it is that person with whom they connect at a very deep level, and consistently operate on the same emotional, psychological, intellectual and spiritual wavelength.

Annica and I embrace the idea of "The One" in the larger context of someone who can be an ideal match for the type of relationship you desire. However, we share different opinions on who "The One" is. I believe that there is only one person made specifically for each one; Annica believes that you can choose anyone and make that person "The One" if you are both reasonable and committed to each other.

It is important to note that the idea of "The One" should not be confused with the idea of a perfect partner. Perfect partners are like unicorns – they exist in our imaginations. In any relationship involving normal human beings, "The One" may not be perfect in all their ways but the two of you could match each other in ways that make you better together, perfectly.

When someone is in a relationship with "The One" or a "better half" or a "soul mate", the two people are often said to complete each other. That idea of completion does not in any way mean either person is incomplete prior to being in the relationship, or that they will be incomplete if the relationship ends. Completion here means being a complement to, or a match, with that person. It also means that person brings out the best things in their partner.

Generally, people are not meant to go through life alone. Most people have emotional, physical, intellectual and spiritual needs that they rely on other people to meet. That is why most of us live in communities and form varied bonds with acquaintances, friends and family members. A romantic relationship is another type of bond that people establish to meet their needs. When that bond appears to be exactly what that person wants and needs, such people could be said to complete each other.

Some people have misused the idea of one person completing the other to perpetuate a notion that a person is incomplete until they are married. That is a mistaken belief based on an unsound argument. A person can absolutely live a successful life as a single person. Spreading the notion that a person is incomplete or deficient when unmarried can be harmful to that person's self-esteem.

The question of whether the person you are with is "The One" tends to be important to many people because of the human desire for security. Most of us have a need to be sure that we are not wasting our time and emotions on someone who will turn out to be a painful experience or simply a waste of our time. For some of us, our past experiences and the things we have read and heard come into play – either consciously or subconsciously – when we are with a new person. On the basis of those experiences and information gathered, the question begs to be answered.

How then could someone tell if the person they are dating exclusively or in a relationship with is "The One"?

Annica and I suggest a three-pronged approach to determining if the person is "The One". First, **determine how you feel about your partner;** second, **evaluate how your partner feels about you**; and third, **examine how well your personal values align**.

When a person is dating or is in a relationship with an individual who could be "The One", that person feels **peaceful** when relating to them. They feel **inspired** and not suffocated; they entertain **hopes** and not fears; they develop **confidence** and not doubts about the person; and they feel like they are on the **same team** rather than in competition with each other. The two of them can **reason together**, enjoy conversations with each other, and be **reasonable** when they disagree.

The second prong, evaluating how their partner feels about them, can be done through observation and attentive listening. **Observation** without prejudice can help a person discover unspoken attributes and intentions of their partner. Observation could reveal how comfortable their partner is both alone with them and together in public. With **attentive listening**, a person could pick up on nuances in their partner's choice of words, hear clearly what that person says, and ask for clarification when something is unclear. The way their partner feels about them could throw light on whether that person has the capacity to meet their needs.

When Annica and I started dating, she had graduated from university with a degree and I had none at the time. There was an instance where someone asked her why she was dating a rapper and not a university graduate. She told the person that I (Kwame) did not have a university degree at the time, but I was smarter than that person with the university degree.

Not only did she say that to shut that person up, but she also believed what she said. She had come to know me and my plans for the future to the extent that she felt confident defending my honour. That was one of the moments that indicated to me that she was "The One" for me. I did not yet have everything she wanted me to have but she publicly displayed confidence in me.

For her second degree, Annica could have obtained a master's degree in Law and then become a lawyer. When she realised how disorganised and financially unstable my career was, she changed her career path to pursue a master's in Marketing with a Branding option. Her research thesis was about finding alternative financial routes for the Ghanaian musician. She was devoted to seeing me blossom. I knew how she felt about me not only because she told me she loved me but rather through the confidence that she had in me when I did not have much.

After being together for as long as we have, she continues to demonstrate in many ways that she believes in me. She is devoted to protecting my best interests and is always willing to make sacrifices to help me develop personally and professionally. Knowing how she feels about me affirms that she is "The One" for me.

Another attribute that uniquely factored into my determination that Annica was "The One" for me was that Annica did not tell lies, and did not appreciate it when other people lied. She was always direct in her dealings with me, and did not make promises that she knew she couldn't fulfil. She was also candid about what she could or could not do and I didn't need to guess whether she meant what she was saying. I did not need to decode her statements.

Integrity is paramount for me and it was refreshing to be with someone who embodies that. That quality in her told me a lot about how much I could trust her and together build a future.

Annica is "The One" for me. I have known this fact for years and I have never had any doubt about that, even though she is sometimes troublesome. I have known she's "The One" for me based on the logical attributes that I have experienced. Also, the way I felt about her from the start contributed to my realisation. The way I felt about her was special, which gave me an early signal that she was meant to fulfil a purpose in my life.

Annica is "The One" for me mainly because we liked each other enough and have decided to treat each other with respect and remain devoted to seeing each other blossom. While many of her attributes and actions convince me that she is "The One", the work each of us puts in to ensure that we're not taking each other for granted is what keeps her as "The One" for me.

Kwame earlier discussed two prongs of the three-pronged approach to determining if the person you are with is "The One". The third prong is **values alignment**. A person's values system indicates the level of importance that person attaches to specific ideas and behaviours. Consequently, a person's thinking and behaviours are largely driven by their personal values. Depending a person's upbringing, life experiences, and goals for life, that person develops their **core values**. Examples of values include loyalty, respect, appreciation, discipline, compassion, ambition, competence, passion, privacy, trust, forgiveness, authority, and accountability. The values that are most important to you become your core values. Your core values guide your decisions and actions both consciously and unconsciously.

While we were dating, Kwame and I discovered that we shared many core values. That alignment made it easier for us to agree on priorities and remain unified in the things we chose to focus on. We recently completed a values-based assessment that confirmed many of the things we already knew about ourselves. The assessment, provided by *personalvalu.es*, revealed which values each of us consider the most important.

From a list of more than 60 values, I selected about 20 and then completed a series of questions comparing the level of importance I attributed to each of the values. At the end of the exercise, my results showed that the values I find most important are **independence** (self-reliance, self-sufficiency), **wisdom** (making good decisions and judgements), **loyalty** (faithfulness), **success** (achieving desired results), and **family** (caring for loved ones). These results were spot on! These values are indeed important to me. I laughed out loud when I saw them because they were so true.

Kwame's results showed that the values he finds most important are **love** (deep feeling of affection), **honesty** (sincerity, frankness), **forgiveness** (willingness to forgive others), **compassion** (empathy, sympathy), and **growth** (physical, intellectual and spiritual development). Once again, those were also spot on! These values are very important to Kwame. Even though we knew most of these things about each other, the exercise gave us a clearer picture of the ideas that drive each other's actions and decisions.

For most of us, we are usually at our happiest when we are able to live according to our core values. Most of us usually feel horrible when we or someone else violates our core values. In relationships, most people tend to get along better with people with whom they share core values. The two people need not have the exact core values. As long as their core values align or are closely related, their relationship can be successful.

For example, a person who has discipline as a core value will take punctuality very seriously. Even if their partner does not have discipline as a core value but has instead has respect as a core value, there will be enough alignment for them to appreciate their partner's expectation of punctuality and show up as scheduled for the appointment.

Each person has a threshold of values alignment that is acceptable to them. People are not perfect, and are likely to have shortcomings. However, alignment on key values such as **trust**, **respect**, **accountability**, **forgiveness**, and **commitment**, is necessary for developing a successful long-term relationship.

It is important to be cognizant of confirmation bias when determining if the person you are dating exclusively or in a relationship with is "The One". Confirmation bias is the human tendency to interpret new evidence as confirmation of existing personal beliefs or theories. That can unduly influence a person's assessment of "The One".

For example, a person may have been told by a prophet or a fetish priest that they will marry a doctor or a light-skinned woman; that person then becomes consumed with chasing that prophecy. He may even become obsessed with getting to meet specific groups of people hoping to enhance the likelihood of that prophecy being fulfilled.

Confirmation bias could also happen when a woman who is particularly focused on financial security become fixated on the type of car a man drives or what kinds of material possessions the man appears to have. Such a woman could ignore the fact that the man is rude and disrespectful to her or that the man does not operate with wisdom.

Being "The One" is about creating balance - the two of you should be able to maintain a harmonious balance. Not only should the other person be "The One" for you but you should also be "The One" for that person.

If you are "The One" for each other, your paths will merge effortlessly. You will not need to rely on another person to tell you when you have found "The One". You will know that for yourself.

Do I Tell Them If They Are "The One"?

Must I let the person I'm in a relationship with know that I think they are "The One"? How often should I say that? Will I be making myself too vulnerable by making such a declaration? Would it change the dynamics of our relationship if I tell my partner they are "The One" but my partner does not reciprocate by telling me I am "The One"? Does my boyfriend or girlfriend have to be "The One" in order for the relationship to continue?

The are some of the questions that may swirl in the minds of people in relationships.

When you are confident that your partner is "The One", sharing that information and citing specific reasons can help your partner understand that you have solid reasons for choosing them. Letting your boyfriend or girlfriend know that he or she is "The One" and offering reasons to support your claim, can inspire confidence in the relationship.

Acknowledging key attributes about your partner communicates to them the things that are important to you. Failing to share with your partner how you feel about them leaves room for them to guess how you feel about them. Instead, pointing out specific reasons why you feel the way you do about them, especially when you are confident that they are "The One", is helpful feedback that reinforces good behaviour. If you don't subscribe to the concept of labels, you can still provide such feedback without labelling your partner as "The One". Once in a while, tell your partner why you chose to be with them.

Beware of the temptation to "sweet talk" your partner with empty statements that have no truth in them. Do not tell your partner they are "The One" if you don't mean those words. That move could backfire. Also, the fact that your partner tells you that you are "The One" for them does not imply you should automatically echo the same.

Before proclaiming to your partner that they are "The One", it will be wise to know whether that person is mature and well-intentioned enough that they will not abuse the "recognition". Some people become complacent when they know they have been designated as "The One". Others develop a false sense of indispensability and believe that their partner cannot exist without them.

In the early stages of a relationship, some people may choose to keep such information close to their vest, even if they know from the start that they are dating "The One". Of course, it is important to pace yourself. Sharing too much information too soon could create an information overload. Know your partner well and share such information at the right time. Keep in mind that while oversharing can create unintended consequences, not sharing enough can starve the relationship.

In a highlife song by Daasebre Gyamena, he says, *"Obi se ɔdɔ wo a ma ɔnkyerɛ mu"*, which translates into "If someone says they love you, let them explain". In other words, it is reasonable to ask your partner why he or she believes you are "The One". Such a question can be a healthy conversation starter for the couple to learn more about what they appreciate in each other. The examples a partner provides to support their statements could further buttress the point.

While it is helpful to let your partner know if they are "The One", it is also important to remember that the two of you may get to that state of confidence at different times. The fact that you are confident that your partner is "The One" doesn't necessarily mean your partner feels the same way about you. Demanding that pronouncement from your partner may put an undue pressure on them. If you feel inspired to share how you feel, share without expecting your partner to automatically do the same.

Kwame is the more verbally expressive one in our relationship. In addition to his actions, he is also generous with words by reminding me of why he chose me as "The One". He started doing that early in our relationship and continues to do so. More than the words he says, his genuineness and the real examples he offers make me believe that he is not just 'sweet talking' me. He rarely misses an opportunity to reinforce his confidence in me as his wife and life partner. On my part, I use generous actions rather than elaborate words to convey to him that he is "The One". Since repetition is always good for emphasis, I do that as often as I can.

When getting into a relationship, the notion of "The One" can get in the way of an objective assessment of the prospective partner. Focusing too much on the concept of "The One" could cause you to miss important signals.

There is often a period of pretence when two people begin to date. Whether consciously or unconsciously, each person is usually on their best behaviour, acts carefully, and is tolerant of the other person. It is not entirely pretence. It is usually because neither is has invested much in the relationship. They are, therefore, not very particular about a lot of things With time, the scales fall off from your eyes and each person reveals their true self. Also, with time, the two people will learn more about each other, determine their feelings about each other, and discover how well their values align.

Instead of focusing on whether or not they are "The One", **focus on developing yourself** into a healthy human being (emotionally, physically, intellectually and spiritually). Start with yourself. Decide what values are important to you and make a list. Determine if the person you are considering for a long-term relationship aligns with enough of your core values. That person may be "The One" from the start or that person may become "The One" with time.

There is such a thing as "The One" or "better half" or "soul mate" but there is not only one individual in the world destined to be your spouse. When you find that special one, it does not mean your partner will be a perfect human being.

You will be setting yourself up for disappointment if you approach a relationship expecting perfection. Finding "The One" does not mean the relationship will be perfect; it means the two people can work well together: discuss any issue and still remain considerate of each other's feelings.

At the end of the day, being in a romantic relationship with someone you feel positively about, who also feels positively about you, and who is aligned with your core values can make the relationship feel balanced. It is highly unlikely that "The One" will be delivered to you packaged with everything you dream of in your ideal partner.

Regardless of who you get into a relationship with or marry, it will take a deliberate effort from **both parties** to get to know each other and treat each other with care and respect for your partner to be "The One".

· 7 ·

WHY ARE YOU GETTING MARRIED?

When word got around that I was married, a GBC TV crew came over to interview Annica and me for one of their programmes. The interviewer, a middle-aged woman, asked us why we got married. I responded that we were already best friends who couldn't have enough of each other; making the marriage official was only a ceremonial step.

The woman immediately said "No, that is not the reason", and then asked her question again. I repeated my answer, and then she shook her head in disagreement. I asked her what she thought was our reason for getting married. She responded, "You're getting married because of children. There must be continuity in the world; that's why you're getting married".

I explained to her that while we were expecting our marriage to be blessed with children, children were not the reason we were getting married. If Annica was unable to bear children or if it turned out that I was infertile, our marriage would still continue because our reason for getting married was beyond having children. She remained unconvinced and tried eagerly to get us to say that our reason for getting married was "because of children". We did not say that. When the interview was aired, they reported that Annica and I said we got married because we were best friends, which was true.

Obviously, if I got married to this GBC TV woman's daughter and didn't clarify with her daughter why we were getting married, I may have found out later that we had gotten married for very different reasons. That could create problems for the marriage.

People get married for various reasons. In the 2019 Family Life Survey of Ghanaians with at least a secondary school education, the respondents indicated the top reason for which people get married as follows:

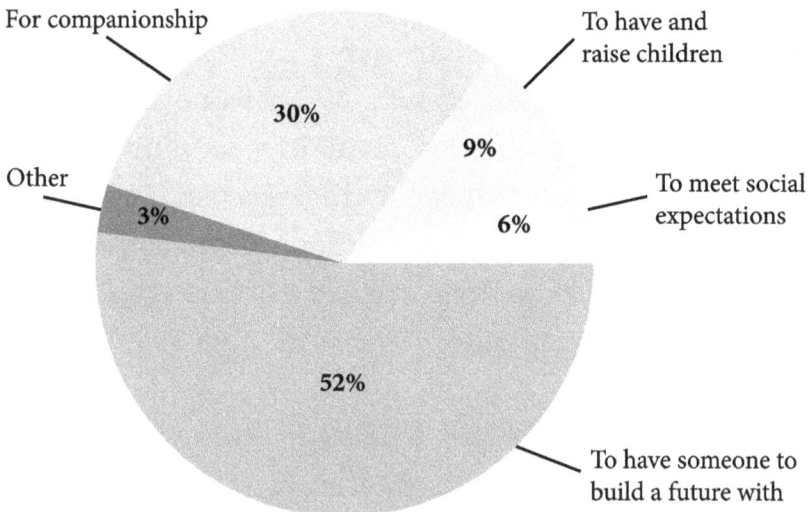

For companionship — 30%
To have and raise children — 9%
To meet social expectations — 6%
To have someone to build a future with — 52%
Other — 3%

Source: Spotlight Creative Group

Some people get married because they may have determined marriage to be the next level for their relationship. Other people get married because they would like to raise children, and believe that marriage would provide the most stable environment for that. Some also marry because they have come of age and are motivated to meet social expectations. Others get married because they would like to be sexually active on a regular basis, and consider marriage to be the appropriate situation for that. Some do it for companionship whereas others do it for economic benefit.

Sometimes, people get married because their sexual relations lead to a pregnancy and the girl's family insists that the two of them marry. In other situations, people get married in response to an ultimatum, where the other partner threatens to leave the relationship if the couple do not get married within a specified timeframe. Others are compelled to marry due to family pressure, peer pressure, and pressure from religious leaders. Some people get married for economic reasons. Others too get married simply because they are in love.

Whatever a person's reason for getting married, it is important for that person to be honest with self. False pretences about your reasons for wanting to get married could come back to bite you eventually.

It is worth pointing out that while love could influence a person's decision to get married, love by itself is often not enough of a reason for getting married. If someone tells you they are getting married because of love, it is possible that the person is only being romantic or has not really thought about why they are getting married. In an extended conversation with that person, you are likely to find out that they have other reasons.

Some of the reasons above seem more ideal than others but a marriage's success or failure will depend largely on the two people involved. Said differently, a marriage entered into for any reason could become a successful one if the two people involved are **committed to the same objectives and are devoted to each other**.

By the way, we recognize that long-term relationships take many forms, and some people may choose to be in unique or unconventional relationships that meet their needs. Since most of the people we know have expressed their preference for monogamous, uncomplicated long-term relationships founded on the idea of love, the primary audience for this book is people who prefer monogamous, uncomplicated, long-term relationships.

If you are in an unconventional relationship, you may disagree with some of the principles we convey here. That disagreement notwithstanding, you are welcome to take any ideas you deem beneficial.

Getting into a relationship can be likened to deciding to travel abroad. When deciding to travel abroad, a person has to decide on **why** and **what they want to accomplish** with that travel. That decision would then be followed by choosing a destination country, and then with working out the necessary logistics for the travel. If the purpose of the travel is for sightseeing, for example, the things that person will take into consideration will differ significantly from another person whose purpose is to travel as an economic migrant.

Likewise, a person deciding to get into a relationship usually does so with a destination in mind. That is why a partner would ask the other, "Where are we going with this relationship?" If the future of the relationship were unclear. Unless the two people have clearly established that they do not have any long-term plans for the relationship, most people get into relationships with the goal of ultimately getting married. By clarifying the purpose of the relationship, the couple can strengthen their connection and prevent unmet expectations.

Annica started her MBA at KNUST while we were dating. She had to pay GHC25,000 to cover the cost of the programme, which was a lot of money at the time. Her father found out that I had paid the money and invited me for a meeting. In his uniquely matter-of-fact style, he asked me if I knew that it was a risky investment for me to pay for the education of a girl to whom I was not married. I confidently responded with a yes. He continued, with the disclaimer that, "I do not want you to complain to me in future if your expectations of my daughter are not met".

Even though making such a significant investment in Annica's education was with the long-term vision of the two of us spending our lives together, I was not oblivious to the fact that she could decide to quit our relationship and get married to someone else. We had talked about getting married earlier in our relationship and had established that we would marry eventually. We were in a place of peace about our relationship and had developed a remarkable trust in each other. Her father's caution was reasonable, and I was not surprised he said what he said, because most parents would act in like manner. Knowing what I knew about how far we had grown in our relationship, making such a significant investment in Annica was worth the risk.

We knew that well-meaning third parties may have their opinions about sacrifices we chose to make for each other. We were, however, confident that as long as our intentions were transparent to each other, our sacrifices for each other would serve us well in the long run.

In the process of moving from dating to being in a relationship, we established clarity about our intentions for being together. During our numerous conversations, we asked what each other's goals were for life and for the relationship. The answers eliminated ambiguity about the purpose of our relationship. The clarity enabled us to go on knowing that investing in the relationship was worthwhile. Needless to say, we eventually married each other.

Marriage has legal, social and cultural implications that make it necessary for each person to clearly answer the question of why they are getting married. Most people have strong personal reasons for wanting to get married. Just as it is important to clarify the purpose of a relationship when getting into one, it is even more important to establish the purpose of a marriage since the stakes are higher in marriage. Two people's lives converge when they are in a relationship but their lives merge in a more significant manner when they get married.

It is absolutely necessary for the two people considering marriage to have a conversation about why each of them wants to get married. "Why do you want to get married to me?" is a fair question to ask of each other. Each person should be able to give reasons, and the couple should discuss their reasons. That conversation will likely be one of the most rewarding they will ever have about their relationship.

It is possible for two people to get married for different reasons. However, having a shared purpose gives the couple a compelling reason to commit to the long-term success of the marriage. Even for people who are not madly in love with each other, having a shared purpose could yield a certain degree of marital success. On the contrary, the absence of a common purpose could become the bane of their existence.

Sometimes, people settle for whoever is available regardless of their own misgivings about that person. Settling (or settling for less) in a relationship is a situation where a person agrees to marry someone that they sincerely know is a less-than-ideal partner. The person may even acknowledge the facts that do not favour a successful marriage, but they may proceed anyway because they deem that person the only option available. For example, a person marrying a serial cheater may be settling for less than their ideal. A person planning to marry a rich man's daughter who belittles him in private and in public is settling for less than his ideal.

When a person settles for less and tries to retrofit it with love (or a common purpose), there will most likely be challenges. The pain and misery some people experience in relationships and marriages are as a result of them settling for less.

To each their own, and people are free to choose relationships that they believe meet their needs. However, taking a shortcut into wealth by marrying a person who humiliates you or succumbing to the fear that you are getting old and should marry whoever is available may come at the expense of your mental health. The notion of *"Fa no saa"*, which suggests that a person should take whatever is available, often leads people into settling for less. While it is necessary to be realistic about your options, it is also necessary to honestly assess your reasons for getting married.

Admittedly, a situation that I may consider as settling for less may be enough for another person to develop into a successful relationship. As long as that person has a sense of peace about who they are marrying, even though the prospective partner may not meet all the "requirements" of an ideal spouse, no one should stand in their way. At the end of the day, a realistic person who commits fully to a relationship with another person who is also fully committed to the relationship will be better off even if it appears to the rest of us that one or both people are settling for less.

Regardless of the reasons for which two people are getting married, what matters most is their confidence in their commitment to a shared purpose and their devotion to each other.

It is absolutely important that each person in the relationship knows why the other person wants to get married to them. The reasons provided for marriage need to be clearly communicated to each other whether as answers to direct questions, or gleaned from observations and attentive listening.

The decision to marry someone is a deliberate one that is accompanied with reasons. If you have not clearly heard your partner's reason for wanting to be married to you, please hold off any elaborate proposal plans. If your partner has not clearly told you why they want to be married to you, you may be waiting in vain if you are waiting for a marriage proposal. The pre-proposal conversation is absolutely necessary.

In the name of romance, some men spend too much time planning a memorable way to ask a woman to marry them, and skip the part about finding out why the woman wants to marry them. In many such instances, both the man and the woman skip the conversation about why they want to get married to each other. There have been situations where men staged elaborate public marriage proposals that were met with blank stares from the women to whom they were intending to get married.

The conversation as to whether the two people would want to get married to each other should have been had thoroughly and conclusively in private before they staged the public display of affection. Then the ceremonial question to pop would be, "Will you wear this ring to honour the conversation we had about getting married to each other?"

Out of fear of irritating their partners, some people may shy away from the conversation. Such an unhealthy fear is a signal of an imbalance in the relationship. It is such fear that could lead a person to think their partner is doing them a favour by marrying them. If you are getting married to someone you fear will change their mind because you asked why they want to get married to you, then that's a red flag right there.

Everything done in fear suffers; everything done in love blossoms. When done in love, asking your partner for their reasons for wanting to get married to you is a very good thing. A conversation with your spouse-to-be about why you are getting married to each other must be a healthy, mature conversation with no strings attached.

Your partner's reason for wanting to get married to you may not be as romantic as "because I cannot see myself with anyone else" or "because we are meant to be together for ever and ever"; it may be a pragmatic reason like "because we have been together for a long time and I want us to take things to the next level", or "we are growing older and I don't want us to remain boyfriend/girlfriend forever". While the romantic reasons may make you feel warm on the inside, the pragmatic reasons may be more grounded in reality.

In most cases, the reasons for getting married are practical and the couple should focus on those. Even in situations where one partner was expecting a romantic reason, it is important for them to welcome their partner's practical reasons.

It is worth noting that the conversation about why you want to get married to each other is not always an easy one. One partner may not be as eloquent in expressing their thoughts; one partner may be anxious that their reasons may not meet their partner's expectation. Regardless of the discomfort, the conversation cannot be ignored.

The most important thing to keep in mind is that the conversation is an exercise to help you align your purpose for getting married. It is not a therapy session; neither is it a means to force a marriage commitment out of your partner. Therefore, ask the question without a defined expectation. Allow yourself to be presented with the truth.

Allow your partner to be as honest as possible. Don't judge their responses even if the reasons seem like they are not substantial enough. Respectfully accept those reasons as a start, and carry on with the conversation. Maintain a well-composed demeanour even when their reasons surprise or irritate you. Remember that it is a conversation and not an interrogation.

It is possible that one or both partners may have never thought of the question, let alone have a good answer to why they want to get married. Thankfully, this is not a pass/fail test but rather a conversation starter. It will be perfectly fine if one or both partners express a need for some time to think about the question. The conversation will be more beneficial should each partner have ample time to think of their reasons. Give yourselves ample time.

While you think of your reasons, also assess your readiness for making this life-long commitment. Some of the questions you could ask as you self-assess your readiness for marriage include the following:

1. Am I willing and capable of making a commitment to only one person?
2. Can I make a life-long commitment to the person I am considering for marriage?

3. Am I making my marriage decision based on sexual feelings or clouded judgement?
4. How can I contribute to the success of the marriage?
5. How forgiving or selfless can I be with the person I am considering for marriage?
6. Do I have the maturity needed to support my partner during difficult times?
7. Do I really understand my partner's needs, and am I willing to meet them?
8. Am I mercurial or emotionally unpredictable, and am I willing to disclose that information to my partner?
9. Am I attached to a certain ideal that is pushing me to make a decision without proper reasoning?
10. Am I shrewdly considering my next step in this relationship?

Commitment requires a long-term outlook. Jesus once asked his disciples, "For which of you, desiring to build a tower, does not first sit down and count the cost, whether he has enough to complete it?" Jesus' question was not about marriage, but it applies to all types of commitments. The long-term nature of a marriage commitment makes it imperative that the couple count the cost before making the leap. The marriage commitment is a deep one and the couple must assess the implications diligently before they dive in.

Getting married before you clearly know each other's reasons for getting married could be likened to hopping on a flight without checking its intended destination. You may be moving but you may not be headed to where you think you are going. Getting off that flight in mid-air may be impossible. You may have to wait until the plane lands and then get on another flight whenever one is available. The waste of time and money for getting on the wrong flight is the reason you should know where the plane is headed before getting on board.

Think of marriage as a one-way ticket to a destination of no return. Rather than imagining yourself as a vacationer having fleeting fun, think of yourself as a permanent resident who will enjoy the benefits and live through the benefits of this.

Your reason for getting married should be a well-thought-out one and not just an uncomfortable compromise. When you believe you have found the one with whom you wish to spend the rest of your life, it is prudent for to ask them **why** they want to enter the marriage. Ask them "Why are you getting married?" and listen to their answer with an open mind. When you both answer that question honestly, you will know whether to proceed or wait.

The most important reason for doing anything is knowing why you are doing that thing. Your **why** will serve as a guiding compass for your journey.

· 8 ·

WHEN ARE YOU GETTING MARRIED?

For various reasons, different people may marry at different times. Some may marry earlier in life; some may marry later in life; others may marry somewhere in between; and others may not marry at all. Unless you are in a relationship with, and planning to get married to the person, please don't ask a single, unmarried person when he or she is getting married. On the contrary, two people in a relationship should at some point ask each other when they would like to get married.

The question of when a person would like to get married is appropriate within the context of a relationship. Everyone else should hesitate to ask that question of an unmarried person.

You may have heard the joke about a single lady in her thirties who always got asked by her three aunties whenever they met at a wedding, "When are you getting married?" Each time, the lady smiled politely and pretended not to be bothered by the constant pestering. At a family member's funeral at a later time, the single lady walked up to the older ladies and asked them, "When are you dying?" Hopefully, the older ladies got a taste of their own medicine from the question the single lady asked them.

Asking "When are you getting married?" of someone, especially if that person is single and has not announced their need to get married, is a very inconsiderate question. The inappropriateness of the question displays the ignorance of the person asking. It is, however, appropriate to ask a person when they are getting married if that person has informed you that they are getting married, and then you ask "When?" as a follow-up question.

Usually, the question of when a person is getting married means different things to men and women. To a man, that question comes across as a compliment, albeit a misguided one. That question may be asked of a man to imply that he is of age, respected and responsible enough to take on a wife and grow a family of his own. Nobody asks such a question of a man who is considered immature and irresponsible (even though such a question could be posed sarcastically as a jab at a person who acts irresponsibly).

To a woman, that same question comes across in a derogatory or insulting manner. That question asked of a woman may imply that there is something deficient about her for which reason no man has found her worthy enough to take her as his wife. That question may be especially uncomfortable for a successful woman when, in a moment of professional or other personal accomplishment, somebody finds the need to remind her that she needs to get married.

No matter your best intentions, there is not much good that can come out of such an enquiry, especially when delivered with little or no empathy.

Understandably, you may be well-intentioned in wanting to know if a close friend or relative of yours is planning on getting married someday. Such an enquiry should be made tactfully and with wisdom if you feel so strongly about asking such a delicate question, especially of a woman. A key reason being that in most societies, especially in the Ghanaian society, a woman does not decide by herself when she is getting married.

If she asks you to help her find a husband, of course, you can ask when she would like to get married. Also, if someone has expressed interest in an unmarried adult with whom you have a close relationship, and you genuinely want to make an introduction, you can respectfully inform them of that interest – without asking the question of when they are getting married.

Due to reasons such as professional development goals, age, financial stability, levels of maturity, religious beliefs, and personal preferences, the couple may be ready to get married at different times. That is why it is necessary for the partners to have that conversation.

Professional development goals for an individual could include learning a trade, obtaining an advanced degree, pursuing a licence or certification in a professional field, establishing a business, or growing their career. Such goals require focus and dedication. For some people, the focus and dedication they devote to the pursuit of their professional development goals leave little room for getting married and attending to the needs of the marriage. Therefore, such people may defer their marriage decision until after they have accomplished their goals.

Age plays an important role for many when deciding to get married. Both the perception and the reality of when most people would like to get married was reflected in responses provided in the 2019 Family Life Survey of Ghanaians with at least a secondary school education. The responses to the questions of ideal age ranges for men and women to get married is provided in the charts below:

What is the ideal age range for a woman to get married?

What is the ideal age range for a man to get married?

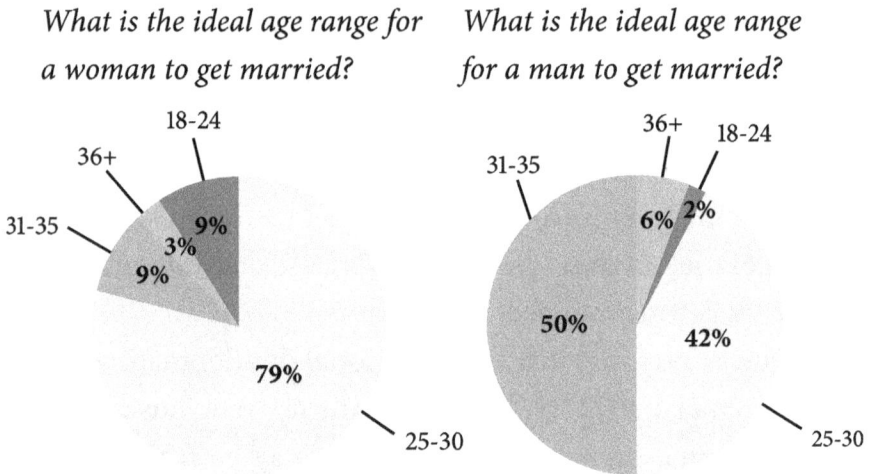

Source: Spotlight Creative Group

From the survey responses, it appears that for a young couple starting a relationship when each of them is 25 years old, the woman may want to get married within a year of the relationship starting, whereas the man may be thinking about getting married five years later. It also appears the marriage timeline for a man or woman over the age of 35 may have more urgency to it than that of someone less than the age of 30.

The reasons for which age is an important factor in the timing of marriage includes child-bearing considerations for women, and financial stability for men. For women who are planning on having children, many intend on doing so after they are married, which ties their marriage timing to their child-bearing goals. Typically, financial stability is a secondary factor for most women when they consider when they would like to get married. Child-bearing tends to rank higher.

The reverse is true for men. For most men, financial stability ranks higher than child-bearing when considering their timeline for getting married. Even for men who would like to get married earlier in life, the reality of their financial situation may compel them to postpone getting married until later in life.

Typically, a man is expected to be the primary financial provider for his household. That expectation includes owning or renting a residence and having an income that could take care of a household that includes a wife and children. For many young men, it may take until their late twenties to early thirties, at the earliest, to achieve such stability. For some young men, additional financial obligations such as taking care of younger siblings or other family responsibilities can further complicate and delay their readiness for marriage.

When maturity is factored into a person's desire to settle down, age and gender tend to play a role as well. Maturity is your emotional and intellectual capacity to relate reasonably with people and events. This does not necessarily come with age. Attaining a certain age happens simply because time passes; no effort is required from you since you only have to remain alive. Maturity, on the other hand, comes about as you develop self-awareness, practice personal responsibility, and become competent at managing relationships with others.

Through various personal development activities, such as reading books, seeking the counsel of insightful and experienced individuals, and learning from the examples of others, a person matures over time. With their inclination towards being nurturers, most women grow up tending to the needs of others and assuming more responsibilities than their male counterparts. As a result, a growing woman tends to mature at a faster pace than a man of the same age.

Maturity often shows up in the person's ability to effectively manage their emotions and seek their partner's best interests. Other ways maturity is displayed include the acceptance of personal responsibility, honouring one's commitments, displaying integrity, and behaving appropriately in different settings. If two people in a relationship differ in their levels of maturity, their timetables for getting married are likely to differ significantly. Marriage might be embraced warmly by one whereas it could seem like an overwhelming commitment to the other.

Religious beliefs and personal moral values may also influence a person's timetable for marriage. Most religions teach their followers to observe a code of conduct that often includes abstinence from sex and not living together with a boyfriend or girlfriend. For a person who adheres strictly to their religion's code of conduct, they are likely to have a sense of urgency about getting married. On the other hand, a person who does not adhere to religious rules prohibiting pre-marital sex or cohabitation may be in less of a hurry to get married.

Personal preference plays an equally important role in when a person may choose to get married. A person might prefer to get married early in life simply because they like the idea of being married, and will jump at the first opportunity to do so. Another person might prefer to wait until later in life to get married simply because they may be very comfortable with the flexibility that comes with being single.

Each of the reasons above introduces a variable into a couple's timing for when each of them may want to get married. That is why the two people need to ask each other when they would like to get married, have conversations about the timing, and then sync up their timetables. In a case where they are working with different timetables, the couple may have to negotiate an adjustment of their respective schedules and find ways to address related issues.

How long the couple has been together is an important factor in two people deciding when to get married. Depending on how much time and effort the two people have invested in getting to know each other, the chronological timeframe for getting married will vary from that of another couple. While less than twelve months might be enough time for one couple to decide they are aligned enough to get married, another couple may need two years of being in a relationship before coming to that alignment. The chronological length of time is important, but the quality of the time spent together is more important. It is the knowledge and understanding they develop about each other that matters, not the length of time they have been together.

Annica and I were in a relationship for four years before getting married. We decided early in our relationship that we would get married and we had no doubts about getting married to each other. We did not set a timeframe for when we would get married. We carried on with our lives and were aligned for most of those four years in the belief that getting married was only a formality to make our relationship official.

It is important to **know each other well enough** and be confident that the person you are getting married to is honest and truly who they say they are. Knowing each other well will also help you know if your partner is mature enough to accommodate your ambitions and flaws, and reasonable enough to weather the storms of life with you.

Human beings are complicated creatures, and they can be difficult to figure out fully. Also, people are dynamic and are constantly changing, which could lead to subtle or drastic changes over time. While each partner would like to know the other thoroughly, it is impossible to do so even after living with them for years. Therefore, do your best to know the person well enough to be at peace with your decision to get married to them. When you have done your due diligence in earnest, proceed in good faith and then learn more as you go.

Each partner in a relationship is likely to have their individual goals. Some individual goals may translate naturally into shared goals. Other shared goals may have to be developed as part of the conversations and process of planning your lives together.

For instance, an individual goal of becoming a mother by a certain age could naturally evolve into a shared goal if both plan on having children in the marriage. By the same token, the timing of that goal may need to be adjusted in order for it to become a shared goal if one party plans on having children soon after marriage and the other plans on having them later. Individual goals are important. When planning on getting married, shared goals are more important.

It is very possible for one party to be ready to get married at a time when the other party may genuinely not be ready. For example, the woman may be genuinely concerned about running out of time on her "biological clock" and may want to get married as quickly as possible whereas the man may have started a time-consuming business and he may not have enough time to devote to a marriage. In another example, the woman may be focused on growing her career and may not be interested in starting a family whereas the man may be eager to start one.

What is such a couple to do since one is ready to get married but the other is not?

Talk about it.

Have honest, considerate and respectful conversations about your readiness and your reasons. Such conversations will allow each person to clearly lay out their reasons or concerns. It will also allow each partner to determine whether there is a middle ground for a compromise.

In situations where the difference in readiness is vast and both partners are unwilling to explore a reasonable compromise, both parties may be better off moving on and finding other people to marry.

As the couple invests time and effort into developing themselves and sharing meaningful conversations, each person will pick up signals about the other person's marriage readiness. If your timetables are in sync, smile and then carry on. If each of you is working to a very different timetable, further conversations are necessary to create clarity.

Either person has to have an opportunity to determine their right time to get married just as their partner deserves to know when that right time would be. That way, the two of them could march to the same beat and keep to the same schedule.

· 9 ·

SEX
BEFORE
MARRIAGE

Aperson's upbringing, religion, personal values, personal experiences, culture, tradition, and outlook on life inform their perspective on the topic of sex, specifically sexual intercourse. Many people are genuinely interested in knowing the right way to handle their sexual desires and how to conduct themselves appropriately in the context of a relationship. When two people share a physical attraction, that physical attraction may translate into a sexual attraction, which may leave them with a dilemma if both of them don't share the same views about sex before marriage.

Sex before marriage covers a broad range of sexual relations but we will focus our discussion on sexual relations between people in long-term committed relationships. While casual sex can be easily dismissed as irresponsible, the same cannot be said about consensual sex between unmarried partners.

Kwame and I have different opinions on the subject of whether sex within a serious non-marriage relationship is advisable. Hopefully, our respective opinions will help bring clarity to people who may be conflicted about how to handle this delicate subject.

My views on sex have been heavily influenced by teachings from the Bible. I learned that the appropriate place for sex is within a marriage. I learned that sex is a sacred act between a husband and a wife for the purpose of pleasing each other and for procreation. As I came into my own as a young adult, I made a vow to myself that the only man that would see my nakedness would be my husband. Therefore, my decision to not have sex before marriage was not only based on the Bible's teachings but also based on a very practical reason.

I shuddered at the thought of running into a man who had seen my nakedness but wasn't married to me. Even if that man was going to be respectful and mature about it, I couldn't bring myself to let a guy who had not promised to be my life partner engage with me in such an intimate manner. Therefore, I chose abstinence and remained resolute about my decision to abstain from sex until I was absolutely sure.

Sex is a good thing. It was created by God for a worthy purpose. The Bible, however, speaks against sex between unmarried people, which is also known as fornication. The Apostle Paul stated in 1 Corinthians 6:9-10 that, "Know ye not that the unrighteous shall not inherit God's Kingdom?

Be not deceived: neither **fornicators**, nor idolaters, nor adulterers… shall inherit God's Kingdom".

The Bible also denounces "sexual immorality" in more than 20 instances in the New Testament. Jesus mentioned sexual immorality when he talked about the activities that defile a person or makes them dirty in the sight of God.

For those who believe in the Bible as God's instructions to human beings on how to live a life that honours Him, the scriptures make it clear that fornication does not fit within the Christian code of conduct. Many other religions, including Islam, Judaism and African Traditional Religion frown upon sex before marriage for good reason.

From a very young age, I internalised 1 Corinthians 6:18, which says: "Flee from sexual immorality! Every other sin that a man may commit is outside his body, but whoever practices sexual immorality is sinning against his own body". From further study of that Bible verse, I came to understand how a sexual sin would go against my own body. I would lose my dignity, possibly get pregnant or catch a sexually transmitted disease (STD) and suffer the consequence of that; or a boy may spread information about having sex with me and bring me embarrassment. Therefore, I abstained from sex not only because I thought God would be upset with me but also because I had realised the practical truth in Apostle Paul's statement. I abstained for my own good.

When I met Kwame, I clearly communicated my views on sex before marriage. He told me that he was celibate and, therefore, he did not have a problem with us not having sex. We continued dating for months and we respectfully maintained boundaries that limited our physical contact to brief hugs and occasionally holding each other's hands. I found him very attractive but that was not enough of a reason for me to have sex with him.

About a year into our relationship, his celibacy pledge had worn off, and he directly and indirectly started bringing up the subject of when we were going to have sex. After more than a year of dating, he had proven himself to be a decent young man and had been very understanding of my preference to wait until I was sure about having sex. The subject kept coming up and we respectfully discussed how each other felt. Our passion towards each other became more intense, our hugs longer and our touches more electrifying. In the months that followed, we could not get our hands off each other.

One of the key reasons for which the Bible speaks against pre-marital sex is that once you have sex with a person you are evaluating for a long-term relationship, the sexual act corrupts your wisdom from judging the person rightly. Your emotions become intertwined with your ability to reason logically, and your decisions become emotions-based instead of logic-based. For a spiritually-inclined person, sexual immorality could render them spiritually numb.

Sex before marriage could also lead an individual to confuse lust for love, and create a sense of attachment to someone they are not really interested in. Without sex, a person is likely to make a clearer judgement call if the relationship needs to end. Furthermore, each person can move on without sexual regrets.

As Christians, we believe in praying for forgiveness. For that reason, some people have argued that even if sex before marriage is a sin, they can pray to God and ask for forgiveness afterward. It is undeniable that God forgives anyone who genuinely repents and turns away from their sin in a large way. God's forgiveness, however, does not make you immune to the consequences of your actions.

Additionally, Romans 6:1 offers wise counsel saying, "What then shall we say? Shall we continue in sin so that grace may abound?" That verse is a word to the wise, and I am sure it is enough for those who have ears and want to listen.

Women tend to be impacted more by unintended consequences from sex before marriage. If there is an unplanned pregnancy, it is the woman who has to carry the pregnancy and then nurture the child while the man usually carries on with his life. Also, women tend to be viewed with disdain if a man they had pre-marital sex with does not marry them.

The Ghanaian society is generally not harsh towards a man who has had multiple sexual partners. On the contrary, a woman who has had the same number of past sexual partners as her male counterpart is often viewed with disapproving eyes by the same society. For these and other reasons, it behoves us women to be extra vigilant about avoiding sex before marriage.

There are moral as well as practical reasons to avoid sex before marriage. My practical reasons are as follows:

10 Practical Reasons a Couple Should Avoid Sex Before Marriage

1. Sex before marriage clouds their judgement on important decisions, especially when there are red flags in the relationship that need attention
2. Waiting until marriage preserves the sacredness of sex between the couple
3. Not giving in to their desires teaches the couple self-control, which also helps them avoid the urge to cheat with others
4. Avoiding sex saves either party from "feeling used" should the other call it quits
5. An unplanned pregnancy and/or STD, which can cripple an otherwise healthy relationship, will not be an issue
6. Avoiding sex helps them focus on building the emotional, psychological and spiritual aspects of the relationship
7. Should a break-up become necessary, soul-tie consequences will most likely be avoided
8. Neither party would have to live with sexual guilt or unnecessary awkwardness
9. Avoiding sex before marriage keeps the couple focused on their marriage plans
10. The discipline and self-control to avoid sex before marriage builds trust for when they are married

The debate about whether a couple should engage in sex before they marry has been around for years and will likely continue for more years to come. After considering the reasons to abstain, each individual will have to make a personal judgement call that they can live with.

Annica believes that sex before marriage is wrong, and I respectfully disagree. I recognise that there could be unintended consequences from having sex before marriage, but I don't see anything wrong with the idea of engaging in sexual relations with a serious boyfriend or girlfriend before the two people get married.

In fact, I think it is a good thing and I support it. Speaking of sex before marriage, let me emphasise that I am not talking about all sex before marriage. I am talking specifically about wholesome, physical and romantic interactions in a serious relationship where the two people know each other well and they are both invested in the relationship.

Since I was celibate at the time Annica and I started dating, having sex with her was not a priority for me. I was fascinated by her intelligence and her gracefulness. Being in her company and having conversations with her was satisfying enough for me. I found her very attractive, but that physical attraction did not immediately translate into sexual desire.

With girls from past relationships, sex came earlier in the relationship. With Annica, it was different, starting with how she clearly articulated her reasons for wanting to defer sex until we were married. A part of me was very comfortable with waiting until marriage because I was crazy about her and was willing to do anything to make her happy. The other part of me was hoping that she would eventually change her mind about waiting until marriage to have sex.

My reason for wanting to have sex with Annica before we got married was not only because of my sexual attraction towards her. I wanted to avoid any surprises after we got married. Making a life-long commitment such as a marriage could be likened to buying a very expensive car. It is very reasonable to want to test-drive the car before buying it. Understandably, the car dealer also reserves the right to demand evidence of my ability to afford the car before allowing me to test-drive the car. As long as the car dealer and I agree that I have what it takes to buy the car, it is only fair that I get to test-drive the car. Likewise, a couple who have demonstrated a high degree of commitment to each other should be able to experience each other sexually.

Too many people have reported getting into marriages only to find out disappointing sexual realities about their partners. A wife finding out, for example, that the size of her husband's penis significantly exceeds or does not meet her expectation could create a major challenge for the marriage. However, knowing such information before getting married would have given the person an opportunity to decide whether to go ahead and get married or not.

Finding out such information after getting married may leave the disappointed partner feeling trapped for life or filing for divorce. I know of many examples of sex-related surprises that people have reported after getting married without having sex prior to their marriage. Many of those reports are too graphic to print or discuss here, and they are about both men and women.

Sex before marriage provides the couple with an opportunity to form a strong connection. When two people have sex willingly and passionately, they release into their blood stream a chemical called oxytocin. While this chemical is released during other intimate gestures like prolonged hugging, holding hands, or kissing, it is released in much larger quantities during sex.

Oxytocin helps increase feelings of trust and produces feelings of love between the couple. It is the oxytocin that makes a couple want to cuddle and connect after sex. For a couple in a serious relationship, the connection they form as a result of sex could create an intimacy that keeps them together.

I know that sex before marriage can create problems like unwanted pregnancy and heartbreak for immature people who are not in stable, committed relationships. I also know that many people, even those who believe that sex before marriage is wrong, are having sex before marriage, and are doing so irresponsibly. Rather than ignoring the reality that people will have sex before marriage, because that is the natural order, families and community leaders should highlight the possible consequences and trust people to make decisions that are best for them.

Below are my ten practical reasons for why a couple should have sex before marriage:

10 Practical Reasons a Couple Should Have Sex Before They Marry

1. Prevents sexual surprises after the marriage
2. Helps the couple not to rush into marriage

3. Makes the couple aware of each other's sexual preferences
4. The decision to marry will not be motivated by the absence of sex
5. Provides physical, emotional and psychological relief and satisfaction
6. Prevents the hypocrisy that comes from engaging in other forms of sexual immorality such as heavy petting and masturbation
7. Strengthens the couple's emotional connection
8. Helps to avoid cheating with other people
9. Enables the couple to get comfortable with their sexual desires
10. Promotes cohabitation, which allows the couple to experience each other in a quasi-marriage situation

Much of the prohibition against sex come from society's desire to maintain order by making everyone conform to a prescribed set of rules. History has shown that rules are often made by the people in charge for the purpose of controlling the behaviours of the masses. What most rules don't take into account is an individual's ability to make decisions for themself, and take personal responsibility.

Some people have not made good decisions or taken personal responsibility when it comes to how they have conducted themselves in relation to sex before marriage. However, the irresponsible actions of some people should not bar everyone else from having the opportunity to make personal choices. Therefore, in a relationship, the couple should thoughtfully discuss the topic and decide for themselves whether or not they want to engage in sex before they are married.

As a matter of respect for each person's dignity, it is extremely important that neither partner engages in sex against their will. If a partner forces the other partner to have sex, whether through coercion or by physically forcing them, that is lust at work and not love. It is also rape. Such an objectionable behaviour is unacceptable and should not be condoned. When a partner forces you to have sex against your will, that is a red flag that should not be ignored. In Ghana and in most places around the world, your partner forcing you to have sex against your will is a crime and is punishable by law.

I am an advocate for couples having sex before they marry, and I am a stronger advocate for consent and respect in a relationship. Anything done in love prospers. Regardless of which side of this debate you land on, please make sure your actions are always grounded in love. Always.

Should Partners Exchange Nude Photos or Videos?

Most people these days have easy access to smartphones and the internet, which allows them to easily record and share photos and videos with one another. With the increased ease that people can capture and share photos and videos, people dating or in a relationship may share pictures with each other. Some people take the sharing a step further and share sexually suggestive or nude photos and videos of themselves. While such actions may add to the excitement of the relationship, it is important that each individual understands the benefits and risks of such actions, and proceeds with caution.

Here are ten things to keep in mind if you decide to share your nude photos or videos (whether you are married or not):

10 Things to Consider Before Sharing Nude Photos or Videos with Your Partner

1. You could accidentally send the photo or video to the wrong recipient or recipients
2. You have no control over where it shows up after the video or photo leaves your phone; when deleting after sending, you may inadvertently delete only for self and not for everyone
3. Your trusted recipient may entrust another person with your photo or video
4. You or your trusted recipient could lose your phones
5. You or your trusted recipient's phones or computers could be hacked
6. Most sharing platforms store a copy of the photo or video in the cloud
7. Hiding your face in a nude photo or video does not mean nobody will know it is you
8. If the relationship ends, you may become vulnerable to harassment or blackmail
9. It's OK to say "no" when you're uncomfortable with the idea
10. In some countries, sharing sexually explicit photos or videos could be a criminal offence

Instead of sending nude photos or videos, some people may consider sharing live videos of their nakedness through video chatting. Such scenarios involve risks as well. The other person could covertly screengrab photos or record videos from the video feed of your naked self. So, before getting naked on camera for live video sharing, even with someone you trust, please consider the ten things to keep in mind if you decide to share your nude photos or videos.

There is nothing wrong with nudity. However, sharing a nude photo or video always poses a risk that may cause embarrassment to you and your loved ones. While it is possible to do so safely, there is also the possibility that sharing such photos or videos can lead to unexpected consequences. As always, it is best to act with wisdom.

Avoiding sex before marriage is not an easy task. It takes a great deal of self-discipline. It is doable and many people have successfully avoided having sex before they married. Many could not or did not want to avoid sex before marriage. The decision of whether or not to have sex before marriage is an individual one as well as a shared one for the couple. The partners must weigh the cost and the benefits of the decision for themselves.

The couple should also discuss the cost and benefits to the relationship, and then decide whether or not to have sex before they marry. Whichever decision the couple arrives at, it is important that it is made with love and out of respect for each other. Always.

10

CRUCIAL CONVERSATIONS: BEFORE YOU SAY "I DO"

A Twi proverb states that *"Wo kɔ aware a bisa"* – translation: "Before you venture into marriage, enquire". This proverb has two meanings. The first meaning has to do with asking people who know your prospective spouse and their families about them. The idea is to find out from third-parties whether there are character traits or family traits that could adversely impact the marriage. Even though the parents of either party may begin such enquiries when they realise that the relationship may lead to marriage, the enquiries officially switch into high gear when the two people announce their intention to get married. Usually, an uncle or auntie on either side assumes the role of investigator and obtains testimonials and other crucial information about the other family to help them decide whether to approve the marriage or not.

The second, less commonly used, meaning of the proverb has to do with each party asking the other. The couple owe it to themselves to ask each other certain key questions because even the most skilled investigator can never obtain all the crucial information in either party's head. There is no way to know a person's intentions for getting married or the kind of marriage they wish to have unless you ask them directly, and give you an honest answer.

People's intentions or plans when entering into a marriage may not be obvious. Without asking, you may never know. Even when you ask, your partner may not tell you the entire truth. It is, however, better to ask and not get the truth than not to ask at all.

The types of questions that could help reveal a partner's intentions and plans can include those about what kind of lifestyle the couple plan on having after they get married, whether to have children, how many, when to begin having children, the key principles they will base their marriage on, and how they plan on relating to third parties, are some of the important questions each party should obtain answers to before the marriage happens.

The questions may be asked directly or indirectly as part of a conversation. The best way to keep a conversation going is by asking open-ended questions, which would pave the way for discussions instead of yes/no answers.

See (a) Topics for Crucial Conversations, (b) the Getting Married Worksheet, (c) the Personal Values Worksheet, (d) the Relationship SWOT Analysis Worksheet, and (e) Personality Assessments.

a) Topics for Crucial Conversations: Before You Say "I Do"

Here are some crucial conversation starters for people who are planning to get married:

- What are your short-, medium- and long-term goals in life?
- What experiences of other married couples would you like in your marriage?
- What experiences of other married couples would you like to avoid in your marriage?
- Do you plan on having children? If so, how many? If not, why not?
- If we decide we want to have children but find we cannot, what will be our next option?
- Are there any sexual preferences, anxieties or no-go areas that you would like to discuss?
- Have you been physically or sexually abused in the past?
- Do you have a child or children from a prior relationship? (If either of you has a child or children from a previous relationship, discuss how that situation will be managed.)
- Is there any history of family health-related issues you would like to discuss?
- Have you ever been unfaithful?
- How do you feel about fidelity now?
- How much involvement would you like our families to have in our marriage?
- Which religion or denomination will we subscribe to in raising our children?

- How do you manage your personal finances now? Have you ever been in debt? Why did it happen and how did you find (or are you finding) your way out of debt?
- How much should we spend on our marriage ceremony?
- What is the most effective way I can help calm you down when you are angry?
- What is your preferred method for resolving conflicts?
- Do you have any criminal history?
- How will we manage our use of social media?
- What are your thoughts on exercising, nutrition and mental health?
- What is your vision for the kind of profession you would like to have in the future?
- What price are you willing to pay in order to achieve your goals in life?
- Where would you like us to live after we get married?

b) Getting Married Worksheet

To facilitate a conversation about why and when each partner would like to get married:

    i.   Answer the questions below

    ii. Discuss each partner's responses

Partner 1	Partner 2
A. Why do you want to get married?	A. Why do you want to get married?
1.	1.
2.	2.
3.	3.
B. What will make you change your mind about getting married?	B. What will make you change your mind about getting married?
C. When will you like to get married?	C. When will you like to get married?
D. List three things you would like to accomplish before you marry.	D. List three things you would like to accomplish before you marry.
1.	1.
2.	2.
3.	3.
E. List three things you would like to accomplish after you marry.	E. List three things you would like to accomplish after you marry.
1.	1.
2.	2.
3.	3.

c) Personal Values Worksheet

Your values system indicates the level of importance you attach to specific ideas and behaviours. To facilitate a conversation about values alignment:

i. Visit **personalvalu.es** and complete the free online test OR choose from below five values most important to you.

ii. Discuss your most important values with your partner, highlighting with examples where applicable.

ACCEPTANCE
being included,
approval

ACCOUNTABILITY
responsibility,
dependability

ADVENTURE
looking for exciting and
risky activities

AMBITION
aspiration, strong desire
to succeed

APPRECIATION
recognition of value
or worth

AUTHENTICITY
truthfulness,
genuineness

AUTHORITY
the right to lead and
control

BEAUTY
aesthetics,
attractiveness

CERTAINTY
stability, orderliness,
predictability

CHALLENGE
testing your own
abilities, competition

COMMITMENT
engagement, support

COMPASSION
empathy, sympathy

COMPETENCE
capability, expertise,
skill

CONTROL
control of the situation
or environment

CONTRIBUTION
helping others to
achieve a common goal

COURAGE
fearlessness, bravery

CREATIVITY
imagination,
inventiveness

CURIOSITY
willingness to explore
and learn

DISCIPLINE
obedience, self-control

DETERMINATION
persistence,
perseverance

ETHICS
moral behavior

EXCELLENCE
mastery, perfection

EXCITEMENT
great enthusiasm,
eagerness

EQUALITY
equal rights and
opportunities for all

FAME
being known or
recognized by many
people

FAMILY
caring for loved ones

**FINANCIAL
STABILITY**
stable income, financial
freedom

FORGIVENESS
willingness to forgive
others

FREEDOM
liberty, freedom of
action and thought

FRIENDSHIP
comradeship,
companionship

GROWTH
physical, intellectual
and spiritual
development

HEALTH
well-being, fitness, not
being sick

HELPFULNESS
benevolence, service,
altruism

HONESTY
sincerity, frankness

INDEPENDENCE
self-reliance, self-
sufficiency

INFLUENCE
having effect on people
or things

INNER HARMONY
balance, self-fulfillment

INTELLIGENCE
logical thinking, quick
learning

JOB SECURITY
not worrying about
losing your job

JUSTICE
fairness, integrity

LOVE
deep feeling of affection

LOYALTY
faithfulness

**MEANINGFUL
WORK**
positive impact on
other people's lives

PASSION
a vocation or loved
hobby

PEACE
calm, freedom from
conflict

PLEASURE
enjoyment, happiness,
satisfaction

POPULARITY
being liked or admired
by many people

PRIVACY
the right to have
secrets, discretion

RELIGION
devoutness, faith

RESPECT
honour and care shown
towards someone

REPUTATION
other people's opinion

SECURITY
being free from danger
or threat

SPIRITUALITY
focusing on intangible
aspects of life

SUCCESS
achieving desired
results

TRADITION
respecting customs,
practicing rites

TRUST
a belief in someone or
something

TEAMWORK
collaboration, synergy

TOLERANCE
acceptance, openness,
open-mindedness

UNIQUENESS
being particularly
remarkable or unusual

VARIETY
frequent change,
diversity

WEALTH
money, material goods,
luxury lifestyle

WISDOM
making good decisions
and judgements

d) The Relationship SWOT Analysis Worksheet

SWOT stands for Strengths, Weaknesses, Opportunities, and Threats. A SWOT analysis is an activity that many organisations and project teams use to understand where they are and to determine how to accomplish their goals. In a relationship, a couple could use a SWOT analysis to determine the relationship's strengths, weaknesses, opportunities and threats, which can be useful in planning actions the couple could take to strengthen their relationship.

- Strengths are positive characteristics of the relationship; these could be strengths that each partner identifies in the other or in the relationship, are within the couple's control and can be used by the couple to enhance their relationship.
- Weaknesses are negative factors that weaken the relationship; these could be weaknesses that each partner identifies in the other or in the relationship, are within the couple's control and can be improved to enhance their relationship.
- Opportunities are factors or circumstances that can be used by the couple to help the relationship grow or become stronger. Opportunities are often associated with the couple's environment and stage in life.
- Threats are factors or circumstances that pose a danger to the relationship and could lead to its breakdown or complete demise. Threats are often situations that call for immediate corrective action and boundaries.

Below are some questions to start you off with your relationship SWOT analysis:

Strengths	• *Which attributes do you enjoy in your relationship?* • *What quality or behaviour of yours can be used to better the relationship?* • *Which areas of your relationship are working well?* • *Which unique differences make you a strong team?*
Weaknesses	• *Which attributes do you not enjoy in your relationship?* • *What personal weakness of yours can harm the relationship if we do not work on it?* • *Which areas of your relationship are not working well?* • *Which unique differences make you a weak team?*
Opportunities	• *What activities could enhance the quality of your relationship?* • *What personal activities of yours can positively affect the relationship?* • *Which people could influence your relationship positively?* • *What events or changes could help your relationship to grow stronger?*
Threats	• *What issues could harm the quality of your relationship?* • *Which people could influence your relationship negatively?* • *What personal previous or current activity can bring the relationship into disrepute?* • *What events or changes could cause problems in your relationship?*

Complete the Relationship SWOT Analysis as follows:
  i. Independently provide your SWOT responses
  ii. Together discuss each partner's response
  iii. Together outline a plan of action

Partner 1			
Strengths	Weaknesses	Opportunities	Threats
1.	1.	1.	1.
2.	2.	2.	2.
3.	3.	3.	3.

Partner 2			
Strengths	Weaknesses	Opportunities	Threats
1.	1.	1.	1.
2.	2.	2.	2.
3.	3.	3.	3.

Specific Actions	When?	Who Will Do What?
1.		
2.		
3.		

The following are some recommended actions a couple can consider for their post-SWOT Analysis action plan:

For Strengths:
- Praise attributes you enjoy in your relationship.
- Prioritise qualities that can help the relationship.
- Celebrate areas of your relationship working well.
- Embrace differences that make you a strong team.

For Weaknesses:
- Assist where your partner has a weakness.
- Show empathy towards your partner.
- Encourage your partner to overcome their weakness.
- Do not criticise your partner for their weakness.

For Opportunities:
- Plan activities to enhance your relationship.
- Share your personal activities with your partner.
- Associate with positive role models.
- Make changes that could help your relationship to grow stronger.

For Threats:
- Discuss ideas for avoiding contentious situations.
- Cut ties with people who threaten the stability of your relationship.
- Avoid situations that could lead you to compromise your values.
- Be transparent to your partner about your past.

e) Personality Assessments

When we describe ourselves or others, we are often sharing the results of informal personality assessments. A personality assessment uses a systematic and scientific approach to place people in categories based on shared characteristics. The assessment evaluates the person's responses to carefully crafted questions and identifies patterns or traits that could help explain past behaviour and/or predict future actions.

Personality assessments are used by researchers, medical professionals and other individuals for various purposes. Provided below are two free online personality assessments that could help you learn more about yourself and better understand both your strengths and weaknesses. You may get access to more assessments by contacting a licensed counsellor or other health professionals.

Important Notes: These URLs were fully functional and free at the time of publishing this book. If they are no longer free or no longer functional, please look around the internet for alternatives. These free online resources are not intended to diagnose any condition. If you need help with a mental health concern, please contact a qualified health professional.

16personalities.com
- Described as "a personality test that gives you a freakishly accurate description of who you are and why you do things the way you do"
- www.16personalities.com/free-personality-test
- Premium services available for those who want to dive deeper into their personality

Openpsychometrics.org

- Described as "an interactive personality test of the 'Four Temperaments'", an idea from Ancient Greek medicine
- https://openpsychometrics.org/tests/O4TS/
- This site contains other interactive personality tests with detailed results

IMPORTANT NOTE

You are at the end of Book 1, about **finding lasting love relationships.** To read about **maintaining lasting love relationships**, please continue with Book 2.

Please see the next page for Book 2's table of contents.

TABLE OF CONTENTS (BOOK 2)

PART III: GETTING MARRIED AND STARTING OUT

PART IV: STAYING MARRIED, STAYING TOGETHER

We will be lost without you mother/wife .
You are gentler, more intuitive, more intelligent
and understanding. You are not behind my
success, you are beside me in all things .

Even though you will not accept,
sometimes you are in front of me .

When two complete people become
one, onward movement is only possible
through alignment.

Photo
Gallery

Photo
Gallery

Even when love grows stronger, the
light in the romance can become dimmer.
Love must be allowed to flower, but the
dimming light in the romance must be
arrested.

www.ingramcontent.com/pod-product-compliance
Lightning Source LLC
Chambersburg PA
CBHW030346050426

42336CB00049B/535

LOVE LOCKED DOWN

II

LOVE LOCKED DOWN:

A GUIDE TO MAINTAINING A
LASTING LOVE RELATIONSHIP

By Okyeame Kwame and Annica Nsiah-Apau
with Kyei Amoako

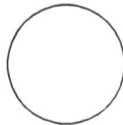

Spotlight Publishing

Columbus, Ohio | Accra, Ghana

IMPORTANT NOTE

You are at the beginning of Book 2, about **maintaining lasting love relationships**. If you would like to read about **finding lasting love relationships** before proceeding, please go to Book 1.

Please see the next page for Book 1's table of contents.

TABLE OF CONTENTS (BOOK 1)

TABLE OF CONTENTS (BOOK 2)

PART III: GETTING MARRIED AND STARTING OUT

PART IV: STAYING MARRIED, STAYING TOGETHER

GETTING MARRIED
AND STARTING OUT

Adinkra Symbol Name:
Ɔdɔ Nnyira Fie Kwan (Love Never Loses Its Way Home)

Significance:
The Power of Love

• 11 •

INTRODUCING THE IMPORTANT PEOPLE IN YOUR LIVES

When your relationship gets underway and you are certain it is for the long term, do you announce it to others? If so, how do you go about it? Do you tell a select few? Do you share cryptic messages on social media to announce the relationship? Or do you deflect the question when asked about your relationship status, and intentionally keep the relationship under wraps for a while longer?

Understandably, different couples take different approaches to making their relationship known to others. On the one hand, some may choose to be quiet about it for a while and not even let their public interactions reveal that they are in a relationship. On the other, some couples waste no time in letting the world know when they become romantically involved. Either way, there will come a time

when the couple will need to introduce their relationship to others, should the relationship continue and become serious.

Confidentiality or secrecy may be necessary at the beginning of a relationship. A couple may need to keep their relationship private to protect the relationship from unsolicited feedback and other interferences. Others may choose to remain quiet about their relationship as a matter of personal preference.

When, how and with whom they choose to share such news is also their choice. In most cases, couples share such news on a need-to-know basis and do so at a time of their choosing.

Couples who announce their relationship (or who do not keep their relationship status hidden from others) may do so to create awareness about the change in their status and let others know they are no longer available; to invite others to share in their joy at having found a partner; or may do so to let the world know that they have an awesome partner. Some announce it to their close friends and siblings, whereas others do so non-verbally through the affectionate ways they relate to each other in public.

Whether a couple chooses to keep the news of their relationship confidential or share it with others, observing best practices could allow the important people in their lives to receive the news in the best possible way.

The important people in each person's life may be important to them for different reasons. They may be close family members, friends, mentors, or other people who provide counsel and guidance. The introduction may be

formal, informal or semi-formal depending on the nature of the relationship that exists between the partner and that person who is important to them.

The approach to introducing a partner to important people in their lives will most likely not be a one-size-fits-all. For example, a recent university graduate who lives in the same house as their parents may have to introduce their partner to their parents much sooner than a middle-aged person living in a different city. In all cases, it is important that the couple discuss and plan the introduction by preparing each other for the introductions, devising a suitable approach, and proceeding in a manner that is agreed upon by both partners.

At the time Kwame and I met, some of the most important people in my life were my parents, my three sisters, my two brothers, and my nephew and niece who grew up in our household. Kwame met most of them the first day he visited the house. When we decided to start a relationship, I preferred that we kept that information between us and only shared it on a need-to-know basis. To them, Kwame and I were just friends. Kwame thought I was being too secretive and for a while called me 'CL' which was short for 'cover lover' (or 'undercover lover'). I didn't think it was necessary yet to announce to all of them that we were in a relationship.

My older sister was the first person I formally introduced Kwame to as my boyfriend. She is more than 15 years older than me and has always been a major positive influence on me. When I was a young adult, I lived with her in Accra. She was my 'eye-opener' who taught me many of the things

I know about becoming a woman. Her opinion mattered in many things I did and I wanted her to 'officially' meet Kwame.

That formal introduction was on the phone since we did not live in the same city. Before introducing Kwame, I spoke to her about how Kwame and I met and developed our friendship into a relationship. I also told her what I liked about Kwame and about my intention for our relationship to eventually mature into marriage. She asked very relevant questions about Kwame's character and if he was congenial enough to get along with our family.

My conversations with my sister were long and enlightening. Her questions helped me think about important things that I needed to consider, and her welcoming demeanour assured me of her support for my decision to get into a relationship with Kwame. At a later time, I arranged for her to have a chat with Kwame over the phone. They had a brief but hearty conversation. They had subsequent phone conversations that led her to conclude that Kwame could be a decent and pleasant life partner.

Even though my older brother is an important person in my life, I intentionally did not introduce Kwame to him in the early stages of our relationship. My brother, who loves me very much, is very immovable in his adherence to Jehovah's Witnesses teachings and was very unlikely to welcome the fact that I was in a relationship with someone who was not an *onua*. As Kwame continued to visit our house and relate warmly with my entire family, my older brother developed a fondness for him. With time, he picked up on the fact that Kwame and I wcrc not just friends. My

brother minds his own business and keeps most of his opinions to himself if unsolicited, and that is exactly what he did. He, however, cautioned that I should use my best judgement in all things.

I did not formally introduce Kwame to my sister Onazia (Sister Ona). She lived in Cape Coast at the time, about three hours outside Accra, when Kwame and I visited her. She is the type of person who instinctively picks up on things happening around me and she figured out that there could be a relationship brewing between Kwame and me. Even though I only introduced Kwame as a friend, she spoke approvingly of Kwame's humility and gracious manners. She implied that I should seriously consider Kwame as a life partner and not be passive about the friendship, as was my usual custom. My sister's reception of Kwame was heartwarming and appreciated.

Prepare your partner to meet the important people in your life. Such preparation involves deciding **who** the important people are, **when** to make introductions and **how** to go about it. In my case, my three older siblings were very important people whose opinions mattered to me, yet it was strategic to formally introduce Kwame to only my oldest sister. The advance preparation and the strategic approach helped me to smoothly introduce Kwame.

Introducing your partner to the important people in your lives often has advantages. That action demonstrates the level of seriousness you accord the relationship, and it signals to your partner how proud you are of them and the relationship. If the person is unsettled about you, meeting some of the important people in your life may refine

their opinion about you or help them with the decision to terminate the relationship. If the person is convinced about you, meeting important people in your life could affirm their reason for choosing you. Each person's thought process is, however, unique to them.

Before announcing your partner to others, it is always a good idea to discuss that with each other. You may start by telling your partner about that person, why they are important in your life, and why you would like to introduce them to that person. If your partner agrees that the relationship is at a stage where it is appropriate to introduce each other to important people in your lives, you may then ask when and how they would want the introductions to occur.

Your partner may be comfortable speaking with your parents over the phone first before meeting them in person. If that is the case, you may want to give your partner a heads-up before handing them the phone to talk with your parents. As a rule of thumb, remember to explicitly ask your partner before taking actions that will require them to take a follow-up action. Wait for a clear affirmative response before you proceed.

Prepare the important people in your life to meet your partner. You can start by simply telling that person that you've met someone that you like, and that you would like them to meet your partner. Expect questions like your partner's name, how old they are, what tribe they belong to, their religious background, their occupation, if your partner has been previously married or has children, how the two of you met, the stage of the relationship, and what plans the

two of you have for each other. The questions may be asked directly or indirectly. You should also arrive prepared to ask questions to keep the conversation balanced. Some curious minds may even ask for your partner's social media handles so they can snoop around for juicy gossip.

When you tell your partner that you are planning to tell your parents about them, their response may reveal their seriousness about the relationship. Pay close attention to that feedback. If it bothers you that their reaction did not meet your expectation, don't sweep that concern under the rug. Have a candid conversation about your observation and clarify how each of you wants to move forward with the introductions.

Whether you are offering to make an introduction or asking to be introduced, it is important to keep in mind that you could scare your partner into thinking you are moving too fast with the relationship if they are unprepared. Another caution couples need to keep in mind is that the person being introduced could become complacent if the introduction happens too early. The right timing and alignment for the introduction cannot be overemphasised.

While the positive feedback from important people in your life can be morale-boosting, your intention for introducing your partner should not be to seek validation or approval. Of course, consider third-party feedback if they share any observations about your partner. However, you should refrain from asking questions like, "What do you think of my partner?" or "Do you think they are good looking?" Such questions put people in awkward positions to have to say things they think you want to hear or cause

them to be candid and possibly hurt your feelings. If feedback is important to you, ask your objective questions of people who are likely to give *constructive* feedback.

For example, you could ask questions like, **"Do you have any advice for me as I move forward with this relationship?"** or **"Would you please let me know when you have any feedback?"**

Introducing your partner to the important people in your life should not be limited to when the two of you are planning the marriage ceremony. It could be done at any point when the relationship has developed a firm footing and the two of you are comfortable with sharing that news.

In the traditional Ghanaian sense, the most important introduction is the one that involves an elderly person from the man's family accompanying him to formally inform the woman's family that the couple are in a relationship and have the intention of getting married within the short term. It is known as "knocking" (kɔkɔɔkɔ). That formal introduction is what lets either family view either partner as a fiancé. Without a formal introduction, either family could intentionally turn a blind eye to the relationship even when they may be fully aware of its existence. A Twi proverb says, *"Akokɔ bedeɛ nim adekyeɛ nanso ɔtwɛn akokɔ nini ma ɔbɔn ansa"* – translation: "The hen knows when day breaks yet she waits on the cock to crow".

Annica and I had been dating for three years before I went with my mother and older brother to formally inform her father of the relationship. I had spent many hours

in their home, I had run many errands for her parents, and they knew Annica and I shared most of our lives together. However, when my mother informed Annica's father that she had come with me to formally inform him of my intention to marry Annica, he told us that he was taking note of the relationship from that point forth. He emphasised that he had not assumed that Annica and I were in a relationship because neither of us had come to him with any such information. He considered us to be just friends until he was formally notified.

It stands to reason that if a disagreement in our relationship required an intervention from Annica's family, her father would have said he did not know a relationship existed and would not have intervened. Prior to that formal introduction, my family could also have pretended that they did not know Annica and I were in a relationship if that stance suited them.

Families tend to hold back their endorsement of the relationship until a formal introduction takes place so that they don't lead the prospective in-laws to make any assumptions about their approval of a marriage between the two.

The significance of the man coming with an older relative to formally notify the woman's family of his intention is so that there will be a credible family member bearing witness to the man's declared intention. Also, the formal introduction signals to either family that they can begin a formal enquiry of the other. Such enquiries may involve one family asking about the other family from credible third parties regarding their history with mental health,

promiscuity, industriousness, and barrenness. It is on the basis of their findings that one family may accept or decline the request for their daughter to marry the man asking for her hand.

While the couple share the responsibility for introducing each other to their families, the onus is on the man to lead in this area. It is a cultural expectation in Ghana that a man who is old enough to ask for a woman's hand in a serious relationship should be responsible enough to facilitate the initial formal introduction. The formal introduction is not only an important protocol but an opportunity for the couple, especially the man, to show leadership and to act decisively in the best interest of the relationship.

When meeting your partner's family, it is important to make a dignified first impression. Whether you like it or not, you will be observed and assessed based on that first impression until they get to know you well. It is important to be self-aware and considerate of the people you meet. For example, if you are a woman who enjoys showing your cleavage when you dress nicely, the day you meet your boyfriend's parents and other family members may be a good day to cover up. If you are a man who talks too much or tends to exaggerate, the day you meet your girlfriend's parents and other family members would be a good day to be measured in your speech. This is not to pretend but to assess the situation before you fully dive in.

During the meeting or visit, you should pay attention to the people you meet and make a mental note of what they say and how they act. That information will be helpful for follow-up conversations with your partner. Meeting your

partner's family is always an opportunity to figure out what values are important to the family, power dynamics in the family, and how to relate to various people in the family.

Being considerate of your hosts and being open to conversation should not mean allowing yourself to be interrogated by everyone in the house. Some families or family members can be very direct in how they ask questions and do not realise or do not care about being inappropriate. In such situations, it is perfectly fine to be assertive and politely put the person in check – unless that person is your partner's father or mother. Better still, your partner should step in quickly and protect the situation from getting out of hand.

The reason preparation before such a meeting is absolutely necessary is so that you minimise the likelihood of awkward moments. You could talk about questions that may come up, and then together decide how you would answer such questions. You should also clarify if there are any no-go topics of conversation. That way, you seem better coordinated in your responses and save you and your partner from strained relationships with the important people in your lives.

With long-distance relationships or in situations where the important people in either partner's life may not be in the same city or even in the same country, the introductions may take place virtually. Additional planning may be necessary if you plan on travelling to meet such people.

In an example of a man living in Toronto, Canada in a relationship with a woman living in Chicago, USA, the introductions to the important people in each other's

lives may require some thoughtful coordination. This is especially true if the man's parents live in California, USA, and the woman's parents live in Ghana, or any other combination in which each family and each partner lives in a different place. In such a situation, the introductions may have to begin virtually, through phone calls and video chats, and then be followed later with in-person meetings when feasible.

For some people, the important people in their lives include their friends and followers on social media. If that is you, it is understandable that you want to update your relationship status on your social media platforms, share pictures of your partner, send messages to one another publicly, and even use each other's pictures as display photos or profile photos. Before any such information sharing happens on social media, it is absolutely necessary to discuss that with your partner.

It is true that making a relationship public on social media may be an effective means for warding off any 'competition' but it may also prematurely expose the relationship to the public's involvement. In a situation where your partner is very big on privacy, posting about the relationship on social media without their consent may create a problem. As with any other introduction, it is necessary for the couple to agree that it's OK to post on social media about their relationship before either party goes ahead.

I realise how private Annica is and mostly ask for her consent before I post content that puts our private life out in the open. While I am very comfortable putting information about me on social media, Annica believes you don't have

to share everything with the world. If social media had been as prevalent fifteen years ago as it is in 2021, I am sure I may have been tempted to post a picture of her on my timeline on Valentine's Day. I am also sure that she would have said "no", being the 'cover lover' that she was. At the end of the day, sharing information about our relationship with a bunch of people that we may not even know personally would not be worth the inconvenience that such an action would have created for Annica.

Related to the idea of sharing information about a relationship on social media is the 'posti me' notion, where one partner may insist that the other partner posts pictures of them on their social media page, and vice versa. To the person asking, being posted on their partner's social media page serves as a public declaration that signals that both of them are 'off the market' and off limits to any other suitors. That approach of exerting pressure to have the relationship announced to the world could work in some situations. In other situations, that approach could backfire if your partner calls your bluff on any ultimatum you associate with that demand. In either situation, the better approach would be for the couple to have a candid conversation about their respective wishes and then arrive at a compromise.

One partner may delay introducing their significant other to important people in their life for good reasons. However, delaying such an introduction for much longer than the other party believes is reasonable could create tense moments for the relationship. Such a delay could lead to the significant other believing their partner is not proud of their relationship, that the partner is unsure of the

future of the relationship, or that the partner is not being completely truthful about other relationships they may have, or the partner may simply not be ready.

When there is a good reason why one partner doesn't want to introduce their significant other to important people in their life, it is advisable that the partner with reservations about such introductions tactfully explain why such introductions cannot happen until later. It is better to let your partner know your reasons than to leave them to assume the reasons or guess your intentions.

Until the relationship is on a solid footing, introducing your partner to important people in your life may complicate matters. If you have unfinished business in a previous relationship, such as an unfinalised divorce or an unhealthy friendship with an ex, the introductions should wait until the unfinished business is resolved. If one party is unsure of the future of the relationship or the relationship is hanging by a thread, it would be unwise to proceed with introductions and then have to go back shortly thereafter to announce that the relationship has ended.

Introducing each other to the important people in your lives is a major step in a relationship. However, it should be done at your discretion and not under pressure from anyone. It should be done after you have had the necessary conversations to clearly establish where the relationship stands and where the relationship is headed. It should be done only after you have both agreed on when and how to introduce each other and to whom.

GETTING MARRIED

With nice gowns and coordinated colours, fancy suits and expensive clothes, elegant Kente outfits, beautiful cars, pretty flowers, elaborate feasts and an assortment of music, getting married is often associated with ceremonial splendour and pageantry involving family members, friends and well-wishers. As extravagant as a marriage ceremony could be, that is only the ceremony. The actual marriage begins when the ceremony ends.

Generally, a marriage occurs when a man and woman reach an age of maturity and full independence and then form a legally recognised union after they have courted for a while. In Ghana, three types of marriages are currently recognised by the country's laws: (1) customary marriage, (2) marriage under the Marriage Ordinance and (3) Islamic marriage under the Marriage of Mohammedans Ordinance.

Marriage has a long history and significance in the Ghanaian society. Preceding the laws that presently establish

marriage in Ghana, marriages were established through agreements between two extended families. A marriage often established a common interest and alliance between the two families, and served as a means for the community to expand and thrive in an orderly manner.

Even though a marriage registration, as prescribed by the Ghanaian government, is all that is required for a marriage to be legally recognised in the country, the cultural foundations of marriage remain a significant aspect of how Ghanaians get married. Over the years, Ghanaians have adopted several foreign practices and have also embraced Christianity, which introduced additional components to the marriage rites that are widely observed by Ghanaians.

Couples often get married in Ghana by observing cultural norms under the auspices of their extended families. The man's family follows cultural protocols to request permission on his behalf from the woman's family so that he can take their daughter for a wife. If the woman's family agrees to the request, the two families and the couple arrange a ceremony where specific items are exchanged and the man and woman are pronounced husband and wife. The families from then on consider them married and accord them the appropriate rights and privileges.

Before or after the customary ceremony, the couple may give notice to the marriage registrar in the district where the marriage ceremony is going to occur or did occur. The registrar publishes a notice of marriage, waits 21 days, and then issues a marriage certificate to the couple if no one raises an objection to the notice.

Religion plays an integral role in the lives of many Ghanaians. As a result, many Ghanaian marriage ceremonies have religious components. Solemnisation of holy matrimony, also known as a wedding, is a popular Christian tradition that is widely practised among Ghanaians. The ceremony often involves the woman wearing a white outfit, from which such weddings have gained the nickname of 'white wedding'. Weddings are often coordinated through religious organisations, where the couple are required to follow rules outlined by the religious organisation, which often include obtaining consent from the respective families and undergoing pre-marital counselling. The religious organisation often coordinates the publication of the 21-day notice of marriage through announcements in the religious organisation and facilitates the signing of the marriage register after a licensed minister officiates the marriage ceremony in compliance with all the steps required for a valid marriage under the Marriage Ordinance.

Marriage ceremonies in Ghana range from modest private events to elaborate public ones that are associated with lots of fanfare. The variations of marriage ceremonies practised in Ghana depend on the preference of the couple, their families, their religion, and their social circles. Some may choose a private ceremony at a private residence with a few close friends and family members or a private ceremony inside a religious organisation with a few friends and family members. Others may hold their ceremony at a secular venue in the presence of a large group of friends, co-workers, family and members of their religious

organisation. Many people combine aspects of a traditional and a religious ceremony into a hybrid ceremony.

Even though white weddings are very popular in Ghana, they are not required by the State for a marriage to be legally recognised. A couple does not need to have a white wedding or a religious ceremony before they can register their marriage with the State.

Some religions require their members to have a wedding ceremony and have it officiated by one of their pastors or priests. Some religious organisations even go to the extent of not recognising customary and legal marriages simply because the couple have not had a ceremony in a religious organisation. Such rules, which put undue pressure on many couples, should not be mistaken for a customary or State requirement. A customary marriage ceremony is a complete marriage rite. A white wedding is optional.

Ghanaian life is structured around extended family systems, making the involvement of the respective families in a marriage ceremony necessary. Cultural norms in various Ghanaian ethnic groups mandate that at a minimum, the parents of both the man and the woman consent to the marriage.

Annica and I chose to have a modest private ceremony. Prior to the marriage ceremony, we had to navigate the part about consent from parents.

Annica's parents liked me and welcomed me into their home. During the years that we dated, her father took an interest in getting to know me better. Her father concluded that he had no doubts about my character and believed I could be an amazing friend, husband and life partner to

Annica. However, prior to the marriage, he was clear that we could not get married if I were not a Jehovah's Witness. He thought it would be best for Annica to follow the protocols of their faith, which prohibits getting married to a non-Witness. That way, he and the rest of Annica's family could participate in our marriage ceremony.

Interestingly, he added that it would be unwise for me to change my beliefs just because I was in love. He advised that I should become a Witness because I was convinced that is what will bring me salvation and not because I want to be married to his daughter.

Jehovah's Witnesses require their members to marry from among themselves. It is their belief that marrying outside the religion could create significant problems for the Witness. Some of the concerns are whether the non-Witness spouse would allow their member to freely practice the religion; whether the non-Witness spouse would allow for their children to be raised with Witness beliefs; and whether the marriage would thrive if the couple shared different beliefs about observing cultural traditions such as performing funeral rites, celebrating certain non-Biblical holidays and birthdays, voting in elections, running for public office, and healthcare practices such as subscribing to blood transfusion.

There is a considerable amount of data indicating that marriages between Witnesses and non-Witnesses have a high failure rate. Annica's parents feared that our marriage would suffer the same fate as many marriages that failed because one spouse was a non-Witness.

To further complicate matters, my family members shared similar fears. My mother knew of people who had married Jehovah's Witnesses and had become alienated from their families. She was conflicted because she had come to know Annica and believed we were a good fit for each other yet struggled with Annica's religion. She feared that marrying a Jehovah's Witness would possibly alienate me from my extended family.

In my father's will, he stated that if any of his children became of age and decided to marry, no one should interfere in their choice of spouse. My mother was well aware of my father's wish and had no intention of ignoring that. She also thought that getting married without Annica's parents' consent could mean Annica's family had washed their hands off her.

Regardless of her reservations, my mother went to see Annica's father on two occasions to seek his consent or request that he delegate a family member to represent the family if he could not participate in the ceremony. His response was very clear – he liked me but could not participate in or consent to our marriage on religious grounds.

We tried to get one of Annica's uncles to represent their family and receive the customary drinks that I was to present in asking for Annica's hand. Her uncle was uncomfortable playing that stand-in role, especially when Annica's parents were not on board with the ceremony. It became clear that our best efforts were not going to change Annica's father's stance.

However, moving forward with the marriage ceremony was inevitable to us. Annica and I were convinced we were doing the right thing by getting married. We had made a choice to get married after getting to know each other over four years.

It was clear that her parents had made a choice to honour their religious beliefs and abstain from participating in our marriage ceremony. There were no hard feelings in either camp.

On the 16th of January 2009, we met with four of our close friends and their wives at the Kumasi Metropolitan Assembly. In attendance were my mother, my older brother, and two of Annica's siblings. One of our older friends, together with Annica's sister, stood in as parents for Annica, and within a few minutes, we were done with the ceremony. We officially became Mr. and Mrs. Nsiah-Apau.

After the ceremony, Kwame and his three friends went to a restaurant to eat and I went with my sister to a convention where my mother was. I had not told my mother that I was planning to get married on that day. As I approached her, I waved my left hand and revealed the ring on my finger. The expression on her face portrayed a combination of mild shock and restrained excitement. Even though she did not verbalise how proud she was of me, she could not hide her genuine happiness about the fact that I was married. I am sure she mentioned it to my father later that day but none of them asked me anything about the marriage ceremony. Each of us carried on as usual.

In almost every Ghanaian culture, extended families are stakeholders in a marriage. When the two consenting adults decide to marry, they carry their families along. It is said that a marriage is between families, not just the two individuals. However, the responsibilities and day-to-day process of being married remains squarely on the shoulders of the couple. As much as possible, they should remain connected to their respective families because there are seasons during the marriage where extended families play key roles.

I had always known my parents were not going to be present at our marriage ceremony, and that was something Kwame and I came to terms with earlier on in our relationship. Our marriage ceremony cost GHS300, not including the cost of the rings, which is the equivalent of $80 today, and Kwame was really happy we didn't have to spend a lot of money just to get married.

I have never liked ceremonies where I would be the centre of attention; so I didn't want an extensive marriage ceremony. It was more important to me that I was getting married to the man of my dreams and did not care for all the pomp and pageantry. As relevant as the ceremony was, it was only a formality.

Generally, marriage customs in Ghana involve the following steps:

- The adult man and woman consent to get married
- The man informs his family of his intentions and his family conducts their preliminary enquiries about the woman and her family

- The woman informs her family that the man and his family are interested in formally requesting her hand in marriage
- The two families meet, the man's family declare their intention to ask for the woman's hand in marriage to their son. This rite in most Akan traditions is known as *kɔkɔɔkɔ* (knocking)
- The woman's family acknowledges the man's family's declaration of intent
- The woman's family conducts their enquiries about the man and his family and make a decision on whether to consent to the marriage or not
- If the woman's family consents to the marriage, they provide the man's family the process and the list of items needed for the marriage ceremony based on their family traditions
- Both families meet on an agreed-upon date and perform the marriage rites, which often involve the man presenting the woman with a ring and items prescribed by the woman's family, a prayer for the couple, and some refreshments

For many people, the customary marriage rites end at this stage. The couple can then register their marriage with the State by applying to the registrar of marriages, completing the required forms and providing a statutory declaration that the marriage is valid according to the applicable customary law.

Couples who choose to have a wedding in addition to the customary marriage often coordinate with their religious

organisations to synchronise their families' wishes with the organisation's protocol. Most religious organisations require that their members participate in pre-marital counselling before the customary marriage ceremony takes place. The religious organisation often participates in the customary marriage and a representative from the woman or the woman's religious organisation often says a prayer over the couple.

Following the customary marriage ceremony, the couple and their families may choose to hold the wedding on the same day or on a different day. The wedding is usually followed by a reception for the guests. Some couples spend the night following their wedding in a nice hotel or may take a trip to an exotic destination where they spend about a week honeymooning. Some couples wait and take a trip a year later to commemorate their first anniversary.

The family members who participate in various aspects of the marriage rites often include a parent and an uncle or auntie at the minimum. Usually, the process involves parents from both sides, uncles, aunties, other relatives and close family friends. In the event that the parents of one or both of the parties are deceased, other close family members may stand in. When the parents of one or both parties are alive but unavailable, the families often designate other family members or respected close family friends to represent the family.

Marriage customs may vary for ethnic groups and may even have nuances within the same ethnic group. It is always wise for the families to consult each other directly to ascertain how things are done according to their respective

traditions. Likewise, specific information about marriages under the Marriage Ordinance, or Islamic marriage under the Marriage of Mohammedans Ordinance, can be obtained from city metropolitan assemblies.

Getting married can be very exciting. The process can be simple or complicated depending on the route the couple takes. There are many practices associated with getting married in Ghana. Some are mandatory customary rites, others are not. Some have reasonable protocols that help ensure readiness for marriage, others are arbitrary demands that may put unnecessary constraints on the couple. Many of the practices are fleeting trends that may wipe out years of savings or leave a trail of debt, whereas others are meaningful experiences that leave memories that are worth the price.

The couple must evaluate every aspect of the process of getting married. If there are parts of the process that place an unnecessary burden on them, they should make every attempt to negotiate with the stakeholders and seek a reasonable compromise. If it is the couples themselves placing the procedural or financial burden on themselves, it is important for them to keep in mind that emotional decisions have financial consequences, and proceed in wisdom.

To us, the purpose of a marriage ceremony and its associated celebrations are to announce the marriage. The actual marriage starts after the ceremonies are done. When getting married, make decisions that you can live with. Observe the protocols and celebrate your union but keep

your focus on maintaining and sustaining a healthy, happy and long-lasting marriage.

• 13 •

MANAGING LIFE
IN A MARITAL HOME

The beauty of marriage is that two people come from different homes and unite to form a unique family unit. Even when the partners come from similar backgrounds, there is likely to be nuances in how each of them was brought up. And from their respective backgrounds, the couple often borrow practices and ideas and then add new ones to establish their own practices by which they will manage their home.

As a result of the partners' different backgrounds, a new marital home is likely to have diversity of thought and personal preferences. Even when the partners agree on how to live together, there will be variations in how each partner does certain things. The two of them may not have the same points of view on everything. That is called diversity, and it is normal in a marital home.

As you continue merging your lives, you will both likely make adjustments. So, embrace your diversity and buckle

up for the ride. Your goal should be to become a strong team where neither partner loses their individuality. Marriage is an opportunity to learn from each other and you can find tremendous strength in your diversity.

The first year for most couples can be very exciting or challenging, or a combination of both. Many couples move in together for the first time. They merge their resources, blend their lifestyles and take their first steps towards accomplishing their shared life goals. They may bask in the glow of being newlyweds and enjoy extended well wishes from others. They discover pleasant things about each other, feel fulfilled and inspired.

On the other hand, the first year of marriage can be frustrating for some couples. Sharing a common living space, blending their social lives, and making joint decisions about big and small things can cause discomfort in the relationship. The couple may need to give up old habits and learn new ones, adjust their personal routines, and accommodate each other's preferences.

Some of those changes may happen gradually or not at all, which may breed irritation. With time, the irritation may turn into frustration and possibly resentment. But things could get better as the two of them learn, adapt and grow together.

The subsequent years will be exciting or challenging or a mixture of the two depending on how well the couple practices **communication, transparency** and **commitment to one another**. The frequency and consistency with which the couple employ these foundational principles will make a huge difference in how their marriage turns out.

Transparency, communication and commitment to one another will be recurring themes in the marriage as they establish a marital home, balance work and family life, nurturing children, create excitement, manage conflict, and practice their faith.

a) Establishing a Marital Home

In the Ghanaian setting, the norm is that a man is expected to have a house that the woman moves into when they marry. It is great if the man has a place of their own where the couple can start their lives. Sometimes, both the man and the woman have fully furnished homes and the couple will have to decide where to live. The couple may even live in different cities or countries before they marry and will have to decide on the place they will live together after they are married. For many couples, such a decision is easy if they have discussed that thoroughly prior to getting married. For others, it could become a sticky point that could cause significant friction between them.

Annica wanted to live in Accra and I wanted to live in Kumasi. She had very good reasons for wanting to live in Accra, just as I did for wanting to live in Kumasi. Based on the facts, living in Accra was going to be a more suitable option for our plans. We lived in Kumasi for a year and a half after we got married, and then moved to Accra.

As insignificant as a discussion about how you will combine furniture, appliances and other household items may seem, it is one that should not be ignored. Deciding on which items to keep, sell or give away should be as much a joint effort as possible. Each person may have important

connections to certain items from their pre-marriage life. So, before one rips out an old painting hanging in the other partner's living room, it would be wise to discuss before taking that action. That painting may be a prized gift from an important person in your partner's life and getting rid of it without care may cause problems in your relationship.

As a young couple, Annica and I established our marital home based on what we had seen from our parents, what we observed from watching other couples, and our vision of the future we wanted for our family. We adopted our parents' practices that we liked and left out the ones we found less desirable. We embraced what we considered the positive examples from other couples and avoided behaviours we believed were unhelpful. We were committed to being a united front in everything we did. We were committed to having fun together, talk about our feelings, look out for each other's best interests, fight fairly, and trust that each person's actions were always with good intentions. We deepened our resolve to resist any unproductive third-party influences, trust our instincts, and relentlessly defend each other in public.

The first year of marriage was one of our best years together. We celebrated Annica's graduation from her master's programme and she started a job she loved. I won the ultimate prize of artiste of the year at the Ghana Music Awards, beating some of the biggest artistes in the country. I subsequently raked in several endorsement deals from national and multinational brands. We got pregnant with our first child and had him on a Saturday (same as the day on which I was born) - very exciting for me. We also moved

into our new home and settled into our routines, sharing roles and responsibilities, and being best friends to each other.

Two primary roles exist in most marriages – one is the gathering and the other is nurturing. The masculine usually gathers while the feminine usually nurtures. Neither role is more important than the other. The masculine role is not limited to men and neither is the feminine role limited to women. In our case, Annica and I took on our roles according to our natural strengths, temperaments and which of us was more available to play either role. Up until today, the roles we play in our marriage are not gender based. For example, I manage many of our third-party relationships because I have the natural temperament for diplomacy. Annica is strong-willed and, therefore, leads in teaching our children how to be emotionally resilient.

In our home we are both leaders, with each leading where they are best equipped to do so. Of course, when we get stuck in a situation that requires one person to lead the way, that person is often me. In other words, I am the Chief Executive Officer. However, I rely on Annica's counsel and support when I have to make executive decisions on behalf of the entire family. It takes true leaders to acknowledge that they cannot do everything by themselves, and to allow a competent team member to lead in other areas. In our home, Annica is the Chief Operations Officer and the Chief Financial Officer. Together, we make an effective leadership and management team.

We are not in competition with each other. Rather, we have an orderly collaboration that recognises natural skills

and uses all of those skills for the benefit of our home. We focus on honing our natural strengths and lead where we are best suited to do so, and we get better by the day.

b) Balancing Work and Family Life

Kwame was a self-employed musician and I was an employee of a multinational company when we first moved to Accra. Our plan was for me to continue on my career path for a while, have one more child, start a business venture, and gradually transition into a situation where we would both have ample flexibility with work and family life. We both believed that our family unit was the reason for everything we did, and we knew that there would come a time when we would need financial and scheduling flexibility in order to take care of our children in the way we wanted.

I chose to make my husband and my children priorities. That meant I was not going to put the management of my home on auto-pilot and I would make choices that fit my personal situation and met my family's needs.

We were in the third year of our marriage and life continued wonderfully without any drama. Kwame drove me to and from work daily for a whole year. We shared many blissful conversations during the four-hour commute – two hours each way. Even though we had a very close relationship before we married, we became much closer after we married, largely due to the considerable amount of time we spent together.

We continued to relate to each other as best friends more than we did as husband and wife. When our children

were with us during the commute, we engaged them with spelling quizzes and Bible studies. We had a lot of fun together as a family.

We compared the income from my corporate career to the income we could generate if I turned my full-time attention to managing Kwame's career and its related ventures. The numbers favoured leaving my corporate career. The prospect of a much-improved work-life balance was a welcomed thought. So, after two years at two companies and the birth of our second child, I made the strategic decision to leave my job at the multinational company. I had no intention of becoming an idle stay-at-home spouse. Rather, I was going to put my natural talents and my professional expertise to use, and take the lead in raising our children.

We acquired an office space and started an advertising and marketing agency, which turned out to be an exciting and rewarding venture. With the flexibility that job provided, I could be with my young children any time I wanted and also get work done. If one of them was sick and couldn't go to school, I was readily on hand to take care of them at home or in my office.

In balancing work and family life, I take challenges in stride and choose to avoid unnecessary drama. We live within our means and do not live a make-believe life. We do what we can with what we have and do not burden ourselves with meeting other people's expectations. Things usually work out because we give everything our best effort. If something doesn't work out, we figure out what next step we could take and try to keep things moving. Above all, I

am able to balance work and family life well because I have a partner who is naturally a collaborator and who enables easy decision-making.

I always knew that Kwame worked in a tough industry where we had to plan ahead at all times, and be resilient and adaptable. Thankfully, we do these things well. We pay attention to the competition but we don't compete with anyone. Just as it is with driving on a road, we pay attention to other drivers so that we don't crash into them, but we don't focus on them. We often remind ourselves to look but not to stare. Staring at others will make us lose focus. Rather, we go at our own pace.

There have been moments when I have had to navigate uncertainty and disappointment. There have also been many moments when I have experienced major business wins and professional success. Over the course of more than ten years, we have made the necessary adjustments that have allowed our respective careers to thrive. Our family unit is firmly grounded and we have the flexibility to dedicate significant attention to raising our two children. In hindsight, the decision to make my husband and children priorities has paid off significantly.

c) Nurturing Children

Annica agreed with me to have only one child. After our son was born, she spent a great deal of effort exercising to shed the pregnancy weight and was on her way back to climbing the corporate ladder when she found out that she was pregnant with our second child. She was surprised. She eventually came to terms with the

fact that having a son and a daughter was going to be a fun experience for her. After our second child, I would have liked to have had a third and a fourth, and maybe a fifth but Annica has informed me that we are done having children.

Raising our children has been a figure-it-out-as-you-go process. We have had to figure out the best way to communicate with them, love them, discipline them, teach them and give them every tool they need to become successful adults. We have adopted a philosophy I call 'transformational technology', which has to do with transforming our family into a balanced and high-performing entity.

As our children have grown up, each of them has been assigned household chores such as sweeping and mopping sections of the house and picking up after themselves and others. We encourage self-directed learning. We provide access to learning websites and guide them to complete academic projects. We have a comprehensive timetable pasted on the wall of our living room to help them effectively and independently manage their time.

Until our son and our daughter were four and two years old respectively, we had a cable-connected TV at home but we realised how much the TV took away from their ability to focus when it came to other forms of learning. We transitioned away from having cable and eventually disconnected all our TVs.

We reintroduced a TV when they turned eight and six years old respectively, but with restrictions. Each of them got a set number of hours of screen time for the week and were responsible for deciding what to watch during that

time and when to watch it. Their screen time covered all leisure content viewed on a screen, be that a TV, a computer or other mobile devices.

Feeding a family consistently and healthily is a major undertaking. As our children grew up, we realised that cooking in bulk saved us time and money. So, we decided to shop for groceries for the week, cook in bulk and store the meals in the fridge. We also made healthy eating a priority. We learned that it is cheaper in the long run to eat healthily to prevent sickness through the foods we eat and those we did not eat. Therefore, we buy organic produce and avoid processed foods, eat lots of green vegetables and drink a lot of vegetable-based concoctions. Annica is very good at juicing natural products into drinks for the household. It is better to nurture healthy children than to fix unhealthy adults.

When it comes to disciplining our children, I don't like corporal punishment. I was whipped often by my parents as a boy, and I wish they had not done that. Annica, on the other hand, believes in corporal punishment and cites "spare the rod and spoil the child" as the basis for her preference. As a compromise, we have agreed that the only offence that warrants corporal punishment is lying. To help our children avoid situations that would warrant any form of disciplinary action, we consistently emphasise integrity as the most important personal attribute. If they live with integrity, they will never have to face their mother's wrath.

Our children have become semi-public figures. Their exposure to the public was never by design but rather something that happened organically. When Annica was

working in her corporate role, I used to take the children with me everywhere I went. I took them to recording sessions, shows, interviews and to many child-appropriate events. They became the centre of attention simply because they were constantly with me. The first time my son featured on a song with me happened because he wandered into my home studio and my producer thought it would be fun to get him to experience the recording process. My son handled the situation well and we helped him polish his rap lines into something presentable. My daughter had her moment too and was excellent singing the chorus to the song. We produced and shared a video to showcase that work. It is a song called *Saucing*, and it is posted to YouTube.

The public reaction was swift with strong and divided opinions across the country. On various radio and television programmes, some pundits criticised us for over-exposing and exploiting our children, while others described our actions as harmless and empowering. We watched in amazement as people argued about the song and video on radio and television. Close friends and family expressed concern about the psychological impact of childhood fame on our children, citing as examples Michael Jackson and other child stars who were adversely impacted by their early rise to stardom.

Even though we never intended for them to become child stars, it was inevitable that the well-produced song and its associated video was going to get the public's attention in a big way. They were eight and six years old at the time, and my son was so confident in the video that many people assumed he was on his way to becoming a

professional musician. We had no such intention for him. It may surprise many people to know that his enthusiasm for music and the arts has not been as great as it has been with Maths, Science and other academic subjects. Therefore, we place more emphasis on helping him develop his strengths in the areas we have observed that he is more gifted, which are his core academic subjects. Our daughter on the other hand is more enthusiastic about music and the arts than she is about other academic subjects. All that notwithstanding, we would not compel them to pursue careers they do not have an interest in.

The *Saucing* project was to give them the immersive experience of bringing a musical idea to life, and we did it together as a family. We were having fun as a family with that project. Even though we received several performance requests involving the children, we declined. That was not the plan for the project.

A few years ago when we put my daughter's name and face on *Sante's Hair for Kids*, the hair extensions product we developed and marketed throughout the country, we heard outcries from the public about that as well. That product came about after we discovered that my daughter cried every time her hair was braided with extensions because of the weight of the hair extensions on her head. Through research and collaborations with people knowledgeable about the hair extensions industry, we developed a product that solved the problem for our daughter. It was a no-brainer to call the product *Sante's Hair for Kids*.

Sante's Hair for Kids hair extensions are lightweight and come in various colours so that parents do not have

to buy other colourful accessories for their children's hair. Since the product is marketed to parents for use on their children, the packaging needed to have an image of a child. When people questioned why we put Sante's image on the product, I sarcastically wondered whose child's image they wanted us to put on the product we had developed.

The concerns expressed by people about our children being in the public light has not been limited to just the general public. I have heard it from my family too. My mother once cautioned me that by exposing our children as much, we are exposing them to spiritual attacks. I love my mother and she is entitled to her well-intentioned opinions. I am sure I am not the only son whose Ghanaian mother would advise that he hides every good thing from the public. Like I often do when my mother makes statements like that, I sarcastically encourage her to keep believing the things that fill her life with fear and allow me to learn from my 'mistakes'. I am sure her concern was out of love but I am also sure it was informed by superstition and an unhealthy fear of things she does not understand.

As my brand and public image has evolved to include more of my role as a father and family-oriented person, we have included our children in projects when appropriate. We intend to help them to develop their full potential and we also plan to remain very selective about the projects we include them in.

d) Creating Excitement

Family life can be boring if you don't make a conscious effort to create situations that you would like to experience.

Annica and I are intentional about every outcome we want in our home, and take the necessary steps to make that happen. We like our home to be a place where we enjoy spending time with each other. We like our home to be a place we look forward to returning to at the end of each working day. Thus, we create excitement by doing activities together as a couple and as a family, as well as individually.

We share true and fictional stories, travel as a family to interesting places within and outside Ghana, have conversations about serious as well as fun topics, and enjoy movie nights where we make our own drinks. Annica leads the kids in trying out new recipes they find on YouTube.

With Annica and me, we look for new ways to make our love life exciting. Among other things, we discuss interesting conversation topics, share thoughts on juicy gossip and trending topics, and text each other throughout the day when we are apart. We also enjoy developing ideas into products and exploring new business opportunities. Brainstorming and research gets Annica's juices flowing and I get a thrill from watching her get excited about ideas.

When I am out of the home and send her text messages, I say nice and playful things to her. She is very good at playing along. For someone who can be very restrained in how she expresses her emotions, she sometimes blows me away with her texts. When I receive random texts from her telling me she misses me, or praising me for something I did or just because she thought of me, I feel well thought of and appreciated. Her texts make me imagine her smiling, and that brightens my mood no matter what kind of day I am having. The following are some of my favourites:

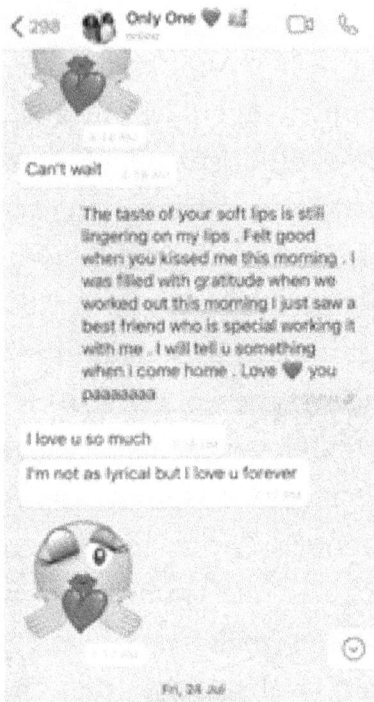

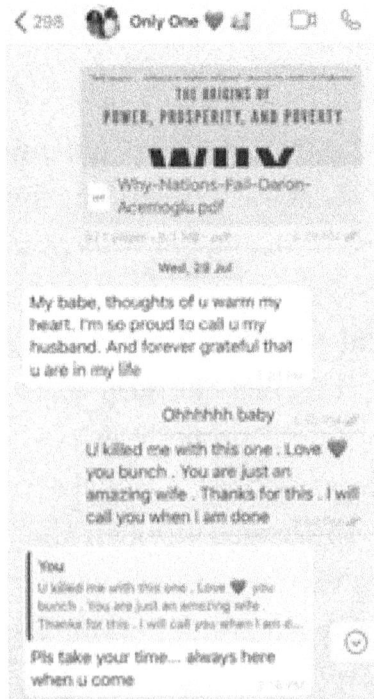

Such thoughtful gestures may seem small but they are very meaningful to me. Random texts from her leave thoughts about her lurking in my mind, and make me look forward to returning home to her. After being together for as long as we have, I get excited whenever I see her. She is a mystery that I am still unravelling.

She also baffles me with how stubborn she can be about getting lost in something she truly enjoys and leaving me feeling ignored. The first big problem we had as a couple was with her corporate workload occupying all of her time and attention. She was the company's employer brand specialist for West Africa. She was responsible for positioning the company as a top choice for prospective employees who were exceptional university graduates or high-performing mid-level professionals. The company had an expectation that employees complete all work assigned and add a self-selected assignment. So, she was working very hard trying to meet deadlines and it was very difficult to get her attention away from her work and onto anything else.

That was a frustrating time in our marriage for me, as she was buried in her work. Our sex life suffered and I was not the happy person that I usually am. I complained repeatedly and sounded like a broken record. Eventually, it dawned on her that she needed to take care of her matrimonial 'business' properly or she would have herself to blame if she gained professional success but her marriage fell apart. We managed through the situation with her consciously shifting her focus from work to the home when she was at home, and things eventually got better.

About a year later after she left her corporate job, we had a different but related problem. It was with her binge-watching of the television series *Suits*. We worked together at the time and usually returned home in the evenings. We would finish eating dinner and take our showers for the night. Around 10 o'clock when we tried to retire to bed, she would get on her laptop to watch hours of *Suits* and sleep only a few hours in the night. That caused domestic friction as well as affected her productivity.

Her father told me that when Annica was a teenager, it was almost impossible to get her attention when she had her head buried in a book. She could read for hours uninterrupted. I realised that the behaviour her father described had carried on into adulthood, with a laptop having replaced the book.

I clearly let her know that her binge-watching of *Suits* was making me and our children feel neglected. She didn't think her behaviour was a problem but agreed to scale back. After agreeing to amend her ways with watching *Suits*, she found another obsession – social media.

Annica uses social media for important work-related research but sometimes veers off into looking around for personal entertainment. We used to have frequent disagreements about that when my attempts to get her undivided attention proved futile. Sometimes, I would want to talk to her about something really important but she would be on her phone deeply immersed in what was going on in Kim Kardashian's world. I was in competition with one of the biggest influencers in the world for my wife's attention, and I couldn't win.

There is a word for when someone ignores their partner because they are paying attention to what is on their phone – it is called phubbing. That word is a combination of 'phone' and 'snubbing'. On my *Made in Ghana* album, I have a song called *Dum Fon No* – translation: "Turn off the phone", which I wrote specifically for Annica.

The chorus includes the lyric, *"Dum fon yi na yɛn ware, na ɛɛyɛ aka wo hɔ"*, – translation: "Turn off your phone so we can truly live like a married couple, for this habit is becoming unbecoming". The verse says, "Since I've been here you don't even look my way; Facebook and Instagram, you're chatting away. Since I've been here you don't even smile at me; smileys and emojis you're sending away".

That song and the daily mentions of phubbing in our conversations brought her attention to the fact that she was spending way too much time on social media. She started reducing the time she spent on her phone and started putting her phone away for long stretches of time when we were all at home. Eventually, she also made a more conscious effort to focus on using social media for work when she was using it for work.

At the time Kwame and our children were complaining that social media had taken all my attention, I didn't think it had. However, with all three of them complaining about the same thing, I needed to take a closer look and make some changes. So, I did.

Social media, especially Instagram with its very visual nature, offers me a way to travel to many places and see many things through the power of my imagination. Social

media is a very important way for me to learn from the people who are blazing a trail in the world. The day that Kim Kardashian leaves social media will be the day I leave social media. She is a brilliant businesswoman and I learn a lot from observing the kinds of businesses she ventures into and how she strategises. There's always something new that she and a few others who play the social media game at the highest level do that is exciting to watch.

When I'm on social media, I'm not vainly and endlessly looking at random people's pictures but usually researching for business strategies and for personal development. I often go on YouTube to watch instructional videos, and dig around on Google for needed information. The combination of Instagram, Google and YouTube can beat any library in the world, as far as timely and relevant information about lifestyle management, wellness and business strategies are concerned.

I take care of my family and do that efficiently so that I have ample time to do the things I enjoy. Without a doubt, I have become better at managing my use of social media after their constant requests. I started to apportion my time on the social media by taking frequent breaks to check in on Kwame and the children instead of being on my phone for long stretches of time. I also talked to Kwame often about the things I was looking at. Keeping him in the loop made him less likely to assume that I had wandered off.

Kwame's complaints about me binge-watching *Suits* were unfair. At one point he watched a 25-hour marathon of Mel Gibson movies. I didn't even know Mel Gibson had been in that many movies until he had his binge-watching

session. Surprisingly, he gave me an earful about how I was spending too much of my time away from the family when I binge-watched a TV series that I loved.

I am not a TV-watching person but when I find a very interesting TV series, I like to finish watching every available episode. *Suits* is an American legal drama with a really entertaining storyline, brilliant dialogue and high-quality acting. With nine seasons of ten episodes each, that was a lot of good content to consume. I cannot say I did not spend a lot of time watching *Suits* but that was my little luxury I carved out for myself after taking care of my family in diverse ways.

We both realise how important it is to make conscious effort to pay attention to each other. We are mindful about eliminating or minimising the use of electronic devices that get in the way of our human interactions. TV tends to be a huge distraction in most homes and we have made a conscious effort to minimise its presence in our home. Consequently, we have never had a TV in our bedroom and we rarely watch the one in our living room.

A TV in itself is not a bad thing but something is definitely wrong in a relationship when a TV becomes such a prominent part of the home that it takes the place of talking to one's spouse. If you are watching more TV (or on the phone) more than you are talking with your spouse, something is amiss.

It is always a blissful moment for me when Kwame and I lie down and enjoy each other's company in silence. We just lie down in a companionable silence and remain grateful

to be in each other's presence. It is always a beautiful and exhilarating experience.

Through all the changing seasons of our life together, we keep in mind that our relationship is going to be as exciting as we make it, and we make it so by being fully present and fully engaged.

e) Managing Conflict

Conflict is an inevitable part of life. When human beings interact with one another long enough, they are bound to experience conflict because they do not always want the same things at the same time, or always share the same points of view. Conflicts happen in most marriages and we have had our share of that. A Twi proverb conveys this idea well – "*Dua a ɛbɛn na etwie*" – translation: "Trees that grow near each other to rub against each other".

People manage conflict differently. Some people are naturally better at managing conflict but everyone can get better at it by recognising the conflict resolution strategies identified in the Thomas-Kilmann Model.

The five strategies, which most people use in managing conflict, are **avoidance** (trying to ignore or sidestep the conflict and hoping it will resolve itself or go away); **accommodation** (taking steps to satisfy the other party's demands at the expense of your needs or wishes); **compromise** (seeking a resolution that will satisfy the concerns of all parties involved); **competition** (taking steps to satisfy your desires at the expense of the other party involved); and **collaboration** (finding a resolution that satisfies the concerns of all parties involved).

In managing conflicts, Kwame and I use all these strategies except competition. While collaboration is ideal, there are many times that compromise and accommodation have been sufficient in getting our conflicts resolved.

Kwame is amazing at managing conflict, and he often takes the lead in diffusing situations and helping bring about a resolution. At a very early stage in our relationship, he realised that I was not as patient as he was. So, we discussed and clearly established some ground rules for how we would manage conflict:

1. **We never hang up on each other**. When we are not in the same place, the phone is often our main way of communicating. Abruptly ending a call deprives the other person of the opportunity to convey their thoughts. If either of us is too angry to continue, our next step is to ask for consent to discuss the subject later. We then mutually agree to end the call. I can hang up on people if the situation calls for it but I will never hang up on Kwame intentionally. He clearly helped me understand how much worse a conflict could become if we were to hang up on each other out of anger.

2. **We practice troubleshooting.** We make up scenarios and discuss how each of us would react if that scenario did in fact happen. We discuss our responses without the intense anger that such a scenario may provoke were we living through it. This exercise allows each of us the opportunity to think about the appropriate response, talk about how such a scenario would

make the other person feel, and deliberate on what could have brought about the scenario.

3. **We don't carry a previous day's anger into a new day.** We may not resolve an issue on the day it happens or may decide to save it for discussion on another day. An issue may have to carry on into the future, but the anger from that issue does not have to carry on into the next day. If Kwame does something that does not sit well with me, I let him know that I am unhappy but not ready to discuss the issue yet. I may not feel very excited about him but I do not withdraw from him. If the issue is so pressing that either of us may have to go to bed upset, then we talk it out before going to bed. When a new day starts, we start on a clean page.

4. **We debate issues and avoid quarrelling.** Wherever there is free will, there is bound to be conflict and conflict must be managed. The words we use when managing conflict are some of the key factors that escalate or resolve an issue. For example, instead of telling Kwame that something he did was foolish, I tell him his action was not very thoughtful. Both statements mean the same thing but the latter is less contentious. Sometimes, the words in a disagreement are best conveyed in silence – some things are better said unsaid. We have established that there are significant differences in objectives when people quarrel, debate or discuss. In a quarrel, the goal is to win at all cost. In a debate, the goal is to make a superior argument. In a discussion, the goal is to

hear and be heard. When we have a disagreement, a discussion gives us the best chance of getting our respective points across without being disrespectful. In a discussion, each of us learns and we both win. Quarrelling is allowed but insults are not.

f) Practicing our Faith

Religion, especially when the couple practice different religions, can be a source of conflict. Fortunately, we have so far avoided such a conflict.

I grew up with a strong biblical foundation and that shaped my moral values. As a teenager and as a young adult, that firm foundation helped me to appreciate the good things in my life and helped me navigate the world with a functioning moral compass. As an adult and as a parent, I have continued in my faith and have been intentional about exposing my children to principles and doctrines that have been helpful to me. Even though Kwame and I have different views on many aspects of religion, we share common ground on the importance of equipping our children with a functioning moral compass. As such, we practice our faith together as a family even though Kwame is very quick to clarify that he is not a Jehovah's Witness but rather a man on a path to enlightenment.

Kwame's religious upbringing started in the Methodist Church. As a teenager and as a young adult, he was without a religion. At the time we met, he had been on a personal faith journey and had been exposed to various faiths, including studying with Jehovah's Witnesses. He was familiar with many of the doctrines of my religion even

though he did not embrace them all. We prayed together and studied the Bible together, and he came with me to Bible studies at my Kingdom Hall. Before getting married, we discussed at length what our family life would be like given that I preferred to raise our children as Jehovah's Witnesses. Kwame welcomed the idea of equipping our children with the skills to study the Bible by themselves and to engage in critical discussions on life and faith, which is typical of the Jehovah's Witness teachings.

In recent years, our personal faith journeys have been independent of each other. Kwame has fully embraced the path of enlightenment, which he very much enjoys. I continue to practice my faith as I have always done. In addition to our individual practices, we engage in prayer and Bible study as a family. On most evenings at home, we hold Watchtower studies, a Bible-based discussion about world events in the light of Bible prophecies, Jehovah's Kingdom and faith in Jesus Christ. On Sundays, we have Bible meetings, which are extended discussions where we examine the scriptures and learn how to apply the Bible's teachings to our life. Kwame joins us in these meetings on Sundays and when he is home during the week.

Kwame and I have been mindful about respecting and supporting each other's personal growth in all other areas of our lives, including our respective faith journeys. With our children, we are a united front in teaching them "the way that they should go so that they do not depart from it when they grow up," as the Bible instructs us to do. We strongly emphasise Bible-based principles such as honesty, fairness, gratitude and service to mankind.

Praying together and studying together brings us closer together as a family. We can discuss current events and take turns in sharing our respective points of view. We can encourage each other in faith and help our children answer questions that young people often have about religion and life in general. Kwame is very good about highlighting the practical applications of the topics we discuss, and that helps keep our discussions lively and relatable. He is also quick to disagree with indoctrinations which he finds segregatory or divisive.

Throughout the marriage journey, couples are likely to go through phases or seasons. Just like a year is filled with seasons, so are the years in a marriage. In a marriage, expect **a phase of discovery**, where you will find out pleasant and unpleasant things about your partner. Expect **a phase where reality will hit you** in a good way and you realise that you are living the amazing love story you imagined. Reality may also hit you in a bad way and you might realise that your fantasy has turned into a nightmare.

Regardless of what phase the marriage is in, it gets better with time if you navigate with wisdom. It is important to keep in mind how much better a marriage gets will always depend on how much **transparency**, **communication** and **commitment** the couple invest in their relationship, in themselves and in one another.

• 14 •

MAKING AND MANAGING MONEY

It used to be the norm in most Ghanaian households that the husband alone took care of financial obligations related to his wife and children. The wife working or contributing financially to the marriage was optional. That is no longer the case. Wives contribute financially and in other ways, and in many instances, their contribution is necessary and indispensable.

Before having children, I was on my way to becoming a lawyer. I was going to start out as a corporate lawyer and eventually branch out on my own to start a private firm. I liked the high professional standards of corporate lawyers, and I wanted to practise my profession at the highest level but did not want to be tied to the strict routine that often comes with a corporate career.

The birth of our second child made it clear to me that I did not want a corporate job. Also, the corporate culture of having to 'play ball' by tip-toeing around issues in order

not to hurt people's feelings did not suit me. Even though I learned a lot at the company and developed many of my technical skills, I was very ready to leave when the time came for me to go. I took my destiny into my own hands and made the leap.

Establishing a marketing and advertising agency gave me the perfect opportunity to pursue my marketing and brand-building passion. I used my brand architecture expertise to make money and help support our family. I took on the role of managing Kwame's brand full time, which saved us the expense of hiring someone else to do so. I also provided consulting services for other artistes and corporate brands, and got paid for my services. When Kwame was not working on his music, we client-hunted or brainstormed marketing strategies for our clients.

Hunting for clients or 'prospecting' was what I enjoyed the least about running the agency. I did that for the first few months but found it draining. The yakking and schmoozing that it took to convince people to give me contracts was no fun for me. I hired a salesperson for that and focused on my core competencies.

We provided solutions for individuals and organisations to develop their brand identity and positioning. We created unique events for launching or promoting products and services. We managed other marketing activities on behalf of our clients. We also offered public relations services to help companies relate with the public through the media and other communication channels. Our clients were happy with the work we delivered and often gave us more business.

With time, we transitioned from developing strategies for other people's products to making our own products, and then used our strategic thinking and marketing expertise to push our own products. Making our own products was a big leap but a very rewarding one in terms of the professional growth and the long-term financial benefits. Making our own products or partnering with others on their products expanded our capacity as entrepreneurs and gave us multiple income streams.

Being self-employed mean we have to make money by ourselves at all times. We do not receive monthly salaries and we are not guaranteed any income if we do not put in the necessary work. We have to plan ahead at all times. We also have employees who depended on our ability to make money. We have to be good managers of money, living wisely according to the times.

Money is a basic resource for managing a household and it can be a touchy subject for many. Discussions on the topic tend to make many people uncomfortable. It is common for couples to avoid talking about finances. Capital Group's 2018 Wisdom of Experience Survey found that people are more comfortable talking about religion, sex, and politics than they are about money.

Before getting married, Kwame and I always talked openly about money. When one of us received money, the other knew how much. If one of us did not have any money, the other knew that and we shared what was available. That system worked for us before we got married and has continued to do so 'til today. The trust we share and the transparency we exhibit in our financial dealings has

helped to make discussions about money a normal part of our conversations.

The open and honest conversations that we frequently had about other topics set the stage for us to develop trust. Each of us endeavoured to tell the truth at all times and honoured our commitments to each other and to other people. We avoided making commitments we could not honour, acknowledged when we did not know something, and admitted when either of us was wrong. These behaviours helped us to establish mutual trust at an early stage in our relationship, which made it effortless for us to be transparent about money. The transparency we had about money while we were dating extended into how we managed money when we got married.

It is true that even when there is trust, a partner may be reluctant to talk about money. It may be because of different levels of financial literacy between the couple. The reluctance about transparency may also be due to a partner's attitude towards money or their history with money. For example, a frugal personal may be slow to share information about a savings account with a significant balance if their partner has demonstrated excessively lavish spending habits.

Kwame appreciated how I managed his resources when he allowed me to manage his finances. Consequently, he entrusted me with more. When I had money, I shared that information with him. When I needed to use his money for my personal expense, I kept him informed. We kept each other in the know about how much was coming in, how much was going out, and what we were doing with what

was left. We continued with that transparency in lean times and in times of abundance.

Ideally, transparency about money should be total, without any exceptions. However, there could be levels of transparency depending on circumstances within the relationship. When transparency cannot be total, the couple could discuss how transparent they would be with each other based on (1) either spouse's history with managing their own finances, (2) the level of trust between them in other areas of the marriage, (3) either spouse's knowledge or willingness to learn about managing personal finances, and (4) whether they will maintain transparency about their individual or pre-marital assets.

Another key factor that contributes to the level of financial transparency in a marriage is cultural orientation. Some people have been groomed to keep financial information away from their spouses.

Couples are more likely to be transparent with each other about money when they both kept their financial houses in order prior to getting married. They are likely to have relatively similar financial circumstances and attitudes towards money, and may be more open to discussing money with each other. On the contrary, discussing money may become awkward or contentious when one party has a history of mismanaging money. That awkwardness could prevent the couple from ever broaching the topic of transparency about money.

It is a basic truth that anyone can spend money but not everyone can manage money. Understanding and using financial skills and knowledge to effectively manage money

is not something most people are born with. Some people, whether educated or not, never learn how to save, invest, budget, pay bills, or manage debt. Such a person may be ill-equipped for a conversation regarding transparency about money in their marriage. For a person who is not financially literate and unwilling to learn, conversations about managing finances could be daunting. Such a person would rather avoid the conversation.

We recognise that transparency about money cannot be forced into a relationship. However, when trust is present in a relationship, and the couple learns to openly discuss money and remain accountable to each other, they are likely to plan and manage their finances well and get better at it with time.

In a situation where one spouse is more competent at managing money, that spouse could take the lead in managing the household income and expenses. Even when one of them is more competent at managing money, it is wise for both of them to take an interest in the process. That participation keeps the lines of communication open and ensures that both partners are abiding by the agreed-upon system. Additionally, the partners should make room for periodic conversations about their finances, which could prevent surprises down the road.

As part of learning to manage money well, it may benefit a couple to attend financial literacy workshops. Learning about personal finance and basic money management from a qualified financial counsellor could help a couple develop the necessary money management knowledge and skills to manage their joint finances. If you are interested

in such classes, you may contact your bank or religious organisation. You may also find helpful resources on the internet.

At the end of the day, it is important to remember that money is spent in meeting short-term needs, and saved for mid-term and long-term needs. Money is only a means to an end; not an end in itself. Therefore, the more aligned a couple is about their approach to making and managing money, the more likely it is that their marriage will thrive.

Money can make marriages thrive or fall apart. In fact, money runs through life like blood through our veins and I cannot think of any circumstance in life that money does not affect. 'Sika' is the Twi word for money and that is also the title of a song I released in 2012.

In the song, I talked about money being an invaluable resource that has been around since the dawn of history, and which has played a major role in the pleasures and strife people experience in this world. The chorus includes the lyrics, "*Me firi wo fie a wo nni asomdwee; me nka wo ho awareɛ nnyɛ dɛ*" – translation: "When I'm absent from home there is no peace; without me marriage is no fun".

Money is needed to be able to afford the basic necessities of life. I need money to pay for the material things that enhance the quality of my life. Treating myself and my family to pleasant experiences requires money. To be generous and look out for people who need help requires me to have a source of income. It is, therefore, good to have money.

Money is *one* of the most important things to have but it is *not the most* important thing. The most important thing in life is life, and money can help me extend my life by paying for good quality experiences, good healthcare and medication. I want to make enough money to take care of my needs and the needs of the people who depend on me.

Annica and I need to work very smartly so that we can meet our most essential needs, which include affording the best hospitals, the best specialists and the best medication. Additionally, quality education for our children, living in a safe and comfortable home and supporting our extended family are essential for us. When we are low on cash, we are honest enough to ourselves about not having what it takes to afford certain things. We don't become frantic. We live within our means, keep working until we earn more money, and then spend or save as we see fit.

Money is the by-product of a job done well. It is the value I receive because I have solved a problem. Every time I think about how I can increase my revenue, I think through problems that I can solve with my skill set and then take steps to solve those problems in exchange for value. As long as I make an impact in the world with my skills and talent, I know the Universe will give me what I need.

Several married couples have had to confront the question of joint versus separate ownership of money, or whether to choose a hybrid model.

Should there be 'my money' and 'your money', or 'my money', 'your money' and then 'our money', or should there be 'our money' only if we were married and shared our lives together? The answer to this question, as you may

have guessed, will vary depending on the couple's unique circumstances.

We have never had a distinction between 'your money' and 'my money' just as we do not have any such distinctions when it comes to our children, our cars, and other assets. We are together in everything we do. We live our lives together, plan for the future together, and manage our finances together. We are a unified entity, and each of us is an extension of the other. When Annica has money, it is for both of us. When I have money, it is for both of us.

Earlier in our relationship, I told Annica that I preferred transparency to secrecy in all areas of our relationship. I wanted us to be transparent about everything, including money. I led by example and kept her in the know of my financial activities.

At the time, I had not established a business structure that kept track of my money. I was making a lot of money from multiple sources and I couldn't easily keep track of the money coming in, what receivables were outstanding, what I had spent, and what the remaining balance in my account should be. The financial aspects of managing my career involved money changing hands so frequently that I couldn't have realised if the person managing my money was stealing from me.

Shortly after Annica completed her MBA, I thought it wise to have her manage my money instead of using a third party. She had studied key principles about managing money like a business should; she had the right temperament for keeping a keen eye on the cashflow, and most importantly, she had my best interests at heart. With her at the helm of

my affairs, I could focus on making more money and be confident that someone else was not quietly siphoning my money for their personal benefit.

Annica receives all payments made to me, keeps the money in a designated bank account, and keeps me thoroughly informed. She knows exactly how much money I am making. She knows about the direct payments, indirect payments and gifts I receive because I maintain total transparency with her. In return, she has been totally transparent with me regarding significant expenses. She has done such a fine job with managing my income that I continue to trust her completely with everything I earn. The trust and transparency we developed while dating continued in our marriage and has served us well.

Our transparency about money makes it more difficult for someone to steal from us without our knowledge. Annica and I have always kept each other informed about things the other person is doing and it is therefore easier to spot financial irregularities when they happen.

Not long after our son was born, I left my ATM card with Annica when I travelled to Italy for about three weeks. We were working on a major project for a multinational corporation at the time so we had a lot of money in the account, and GHS30,000 disappeared from the account in a week. That caught my attention. It was really strange that Annica would spend that much money.

One of her sisters had been staying with her, helping her take care of the home in my absence. Annica had given the ATM card to her sister to purchase items for the household but it was baffling that she would spend anything close

to that amount on such a short leash. We both became very worried but thought it unwise to ask her sister if she withdrew extra money with the card.

I asked my private banker for help figuring out the transaction. He insisted that it was a legitimate transaction performed with the card and that I should check with the person I gave my ATM card to. Since he knew I was travelling and Annica was a new mother focused on nursing our son, he had seen an opportunity to enrich himself at our expense. He had devised a way to adjust the transactions on my card by covertly increasing the withdrawal amount and keeping the extra for himself. Annica's sister had taken out GHS300 and my private banker had added two zeros to that amount and paid himself the difference.

When presented with the transaction receipt from Annica's sister's withdrawal, my unscrupulous private banker had no option than to come clean. He admitted taking the money, promised to pay me back, and begged me not to tell his boss. He paid back most of the money until he was fired for committing a different fraud at the bank.

Had it not been for the transparency Annica and I had about money, I would have assumed that Annica and her sister had connived to steal from me. That assumption could have led me to behave very badly and ruin my relationship with Annica and her sister. Following that experience, we had a comprehensive discussion about keeping each other clearly informed before involving any third party in the handling of our finances, so as to maintain our culture of

transparency. We stopped using ATM cards from that point on.

Earlier in our marriage, my mother noticed from a cheque I wrote to her that Annica and I had a joint bank account. She wondered aloud about why we chose to combine our resources. She explained that her attempts to do so with my father almost cost them their marriage. She believed that a husband should keep his money separately from his wife, and for the husband to take care of certain expenses and the wife to take care of others. In her view, it is not necessary for the right hand to know everything the left hand does.

My mother is not alone in thinking about household finances that way. That is the advice many married couples receive and many keep their money separate from one another. Some people do that to maintain their independence to spend on the things they deem appropriate while others do so to avoid accountability to their spouse. Others do so out of fear of having to walk away empty handed in the event that the marriage ends.

Ten years later, I wrote another cheque to my mother and it showed both of our names on it. She admiringly remarked, "You and your wife are an exceptional couple in the way you manage your marriage". I smiled and did not say anything. I should have asked if she would still advise a married couple to keep their money separate from each other. Her statement left me with the impression that she still would since she believed Annica and I are an exception to the norm.

We have a system for managing our money and every marriage needs a system that works for them. Some couples have a hybrid system where they set aside two individual spending accounts for either partner to use as they please and keep the bulk of their money in a joint account for mutually agreed-upon expenses. Some keep a small percentage of their income in a personal account and deposit the remainder in their joint account. In some marriages, they do not combine their money but agree on who will take care of which expenses.

In other marriages, especially when one party makes significantly more money that the other, the partner who makes significantly more money may take on all the expenses and give the other spouse a monthly stipend. They agree that each party owns their own money and uses it how he or she sees fit.

Regardless of the system they decide on, the most important thing is for the couple to practise that system transparently and to keep the lines of communication open at all times. If you decide not to share the details of your finances with your spouse, clearly communicate why and how you plan to go forward.

We work hard for every cedi that is due us but are also content with what we have. We do not chase after money at the expense of our integrity. We know we need money in order to live well and we also know that there is always a price to pay to make that money. We always assess if the sacrifice is worth the reward.

We are willing to walk away and leave money on the table if an opportunity is not a good fit for our family or if it could tarnish our integrity. We have turned down opportunities that did not meet out family's needs nor align with our family values.

Our lifestyle, family's goals, individual aspirations, and career choices have determined how we make and manage money. We constantly reinvent ourselves and keep our eyes out for problems that need solutions, and then apply our creativity and expertise to solving those problems. When we deliver a valuable solution to the appropriate audience under the right circumstance, we can expect to be rewarded appropriately for our efforts.

The closing verse of *Sika* is, "*Hwehwɛ me kwan pa so, na mɛma wo anidasoɔ; na ma ka wo ho, mi nfiri wo ho. Nanso kae hunu sɛ mebɛ tena a mennkyɛ koraa; enti di bi, na sie bi, na boa obi. Na dabi dabi wo nso wo bɛ yɛ yie*" – translation: "Seek me through noble means, and I will give you hope; I will abide with you and not leave your side. However, remember that when I come, I will not stay for long; so, spend some (of me), save some, and help someone. One day, you too will be wealthy".

Our goal is to manage our money well so that we remain financially independent, especially in our old age. We keep in mind that abundance is not perpetual, and set aside some of the bounty for the seasons of scarcity. We will continue to work hard and enjoy the fruits of our labour.

• 15 •

CRUCIAL CONVERSATIONS: GETTING MARRIED AND STARTING OUT

The decision to marry is a major milestone in a relationship. By the time two people decide to marry, they have likely come to know some key things about each other and have determined that marriage is the best next step for them. Regardless of how much they know about each other, the couple should have specific conversations about why, when, how, and where they want to get married.

If you are planning on getting married and have not thoroughly reviewed the crucial conversations topics and the worksheets provided earlier, please consider doing so before proceeding with the conversations and exercises that follow.

a) Topics for Crucial Conversations: Getting Married and Starting Out

For couples who have decided they are getting married, below are some crucial **conversation starters** about confirming the decision to marry, introducing the important people in your lives, the marriage ceremony, and life after the marriage ceremony.

- How sure are you about your decision to get married, and how do you know?
- Have you made any changes to your mid-term and long-term goals?
- What does the type of marriage you would like to have look like?
- How would you like to maintain excitement in our marriage?
- What about sex would be most important to you in our marriage?
- Do you have any sexual fantasies you would like to explore when we are married?
- How will we maintain our physical attraction towards each other?
- How will you let me know if you are not satisfied with our sex life?
- What are your thoughts about contraception?
- Where will we live after we are married?
- Do you want to have children?
- When would you like to begin having children?
- How many children would be ideal for our family?
- What would you like to do if we are unable to have any children?

- How will we take care of our children while we both work?
- Will we let our parents take care of our children while we are both working?
- How do you feel about having a househelp?
- When we give birth, whose parents will help take care of the new mother and the newborn child in the days immediately following the birth? Will the new mother go live with her parents for a while, or a parent will come live with us?
- What level of extended family involvement will we allow in the relationship?
- How will we manage conflict?
- Will we have an experienced married couple we will lean on for mentoring?
- Are there any topics about our relationship that we should not discuss with others?
- Which important people in your life would you like to formally introduce me to?
- How would you like to carry out such introductions?
- Will we participate in pre-marital counselling?
- What type of marriage ceremony would you like to have?
- How much would you like to spend on getting married?
- How will we pay for the cost of getting married?
- Would you like to go somewhere for your honeymoon?
- Will both of us continue with our current jobs after we are married?

- Under what circumstances would one or both of us need to change jobs?
- Where do you see yourself professionally in about ten years?
- How would you balance your professional aspirations with the needs of our family?
- Do you have any debt?
- If you have debt, what is the plan for paying it off?
- What will we do if we want something we cannot afford?
- How will we manage our finances?
- Would you like to have a household budget and periodic meetings to talk about money?
- What are your thoughts on the wife taking her husband's last name?
- How important is it to you that each partner wears a wedding ring?
- What changes do you anticipate in your involvement in social and community activities?
- What aspects of your parents' relationship would you like to emulate or avoid?
- Do you have any concerns about the relationship with each other's extended family?
- Are there tribal or cultural stereotypes that our relationship may have to confront?
- How would you manage relationships with negative or toxic close friends and relatives?
- Do you have any unresolved differences in religious views and beliefs?
- What is your biggest fear about marriage?

For newly-married couples, below are some crucial conversation starters about managing life in a marital home:

- What do you like most about being married?
- In what areas of our marriage do we have room for improvement?
- What one thing have you discovered about me after we got married?
- Is there something I do that you would like more or less of?
- What are your thoughts on our sex life?
- What has surprised you most about being married?
- Are there things we can do to enhance our sex life?
- Are there daily activities you would like us to do together?
- Are there things we could do to enhance our communication?
- Do we have enough transparency about money?
- How well are we doing with our system for managing money?
- Are there things we could do to enhance our system for managing money?
- How well are we doing managing conflicts?
- Are there things we could do to enhance our conflict management approach?
- Are there items in our household you would like to get rid of?
- Are there things we don't own that you would like to buy?
- Are there ways I could be more helpful in managing the home?

- Are there ways we could be more efficient with household chores?
- What are your thoughts on methods for disciplining children?
- What are your thoughts on lending money to others?
- What are your thoughts on honouring our rights to privacy?
- What are your thoughts on my engagement with social media?
- How often would you like to visit our extended families?
- How often would you like our extended families to visit us?
- What are your thoughts on financially supporting our parents or older family members?
- How has our relationship with friends changed in your opinion?
- Are there people we should consider spending more or less time with?
- Which marriage milestones are you looking forward to the most?
- How would you like to commemorate those milestones?

b) The Marriage Creed

A creed is a set of fundamental beliefs or guiding principles that a group of people agree to abide by. A marriage creed serves as a reminder of the most important things for the couple. It establishes the core ground rules for how they will honour each other, and reflect their aspirations. It could take the form of a list, a poem or a brief statement, and it should be written down. Here is ours:

Our Marriage Creed

In this house, we tell the truth and we show the proof
We live fully, and we love truly
'Fear' is the only thing that is afraid, integrity is praised
We speak freely and we are allowed to be silly
We make no assumptions and we pay full attention
We love nature and we nurture 'nurture'
We weep when we must; we fly our happiness flag at full mast
We are proud of ourselves in good and bad times
We value millions but are perfect without a dime
When we make mistakes, we apologise
No matter the stakes, love is what we eulogise
We are powerful but merciful; we are colourful and fanciful
Our playfulness is in our seriousness
Our carelessness is to see what's next
We are perfect not because we do not make mistakes
But because we forgive no matter what it takes
In this house, honesty is our bedrock.
In this house, we rock!

You might like to use the following prompts to write your marriage creed.

- What are the fundamental principles your marriage is built on?
- What will you do to help each other blossom?
- What do you want your partner to never forget?
- In difficult times, what would you like your partner to remember?

c) Family Balance Sheet

A balance sheet is a financial statement a company uses to list all of its assets and liabilities. Many companies do that monthly, quarterly, and annually. If a company has shareholders, it is required to make the balance sheet available to them. This statement helps the company and its shareholders to understand how much they actually have versus what they think they have.

For a household, a balance sheet can be helpful in taking stock of major assets and debts you have. Most of us have our balance sheets in our heads. It would be more useful if it is written down. That way, you would have a clearer picture of what you own and what debts you have to repay. **Whether or not you are combining all your individual pre-marital assets should be discussed prior to beginning this exercise.** Your family balance sheet can be as simple or detailed as you would like for it to be. Consider doing this within your first year of marriage.

Here are some steps to creating a basic family balance sheet:

1. Make a list of all your major assets (e.g. houses, cars, money, electronic devices, appliances, furniture, etc.) Include the actual or estimated value of each asset.

2. Make a list of all your major liabilities (e.g. personal loans, student loans, car loans, credit card balances, mortgage balances, etc.). Include the actual or estimated balance of each liability.

3. Classify the assets into short- and long-term assets. Short-term assets include cash and small assets that can easily be exchanged for money (e.g. laptops,

mobile phones, jewellery, short-term treasury bills, etc.). Long-term assets are high-value items that are meant to be used over a long period of time.

4. Classify your liabilities into short- and long-term liabilities. Short-term liabilities are outstanding debts that needs to be repaid within 12–24 months. Long-term liabilities are debts that can be repaid over a longer period.

5. Add up all the short-term assets and record their total. Add up all the long-term assets and record their total. Add the totals for the short-term and the long-term assets and record the answer under total assets.

6. Add up all the short-term liabilities and record their total. Add up all the long-term liabilities and record their total. Add the totals for the short-term and the long-term assets and record the answer under total liabilities.

Notes:

1. To keep this exercise simple, Shareholders' Equity is not included in the Liabilities section of the balance sheet.

2. The difference between your Total Assets and your Total Liabilities is your net worth.

_____ Family
Balance Sheet
As of _____

Short-Term Assets

_____	_____
_____	_____
_____	_____
_____	_____
_____	_____
_____	_____
_____	_____
_____	_____

Total _____

Short-Term Liabilities

_____	_____
_____	_____
_____	_____
_____	_____
_____	_____
_____	_____
_____	_____
_____	_____

Total _____

Long-Term Assets

_____	_____
_____	_____
_____	_____
_____	_____
_____	_____
_____	_____
_____	_____
_____	_____

Total _____

Long-Term Liabilities

_____	_____
_____	_____
_____	_____
_____	_____
_____	_____
_____	_____
_____	_____
_____	_____

Total _____

Total Assets _____

Total Liabilities _____

PART IV:
STAYING MARRIED, STAYING TOGETHER

Adinkra Symbol Name:
Boa Me Na Me Mboa Wo (Help Me and Let Me Help You)

Significance:
Cooperation and Interdependence

$$\cdot \quad 16 \quad \cdot$$

KEEPING THINGS HOT WITH ROMANCE, SEX AND INTIMACY

In a 2016 interview on the Delay Show, a popular Ghanaian television talk show hosted by Deloris Frimpong Manso, Annica was asked if it was true that we had sex every day. She looked into the camera, pointed a finger and she coyly said: "Okyeame, you have let out our secret!". She went ahead to explain how attracted we are to each other, how often we had sex and make out, and how we keep our relationship exciting. That interview made national headlines: "Okyeame Kwame and His Wife Have Sex Everyday", "We Have Sex Everyday Unless I'm Menstruating, says Okyeame Kwame's Wife" and "Okyeame Kwame's Wife Claims Sex is a Habitual Thing for Them".

Sex was very frequent and euphoric at the beginning of our marriage. In later years, sex declined and even became rare at a point in time. To keep our relationship exciting, we

had to be intentional about being romantic and developing intimacy in addition to having sex.

A popular Twi saying: *"Mpenatwe yɛdɛ sen awareɛ"* translates into "Dating or courtship is more exciting than marriage," and that is often quoted by some people to advance their argument that dating or courtship is more exciting than marriage. That statement is informed by the reality that people tend to bend over backwards to express their love to their partners when dating or courting, but become complacent after they marry. After they get married, they may slowly cease to say the nice things they used to say to woo each other, and neglect the thoughtful actions they used to employ to show extra care and attention. Consequently, their marriage becomes dull and the statement above typifies their reality.

Fortunately, I come bearing very good news – marriage is very exciting and can be more exciting than dating or courtship. More than a fleeting excitement, the deep-rooted bond and trust that couples share in a marriage provide a unique enabling environment for exploring a higher level of excitement beyond what dating or courtship could ever offer. If a couple invests the same amount of time, attention and empathy towards each other in a marriage as they would have done while dating or courting, there is no arguing that the return on that investment will be much greater in the marriage.

Many people assess the excitement in their relationships based on how much **romance**, **sex** and **intimacy** they experience. Excitement in a relationship could also come from experiencing security, comfort, authenticity, devotion,

and the thrill of a challenge. In our relationship, excitement is ensured by having peace of mind. For the purpose of this conversation, romance, sex and intimacy offer us a lot to talk about, and we will stay our focus on these.

Romance

A gentleman on a white horse comes to save a damsel in distress; she resists his help but he persists; he brings her flowers and sings to her until the lady finally gives him her hand; he carries her on his horse; she gratefully embraces him from behind as they ride off into the sunset to live happily ever after.

That is an 1800s European concept of how a man showed a woman that he was going to care for and protect her if she accepted his proposal of love. In this example, the woman reciprocates by giving the man what he wanted – her attention and affection.

People in other cultures did the same thing differently. In a hunter-gatherer society, for instance, a hunter may bring the choicest portion of the game he killed to the lady he is fond of as a way of signalling to her that she is special to him. The lady would cook a delicious meal with the meat, pack it in her finest bowls, take it to the hunter's house, serve him the food, wait for him to finish eating, pack the bowls and then return home to wash them. That would be the lady's way of showing her appreciation for the hunter's gesture.

Romance in a marriage is key and it is important to remember that different people express romance differently. Each of the people, in the scenarios above, was expressing

a degree of affection, attention and care. Each of them was being romantic in a context that fits their way of life. If you were to swap the characters in the two scenarios, the hunter may have shown his care and affection differently – because his choicest meat would have been of little interest to the damsel in distress.

On her part, the damsel may have showed her appreciation by carrying some of his game to help lighten the hunter's load. The guy on the horse may have had to get off his horse to sit next to the lady and help with the cooking as a way of expressing his affection. The lady, in return, may have fetched water for his horses and cleaned his clothes before he set off again.

Romance is expressed through actions and words. Romance could be very overt with the couple calling each other pet names, creating moments of pleasant surprises for their spouse, or engaging in public displays of affection. Some employ subtle or practical ways such as taking care of their household with dedication, treating their partner with respect, or making sacrifices for their partner.

Since each person may have their own perception of romance, it is important to know what your partner considers romantic and operate with that in mind. Annica and I, for example, exchange texts throughout the day and verbally acknowledge it when one of us does something well. We have found these seemingly simple actions to be effective in keeping romance alive in our marriage.

Romance happens when performance meets or exceeds expectation. Your partner may have their own context of affectionate behaviours that express love, care and

appreciation. Knowing your partner well and knowing what floats their boat is what keeps romance alive in a marriage.

Whenever I travel out of the country, I buy panties for Annica as a gift. The process of entering a lingerie shop, making my selection, and then bringing them to her engages all my senses. I like that. She likes receiving such intimate gifts from me and she smiles each time I bring her such exciting gifts, even though she rarely gives me credit for being romantic. Her reaction to my intimate gifts give away the fact that she secretly thinks I am romantic.

I was returning from the US and could not find a Victoria's Secret store at the airport. So, I headed into New York City in an Uber, picked up some of the finest pairs of sexy underwear, and nearly missed my flight. When I arrived home and handed Annica the nicely-packaged bag of panties, she thanked me and casually told me to place them in her underwear drawer.

I was expecting that she would get excited and maybe model one of them on her for me, which would have been very romantic on her part. Obviously, I was disappointed since her actions, in that moment, did not meet my expectation.

When I later drew her attention to that incident, she laughed and carried on like it was no big deal. She had grown used to my buying her panties and wasn't wowed. I am going to have to be creative next time with my presentation. I think buying a gift of panties, not only on Valentine's Day or on special days, is one of the most romantic things a man can do for his wife. Rather than simply handing it to her, I may have to come up with a different approach that grabs

her undivided attention. I will then deliver the gift and wink at her with an expectant smile.

The essence of romance is making your spouse feel loved, and it is important to not restrict your perception of romance to a preconceived notion. If, for instance, your spouse is not interested in flowers, buying them the prettiest arrangement may not do anything for them. On the other hand, if your spouse loves flowers, even a single stalk of their favourite flower may light up their world. So pay attention to what your partner likes.

Some people find it romantic when their spouse randomly compliments them, whereas others find a routine affirmation of love more romantic. Thus, a spouse may often, spontaneously compliment their partner about big or small things and rarely utter the words "I love you", whereas other people may find it romantic to end every phone conversation with "I love you, honey". As nice as each of these actions and words are, what matters most is whether the gesture meets or exceeds your spouse's expectations.

Being romantic means conveying to your partner the attraction, enthusiasm, devotion and general feelings they stir up in you. Doing so sincerely and creatively can deepen the attraction and emotional feelings you share. The warm and fuzzy feelings that romantic actions generate in your spouse can stir up sexual desire and passion, transforming the romantic attraction into a sexual attraction.

All things being equal, they may, as a result, engage in physical contact that could range from a gentle hug to intense intimate sexual activity.

Even though romance is not necessarily about sex, it can pave the way for a vibrant sexual experience. Romantic behaviours generate emotional goodwill that can significantly enhance a couple's sexual bond. That emotional goodwill is what elevates sex from being merely a physical act to a meaningful affirmation of their shared connection.

Sex

Sexual activities, and not just sexual intercourse, can be to a marriage what music is to a party. Just as the right music can make a party come alive, sexual activity can create an elevated sense of satisfaction in a marriage. As the primary means for bonding physically and emotionally, sexual activities include all interactions that convey sexual desire for your spouse. Generating arousal through the gentle and sensual physical touches, foreplay elevates each blood flow which gets the partners ready to engage.

Marriage exists on the concept of balance – seemingly opposite forces being complementary, interconnected, and interdependent as espoused by the Chinese philosophy of ying and yang. The husband and wife are seemingly opposite forces with unique characteristics designed for collaborating with one another. When a couple in love engages in sexual activities, that collaboration creates a unison that brings their physical, emotional, mental and spiritual selves into harmony. Like two different melodic parts combining to produce a soothing duet, a couple engaging sexually with one another can create a surreal sense of pleasure and fulfilment.

Sex is the most intimate of physical contacts. One partner's body enters the other, they exchange bodily fluids and become unified in a way that causes the couple to form strong emotional bonds. Sex, specifically, orgasm from the sex, and cuddling release oxytocin in the brain. The increased levels of that hormone prompts each of them to associate that good feeling with each other. To sustain the nurturing feeling that the hormone produces, they draw closer to each other.

The bonding is enhanced by a range of sex-related activities. Looking into each other's eyes in the middle of the act can provide emotional reassurance without any words being said; seducing each other with enticing gestures can amplify each partner's sex appeal; graciously appreciating your spouse's nakedness can nurture a sense of comfort and security; experiencing genital stimulation and copulation can generate an out-of-body experience that could culminate in an ecstatic sensation; and sharing feedback about what you like, what you do not enjoy, and how sexual activities make you feel can strengthen your bond.

In a 2013 survey conducted by Durex, more than 90 percent of respondents indicated that sex was more fulfilling when there was an emotional connection with their partner. More than the frequency of sex, it is the bond that drives a sense of sexual satisfaction for most couples. Many women have reported having difficulty reaching orgasm when they were not emotionally connected with their sexual partner. However, when sexual partners share chemistry beyond physical attraction, they let down their emotional guards

and suspend their inhibitions. They allow themselves to feel their partner's sexual energy and often experience explosive orgasms that leave them wanting more.

Along with the emotional connection is the intellectual or mental connection. For most women, sex is fulfilling when their minds are tuned to it. One of the significant differences between men and women is that men can generally turn on their sexual appetite at the flip of a switch, whereas women usually need to build up to it. That is why a husband can be ready to go at a moment's notice, but his wife may need to be stimulated with seductive signals throughout the day in order for her to be ready.

Some married men operate with the notion that their wives should be ready to have sex anytime they are, simply because they are married. Unfortunately, it doesn't work that way. At least, I know that fact to be true for my wife and many women I have discussed this subject with. Of course, some women would partake in sex with their husbands and be mentally absent. That physical sex may be sufficient to release sexual pressure, but would not be contributing to a lasting bond between the two of you. Some people ignore the fact that sex requires a person to take off all their clothes and be in their most vulnerable state, and for most people, that cannot happen at a flip of a switch.

Spontaneity is great for romance, but not so great for sex – unless that couple has previously built up romantic goodwill they can draw from. Otherwise, the sex may turn out to be merely a physical activity that leaves one partner, usually the wife, feeling unsatisfied.

While many people may instinctively know the basics of sexual activities, most couples will have to learn what sexual activities their partners like or do not like. They would also have to learn how their partners feel about various parts of their bodies, and how they could facilitate pleasurable sexual experiences for each other. Learning these things create room for adapting your sexual activities to meet each other's needs. The learning may be effortless and instinctive, depending on your personalities and communication styles. It could also be frustrating and time consuming as it requires patience, practice and dedication.

Learning about each other's sexual preferences and history could help create the awareness that your spouse is unique from other people you may have been with in the past. That could help you revise any preconceived ideas you may have had about sex. Learning about each other's sexual history needs to happen in a responsible manner – not an unwarranted sharing of sexual conquests, but a mature conversation about relevant events that help convey important information that will help your partner better understand your sexual needs.

As a note of caution, avoid the temptation of measuring yourself against your spouse's past sexual partners. That may not end well. If your spouse shares an aspect of their past sexual encounters that they enjoyed, take that as invitation to learn. If you do not know or are not accomplished at performing that specific activity, find out. Instead of letting your mind wander and becoming jealous and insecure, inspire yourself with the undeniable fact that you are the lucky one to have married your spouse, and the one who

gets to share every aspect of sex with them now and in the future. Even if you have been told you are not as competent as your partner's pervious lovers, you can always get better with patience, practice and dedication.

In the same vein, do not measure your partner's sexual capacity by that of your previous sexual partners, or expect the same experience that your past lovers may have provided. Apart from the fact that such a comparison or expectation is unreasonable and unfair, it could lead you to focus unhealthily on the past and deny yourself the opportunity to enjoy the present as well as tap into the future possibilities.

Talking about sex with your spouse should be a standard practice in a marriage just like it is with talking about what you eat, drink or wear. Talking about sex, especially when you are not having or trying to get your spouse to have sex, is an effective marriage-enriching exercise that enhances sexual activities. Admittedly, the conversation about sex can feel awkward, because many of us grew up not talking about sex.

People who are sexually eloquent or expressive often suffer a stigma of being considered 'spoilt' or immoral, which leads most people into shying away from sex-related conversations. However, a healthy marriage provides a safe space for the couple to share their innermost desires and sexual needs. Open and honest conversations are what it will take to convey your desires and needs to your spouse.

Start slowly with brief conversations about what you both like about each other's naked bodies. You could describe to each other how specific sexual acts feel for

you and talk about what activities you would like to have more of. As time goes on, the awkwardness will wear off and the stigma will lose its hold on you. For some spouses, becoming comfortable with calling your genitals by their real names, instead of calling them "your thing", may be a small victory that should not be underappreciated. Take that victory, carry on, and be patient with each other: the two of you may become comfortable with talking about sex at different paces.

With the demands of work and life, many couples' individual schedules are not always in sync. When the couple have children, that adds an extra component that takes the couple's attention away from each other. After a stressful day at work, a tired partner may not respond well to sexual advances from their spouse, leaving the other spouse feeling emotionally rejected. For some spouses, it may be complacency that leads them into ignoring their partners' sexual needs.

For sex to maintain its standing as one of the most important bonding activities a couple shares, a conscious effort from each partner to make sex a priority is necessary. Otherwise, sex will become an afterthought. Some licensed marriage counsellors recommend scheduling sex to allow for preparation and anticipation.

By communicating your desires with each other and clearing your calendars on specific days, you would be allowing each other enough time to feel frisky and be turned on for the explosive sex. While sex may be practical for most couples around bedtime, sex in a marriage should not only be around bedtime. Sneaking in a Saturday afternoon

rendezvous or a mid-week daytime action can make all the difference in a couple's sex life. Such sexual encounters, of course, would require some advance planning, hence the need for scheduling.

"How to Have a Better Relationship" is a New York Times feature by Tara Parker-Pope, a health and personal wellness author. Based on aggregated research findings from sources, including the General Social Survey and the International Social Survey Programme, she shared that

- Married people under 30 have sex about 112 times a year; single people under 30 have sex about 69 times a year.
- Married people in their 40s have sex 69 times a year; single people in their 40s have sex 50 times a year.
- "Very Happy" couples have sex, on average, 74 times a year
- About 5 percent of people have sex at least three times a week.
- The average sexual encounter lasts about 30 minutes.

The data above gives a peek into what goes on behind closed doors and gives married couples a yardstick with which to assess the frequency of sex in their relationships. For what it is worth, the frequency of sex in a relationship should be an open conversation between a couple since interest in sex may vary over time for each of the partners.

What if your spouse is not as excited about having sex as you are? What if you want much more sex than your partner does? What if your partner does not respond enthusiastically enough to your sexual advances? What

if you feel emotionally rejected by your partner's low sex drive?

As your relationship evolves, your sexual desires and interest may change. Age, for instance, may change your sex life. Adverse health conditions may impact a partner's sexual vitality. Communicating openly about sex would not only let your spouse know what you do or do not enjoy about sex, but could also make it easier to open up about sexual health problems when those arise.

Sexual problems such as premature ejaculation, erectile dysfunction, orgasm disorders, and lack of sexual interest could create tense moments in a marriage. Thanks to scientific advancements, many sexual disorders can be treated by qualified doctors. Start with a candid and empathetic conversation about how each partner feels about the situation. Be mindful of the words used since the affected party may be already feeling drained about it. The mutual awareness may improve the situation. By all means, do not ignore the problem. Where necessary, consult a qualified health professional.

Do not conclude that your partner wants too much sex and coldly turn them down just because you are not interested in sex. Just like you manage other areas of your household such as finances, conflict, and children, your sexual life needs to be managed. Make a conscious effort to address issues and invest in more than one way of sustaining sexual excitement between the two of you. For example, touching your partner sexually or engaging in oral sex or making out may be options you could consider.

As important as sex is, it is possible for couples in low-sex or sexless marriages to be totally satisfied. A wife's low sex drive may match her husband's and they could both carry on happily with simply talking, laughing and sharing social activities together. It is when one partner is fine with a sexless marriage and the other is not that problems arise. In such cases, an open and honest conversation is necessary. In some cases, a conversation with a doctor or a qualified licensed therapist could be helpful to the marriage.

So, make love and make each other happy. Sometimes, you could be gentle and tender in making love and, at other times, you could let out your wild, freaky sides. You could share humorous moments that create a frisky atmosphere or try new ideas that both of you are comfortable with. Whichever way you choose to do it, just do it as long as you are comfortable.

Intimacy

About five years ago, Kwame was on a working trip in Anyinam in the Eastern Region. He called and his first words were, *"Me pɛ wo saa!"* – translation: "I like you just the way you are!". Those words melted my heart. Even though he was hundreds of miles away from me, I felt very close to him in that moment.

Intimacy is the feeling of closeness, trust and empathy that a couple develop as they get to know each other through the sharing of life's moments and experiences. As intimacy grows, a couple develops more trust for each other and they willingly make themselves vulnerable to each other. Kwame likes to hug and I know physical touches make him feel

really close to me. When I am thinking about his wardrobe or looking out for his best interest, I feel very close to him. Being in the same physical space with him, of course, makes me feel closer to him, but it is the bond we share that makes all the difference.

Intimacy between a couple can be experienced in five areas:

- **Physical Intimacy** involves all physical contact that a couple use to express their affection towards each other. These include hugging, kissing, cuddling, sexual intercourse, holding hands, and standing or sitting close to each other.

- **Emotional Intimacy** is what makes partners share their feelings and emotions without fear of judgement or ridicule. This makes partners interested in each other's feelings and then respond with care and affirmation.

- **Intellectual Intimacy** refers to freely sharing ideas with each other, valuing each other's opinions and accepting differences in opinion. This makes partners share values and interests, and enable them to hold meaningful conversations.

- **Spiritual Intimacy** exists when the couple can share their deep thoughts and beliefs about matters of faith and the non-physical world, allowing partners to acknowledge each other's spiritual journey and remaining respectful of their differences.

- **Recreational Intimacy** is when the couple can play and have fun together with activities such as picnics, movies and shopping. They have some shared

interests, show interest in the things their partner enjoys, and create experiences that they could enjoy together.

Intimacy cannot be forced into place – just as trust and vulnerability cannot be forced. Intimacy happens while the couple invest in learning about each other and allowing their partner to know their innermost thoughts, fears, insecurities and desires. As intimacy grows, the couple sees each other as extensions of themselves and become comfortable with being naked with each other, both literally and figuratively. Each of the areas of intimacy helps the couple establish and maintain their connection to one another.

As intimacy grows, the couple become attuned to sharing non-verbal communication. They feel their partner's feelings; they learn to anticipate what is on their partner's mind; and they develop signals that allow them to communicate with something as simple as just eye contact. As a couple increase their intimacy in all five areas, they become more understanding of each other and allow each other the room to grow.

When a couple share a strong intimacy, they make each other a priority. They stay in touch even when apart. Most of what happens between them stays between them. They maintain a high level of privacy that keeps third parties out of their relationship. They view each other with oneness and willingly make sacrifices for each other. They regularly show appreciation for each other. They also pay more attention to each other's love languages and become better equipped at communicating their love.

Love languages are the five ways, according to family life expert Dr. Gary Chapman, by which people prefer to show love and receive love in intimate relationships. They are Words of Affirmation, Acts of Service, Physical Touch, Quality Time and Gifts.

- **Words of Affirmation** are the things you say to acknowledge, encourage and appreciate your partner.
- **Acts of Service** are the helpful actions you take to relieve your partner of tasks they may have had to complete by themselves.
- **Physical Touch** has to do with the non-sexual contacts that remind your spouse of your presence.
- **Quality Time** involves sharing meaningful activities that involve only the two of you and giving your spouse your undivided attention.
- **Gifts** are physical items that show thoughtfulness and effort.

The love languages help explain why some loving actions by a spouse may be more meaningful to their partner. They also remind us that one size does not fit all when it comes to showing love to our spouses.

Knowing and speaking each other's love language enables the partners to show love in ways that their spouse could identify with the most. You can learn more about the love languages from the book "5 Love Languages" by Dr. Gary Chapman. You and your spouse can find out about your love languages by completing an online assessment at 5lovelanguages.com. The following is a summary of the love languages and how to express them.

	What it is	**How to express it**
Words of Affirmation	Things you say to acknowledge, encourage and appreciate your partner	Tell your spouse what you like about them; recognize and encourage their efforts often.
Acts of Service	Helpful actions you take to relieve your partner of tasks they may have had to complete by themselves	Help with household chores and errands; do things you say you are going to do.
Physical Touch	Bodily contacts that reminds your spouse of your presence	Hug, cuddle, make love, hold hands, sit or stand close, wrap your arms around each other.
Quality Time	Sharing meaningful activities that involve only the two of you and your undivided attention	Make time for just the two of you; turn off electronic devices, make eye contact and have conversations.
Gifts	Physical items that show thoughtfulness and effort	Give big and small items that reflect you know what your spouse likes; remember special dates and events.

Even though your spouse would have a dominant love language, which is how they prefer to receive love, all the other love languages apply too. Using all the love languages in expressing love to your spouse would help create more intimacy in your relationship. As Kwame likes to say, love language, body language and verbal language are all competencies you need in order to be successful in a relationship.

Sexual Rejection

I woke up at dawn to see my beautiful wife up as well. I stared at her as the soft light piercing through the window hit her skin, revealing the contours of her naked body. As my mind and body got stimulated, I thought to myself: "Oh my God, my wife is beautiful!". My ego reminded me that what I had started could lead to disappointment but I dismissed my ego's caution and proceeded with great expectations. I gently approached my wife from behind, softly kissed her on the neck and whispered into her ears: "You are the sexiest woman on earth!".

Startled, she quickly wiggled herself out of my gentle embrace and, dismissively, with a harsh tone said, "Not now! Not now! You know I have a presentation in a few hours!". She looked away and carried on like nothing major had just happened.

Sexual rejection happens often in many marriages as a spouse turns down a sexual advance from the other spouse often with emotionally-distant comments like "I am sick" or "Today too?" or "Don't you know I have work tomorrow?". Sometimes, the spouse may bring up an unresolved issue

as the reason they are not going to partake in sex with the spouse; some wives go the extra mile and falsely claim to be having their menstrual periods. Some spouses have been known to make comments like, "Go to that woman (or man)!", as a way to protest an acquaintanceship that the spouse is unhappy about. Some husbands have been known to tell their wives they are not interested in having sex with them because they are fat, whilst some wives have been known to dismissively tell their husbands: "Take your erection somewhere else".

Much more than the denial of sex, it is the statements and actions of the spouse turning down the sex that could be most painful and even harmful to the marriage. An insensitive comment can bruise or damage a spouse's ego and self-esteem.

Couples are not always going to be in the mood for sex at the same time. One may want sex more often than the other. The spouse not interested in having sex at any point in time may have a legitimate reason, but the manner in which the denial of sex is conveyed is what makes all the difference. Tact and empathy go a long way in such situations.

The spouse, not in the mood for sex, could empathetically embrace the other spouse and explain why they are unable to partake in sex at that particular time, promise to be available at a later time, and honour that promise. Let down your partner gently. Consider using **the Four-G method** by being: Gentle, Genuine, Generous, and Graceful.

The following are some statements to consider when you cannot honour your spouse's request for sex:

- "Honey, you know I love you and would wish to go down this orgasmic road with you, but I am totally out of energy; you will not get my full involvement. So, let's try for tomorrow and I will rock your world."
- "I have a lot on mind right now. Could we wait till tomorrow when we can build up all day to be in the mood by the end of the day?"
- "I am so fortunate to have you, such a romantic and sexy partner with such drive. Could you please teach me how to be turned on as frequently?"
- "Babe, can I give you a hand job instead, since I'm not feeling great for sex tonight?"
- "Instead of a full performance, can I just rock your mic?"

For the spouse who would like to have sex when your partner is not in the mood, here are some things to keep in mind:

1. Do not beat yourself down for wanting sex at a time when your partner is not in the mood. Desiring sex from your spouse is normal even if you want it more than they do.

2. Seek to understand your partner's sexual patterns. Know her menstrual cycle, understand what it means for her to be in her ovulation period, empathize when she honestly says no and partner with her to address any underlying problem together. Your partner's interest in sex may follow a pattern and you may choose to match your sexual advances with when your spouse is most likely to be in the mood. Also,

seek to know what satisfies your partner sexually, and not only what satisfies you.

3. Minimise your expectations. The fact that you are ready does not mean they will be ready too, so don't expect them to be ready.

4. Make no assumptions. Do not assign reasons to your partner's lack of interest without talking about the situation. Also, do not take all intimate and romantic gestures from your partner as invitation to have sex.

5. Seek a compromise. One partner may need to tone down the frequency with which they may want to have sex, whereas the other partner may need to ramp up the frequency with which they may want to have sex.

6. Gently prompt a discussion about your spouse's sexual interest. Sex may not be a pleasant experience for your spouse and you may need to help them revive their interest in sex.

7. Find a new exciting hobby or join a recreational club.

8. Talk to a qualified therapist if the problem persists.

Enhancing Sexual Appeal

To increase your sexual appeal to your spouse, consider doing the following:

- **Invest in physical exercise.** Very few human bodies look attractive without any exercise. It is very likely that if you eat regularly and do not invest any time exercising, you are bound to, eventually, get out of shape, especially as you get older. This is true for both men and women. If you don't find yourself attractive

when you look at yourself in the mirror, it is unfair to expect your spouse to find you attractive. So, hit the gym and break a sweat. Join a fitness club or hire a personal trainer. You will be amazed at how much better your body will feel with a renewed confidence that will boost your sex appeal.

- **Fulfil your promises.** Annica often tells me that a reliable man is a sexy man. I am perpetually sexy to her because I make promises I can keep. I believe most people will find it difficult to say "no" to their spouses when that spouse keeps their word in all areas of their relationship. That habit of fulfilling promises increases intimacy which, in turn, increases attraction. Deliver whenever you promise.

- **Become great companion to yourself.** People love to spend time with partners who are daring and full of character or partners who are simply themselves. Ask yourself if you would frequently make love to yourself if you were in a relationship with yourself. If your answer is an honest no, work on your daily habits and attitudes that would make you attractive to yourself. Strive to become as irresistibly charming as you can be and enjoy being with yourself.

- **Refresh your looks and involve your partner in the process.** Let your partner help upgrade you. I wear facial hair because Annica recommended that I try it. When I return from my weekly barber visits with my extra-clean shave and stylized beard, I am "Prince Charming" in her eyes. When she wears tight clothes that reveal her curves, I get excited. We often talk

about what aspects of our respective appearances turn each other on; and we endeavour to keep that up. Ask your partner about their favourite colours and wear it for them especially. Ask for their feedback on what looks good on you and let them help you pick them out.

- **Take personal grooming seriously.** Brushing your teeth twice daily is a necessity for all. Your breath does not stink as much in the morning when you brush the night before. Clip your finger nails and toe nails and, occasionally, pay a professional to give you a manicure and pedicure. Keep your pubic hair neatly trimmed or shaved. Take extra care of your genital areas. Bath often, at least twice a day. Wear clean underwear. Taking personal grooming seriously will make you feel good about yourself and could also make you a rock star in your bedroom.

Sexual activities in a marriage can be playful and fun, gentle and tender, flirtatious and lustful, experimental and adventurous, as well as various combinations of all these sexual approaches. Even though a couple may have a preferred sexual approach, mixing things up could be an effective way to inject variety into their sex life to keep it interesting.

Falling in love is the easiest part. Not much effort is required to fall in love. Everything else related to developing and sustaining a lasting relationship requires effort. It certainly takes effort to experience the

joy of being married. Romance is necessary to keep the spark alive; sex is essential in providing each other physical pleasure; intimacy is vital to ensure ongoing closeness.

When there is romance, it inspires sex and breeds intimacy. When there is sex, it affirms romance and nurtures intimacy. When there is intimacy, romance is natural and sex is meaningful. Intimacy is the tie that binds and you need sex and romance to keep things hot in a marriage.

· 17 ·

MANAGING RELATIONSHIPS WITH THIRD PARTIES

Who is the first person you usually think of talking to when something important happens to you? Who do you often turn to for guidance when in a dilemma? Who do you confide in with sensitive information about you? How much of your free time do you spend virtually or in-person with people other than your spouse? Do you share more emotional, spiritual, intellectual, physical or recreational intimacy with anyone other than your spouse?

These are not rhetorical questions – you should ponder over them and answer truthfully. If you need some time to think honestly about your answers to these questions, that is perfectly fine. You may even have to periodically revisit these and similar questions in order to assess how you are

managing your relationships with people other than your spouse.

For a married person, everyone, other than your spouse, is a third party. Your parents, siblings, in-laws, best friends, pastors, co-workers, business associates, neighbours, social media friends and followers, exes, and acquaintances are all third parties. They are third parties because they are not directly involved in the marriage. Even your children who are members of your family are technically third parties to the marriage. While some of these individuals or groups may view themselves as stakeholders due to the fact that you may have given them reasons to believe they have a seat at the table of your marriage, each is still a third party.

You may directly or indirectly relate with each third party at different points in time, some more regularly than others. Some may be people you relate to by choice, while others may be those you relate to as a matter of necessity. Regardless of how they came into your life, you owe it to yourself and to your marriage to define the **purpose** and **nature** of your relationship with each of these third parties.

Without defining the purpose and nature of your relationship with third parties, you may forget to establish the healthy boundaries that need to be in place to ensure such relationships do not suffocate your marriage. Third parties may act with good intentions based on what they think is the purpose and nature of their relationship with you and your marriage. Their definitions may not be the same as yours and their actions may therefore not align with your expectations. As a result, they may act in ways that seem reasonable to them, but their actions may offend

or leave you frustrated. Some may even act in ways that protect their best interest at the expense of your marriage, and that is why you need boundaries.

Without boundaries, you may, consciously or unconsciously, hand over control of your marriage to other people. With boundaries, however, you clarify how you want others to relate with you; what actions you will accept; and which ones you will not tolerate.

Most people will respect boundaries if they knew there are boundaries in place. Some will know, but still ignore the boundaries. That is why it is not enough to communicate those boundaries; you must also enforce them. Granted that the tact and urgency required for establishing, communicating and enforcing boundaries with third parties would vary based on the nature of that relationship, the goal would be the same in each situation – to be clear to yourself and to others about your expectations.

Boundaries are not barriers. A **boundary** is a line that marks the limits of an area, whereas a **barrier** is a structure that prevents access to an area. A boundary is for defining the limits of an area while a barrier is for walling off that area. Boundaries do not always need barriers, even though barriers may sometimes be necessary to enforce the boundaries and prevent trespassing. When managing third-party relationships, boundaries are always necessary to ensure accountability and respect. In extreme cases, barriers may be needed to enforce the boundaries.

Third-party relationships that may pose the biggest challenge for couples include relationships with in-laws, relationships with friends, and relationships with religious

leaders. Another situation involving third parties is when one or both spouses are unfaithful. While the "other woman" or the "other man" would be an unwelcomed third party, preventative actions are necessary to prevent such third parties from showing up in the first place.

a) Managing Relationships with In-Laws

When you marry a person, you inherit their family members. Marriage in Ghana is considered not only as a union between two individuals, but also between their two families. Therefore, each partner gains new relatives called in-laws, that is, everyone in your spouse's family who has become related to you by virtue of the marriage. They may love, care and respect your spouse very much. In many cases, that love, care and respect would extend to you. Your in-laws may welcome you into their family with open arms and treat you as one of their own. Your in-laws could be people you learn new things from and they may become a part of your support system, especially in a closely-knit and communal culture like we have in Ghana.

It is also true that many in-laws have behaved very badly throughout history. Many people associate "in-laws" with negative sentiments such as unwarranted interference, lack of empathy, lack of respect, manipulation, and a variety of dramatic behaviours that create toxic relationships. As the saying goes, some in-laws are "outlaws".

Marriages have ended or are on the verge of breaking up because of interferences and demands from in-laws. On the other hand, some marriages are thriving and have not fallen apart because of interventions and support from in-laws.

The reality for most people is that in-laws are like their own extended family – a group of human beings, some of whom you may love, respect and get along with, and vice versa. As a result, you may share a very cordial relationship with some in-laws and only relate with others at an arm's length.

Different in-laws have different levels of influence, and the manner in which they exert their influence vary. In some families, the mother-in-law may be the peacemaker whose effectiveness at diffusing conflict makes her the ideal adult in any room at all times. In other families, the father-in-law is the voice of reason who injects common sense into situations. Some brothers-in-law are the ones who can call family members to order when someone gets out of line. Some sisters-in-law may be the ones who have the final word on most family matters.

Just as these individuals could use their influence to your benefit, some of them could use their influence in ways that work against your best interest. That is why all your dealings with your in-laws require **clear boundaries**. You will also need to employ wisdom and boldness to enforce such boundaries.

Kwame and I have always had good relationships with our respective in-laws. This has been the case largely because even before we were married, we both comported ourselves in ways that prompted our respective in-laws to treat us with respect. Of course, we do not share the same views on everything and have, on occasions, had to be assertive and respectfully insist that others stay in their own lane.

We have excellent relationships with our respective in-laws because we have made a conscious effort to treat them

with love and respect. Kwame maintains a great relationship with all my family members and he genuinely relates to them like he does to his own family. With my father, for instance, they share phone calls and text messages multiple times throughout any given month talking about religion, current affairs, history, traditions, enlightenment, and much more.

On my part, I embrace all Kwame's family members as mine too. With his mother, for example, her counsel is never with pressure. She patiently shares her suggestions and leaves it up to me to apply her suggestions as I choose. We share a warm interaction even when we go for months without speaking with each other over the phone or in person. Our authentic and unforced relationship allows each of us to relate freely and exist peacefully.

As sensitive as relationships with in-laws can be, speaking up when people from your spouse's family treat you in a way you do not like requires **straightforward communication**. Straightforward communication does not have to be rude or disrespectful, but rather assertive and unapologetic. Otherwise, that person may continue treating you in the way you do not like or appreciate which can inevitably ruin your relationship with them.

Sometimes, it is your spouse who may have to step in to establish the boundaries. If your father-in-law, for example, has a habit of yelling at your children in a way that is unhealthy, your spouse may have to tell him that his method of relating to your children is not appreciated. Or, if your sister-in-law has a habit of showing up unannounced, your spouse would have to let their sister know that she is

welcome only when she calls ahead to check that it's OK for her to come over. In the event that your spouse is unwilling or ineffective at enforcing boundaries with their family members, you may have to do that yourself. Remember to do so clearly, firmly and respectfully with your spouse fully aware of the action you are about to take.

It goes without saying that you and your spouse must be on the same team when it comes to establishing boundaries for your respective in-laws. Kwame and I have established and clearly communicated the boundaries to our respective families as far as our relationship is concerned.

Our families know their love and support is welcome as long as they respect the fact that we are building our own family and may not do things the way they want. From either side, there are people who have attempted to overreach and we have vigilantly addressed such situations.

In managing your relationship with in-laws, you will need to **respect their boundaries** just as much as you would want them to respect yours. Actions like taking money from in-laws to pay for a wedding or living in their home for an extended period of time blurs the boundaries. You could further blur the boundaries by asking to borrow money from your in-laws, displaying a lack of independence, displaying a lack of self-respect, and unnecessarily inserting yourself into their matters or inviting them into yours.

When you ask people for money, you give them the right to ask you what you are going to use it for. You open the door for them to assess you financially. Even when you have the best of relationships with your in-laws, you would want to think twice about taking money from them. Some may

talk about you unfavourably in your absence and trample on your dignity. You do not want that.

When you display a lack of independence with your in-laws, you open the door for them to make decisions for you. When you display a lack of self-respect, you give them cause to question your character. When you unnecessarily insert yourself into their matters, you sow the seeds of complication that would eventually make you an unwelcome guest; and when you unnecessarily invite them into your matters, you would have issued an open invitation for them to weigh in on your matters whenever they feel like doing so. For instance, don't be too quick to run to your in-laws with a report when your spouse wrongs you. Once you blur the boundaries, you give up your right to be your own person as far as your in-laws are concerned.

Your respective families played important roles in your lives when each of you were growing up and their roles sometimes change when you become adults. Again, their roles change when you marry and it is important for you and your spouse to be clear about those transitions. Sometimes, your extended family members will play their roles near you and, at other times, they will play their roles from a distance; but at all times, they must play their roles according to the boundaries that you and your spouse have established for your family unit.

Whether it is with how frequently they visit your home or you visit theirs; whether it is with their opinions on matters concerning your spouse or household, having clear boundaries would ensure a respectful and cordial

relationship with your in-laws. At all cost discuss their role with your partner before you get married.

b) Managing Relationships with Friends

Friends are often important in good times and in the bad. Many people celebrate happy moments with friends, count on them for guidance when making key decisions, and lean on them for emotional support in difficult times. You may have had friends before you got married and will likely have new friends after you marry. Those friends may serve different purposes and may share different levels of closeness with you.

The dynamics of your relationship with your close friends is likely to change over time. The changes will be determined by whether your friends are married or not, their perspectives on marriage, and what impact their behaviours have on you or on your marriage.

As a married person, your priorities are likely to be different from those of your unmarried friends. You will have a spouse as a priority, whereas your unmarried friends will not. Even when they have significant others in their lives, the priority levels will be significantly different. Consequently, the amount of pre-marriage free time you had to spend with your unmarried friends may be reduced once you get married. Also, your focus on establishing a home with your spouse may leave you with fewer topics of mutual interest to discuss with your unmarried friends.

Don't feel bad when you have to pull back. Depending on the person or the situation, you may have to pull back gradually or abruptly. Make it abrupt if the situation calls for

it. If it has to be gradual, use your best judgement and don't drag the process unnecessarily. But by all means, cut the ties if you have to. If you are fortunate, some of your most understandable friends, both married and unmarried, may even voluntarily pull back to allow you the needed space to focus on your marriage.

Your friends' perspectives on marriage, whether they are married or unmarried, will affect the dynamics of your friendship after you get married. Their opinions about marriage, in general, and about yours, specifically, would impact the kinds of conversations you would have with them. That would also determine if you would turn to them for counsel. If you continue to have fewer and fewer subjects to discuss with a friend and would not turn to them for counsel, they may go from being a close friend to being an acquaintance. That is perfectly normal.

Among your friends, you are also likely to have differences in opinions. Some differences in opinion, especially about marriage, may be significant enough to merit an end to that friendship. For example, if a close friend of yours does not believe in the idea of marriage or believes that it is not a big deal for a spouse to cheat or that you should never trust your spouse, your closeness with that friend would need to be reassessed in the best interest of your marriage – if you do not share their opinion.

I don't have many close friends. My sisters have been my closest friends for most of my life and that has been sufficient for me. The nature of my work brings me into contact with many people, and I am as friendly as I need to be in order to accomplish the purpose of our meeting.

As a personal preference, I am careful about extending the "friend" label to acquaintances. With the people I consider my friends, I do not discuss my marriage or what is going on in our household with any of them. I don't think it is necessary to do so. We may have general conversations about marriage or relationships, and that's the extent of it.

Understandably, Kwame has many acquaintances as a result of his work and interactions with fans, colleagues and business associates. He also has a few people he considers his close friends. These are people who have provided him with wise professional and personal guidance through the years. These are knowledgeable and insightful people whose opinions he trusts. I have come to know these people and I am confident that they are positive influences in Kwame's life. These people also know the boundaries, and they are respectful of those.

Healthy friendships with people other than your spouse are a good thing, and we recognize the importance of friends to us individually and to our marriage. We also recognize that our relationships with friends need to be actively managed in the best interest of our marriage. Thus, we have ground rules in place for managing our relationships with friends and they are guided by transparency and accountability.

We both know the people each of us considers as friends and each of us has a say in the people with whom we keep close company. We keep no interactions with our friends away from each other deliberately. We do not discuss each other negatively with our friends. We keep our marriage between the two of us, and all the ground rules apply

whether the friends are of the same or opposite gender. By establishing clear boundaries for our friends and being transparent and accountable to each other, our marriage has benefitted from productive friendships. We have successfully warded off interferences and undue influence. Stay friends with people who are serious about life and about their relationships, and those who are seriously married, as our friend Kafui Dey advised when we got married.

Some friends inspire you to do the right things and bring out the best in you. Such friends do not only influence you with their words, but also with their actions. For the benefit of your marriage, you need people like that around you – whether they are married or unmarried. On the contrary, friends who inspire you to behave badly are a danger to your marriage. A friend who inspires or encourages you to behave badly will most likely not be the voice of reason you need when you are in a moral dilemma. That friend may even be the cause of your new unhealthy habits that eventually jeopardize the future of your marriage.

While you do not need to isolate yourselves from your friends when you are married, you need a highly-developed ability to recognize when a friendship starts trespassing. Taking appropriate actions in a timely manner to clarify or re-establish the boundaries is how you would get the most out of your friendships without sacrificing your marriage. The boundaries will reflect the kinds of information you share with your friends and the kinds of access you grant them on matters related to your marriage. Limit the information and access if you want to limit their involvement in your marriage.

c) Managing Relationships with Religious Leaders

Other than medical doctors, religious leaders or the clergy are some of the most trusted people in many communities. The clergy is one group of people that most people are likely to give a benefit of the doubt or trust with confidential matters. Many who believe in God view religious leaders as representatives of God and treat them with reverence and devotion. When confronted with important life decisions, religious leaders often provide a safe space for some to discuss and seek guidance for the best course of action.

For married people, the boundaries you establish with your pastors, prophets, imams, elders, pastors' wives, deaconesses, and other religious leaders will determine the degree of their influence. Furthermore, their influence may work to your benefit or to your detriment depending on their emotional intelligence, their ethical standards and the soundness of the doctrines they preach.

Among Ghanaians, the counsel and general utterances of religious leaders have had a mixed effect on the lives of the people who have turned to them for counsel and direction. Many people have benefitted from the insight, good judgement and empathy of their religious leaders. Others too have acted upon the uninformed or misguided opinions of their religious leaders to the detriment of their marriages.

In many instances, people turn to religious leaders because they believe such individuals have advanced

spiritual discernments or have a special access to God. As a matter of fact, many pastors position themselves that way and encourage their followers to turn to them with all their problems. As a result of the direct and indirect statements that many religious leaders make to that effect, and the typical Ghanaian's tendency to associate a spiritual dimension to almost every situation, religious leader tend to feature prominently in many people's lives and in their marriages.

When a husband and wife have opposing levels of trust or closeness with a religious leader, that religious leader's influence is very likely to compete with that of the other spouse. Such situations are very common, especially when the couple subscribe to different religions or have very different religious beliefs. Divided loyalties emerge when a spouse shares information with their religious leader and not with their partner, or think of their religious leader and not their spouse as the first person to call when something good or bad happens in their life.

There should not be anything that you share with your religious leader that you shouldn't be able to share with your spouse. You may need to have an extensive discussion with your spouse about the level of influence you both let your religious leader or leaders wield over your relationship. All things being normal in your marriage, your spouse should be the first person you think of calling when something good or bad happens to you. If you and your spouse have opposing levels of trust for any religious leader, you may need to distance yourself from that religious leader in the best interest of your marriage.

Radio, TV and social media has provided wide-reaching platforms where people sit in the comfort of their homes and relate virtually with pastors and spiritualists they may have never met in person. For example, a Ghana-based pastor, who has no idea about the realities of living in America, offers one-sided marriage counselling to a Chicago-based spouse desperately looking for ways to address problems in their marriage. Instead of getting to the real issues, of which that spouse may be guilty, the pastor may feed the person's ego and encourage them to focus on "doing warfare with the devil". As long as that spouse in this hypothetical scenario keeps giving the pastor money, that pastor or prophet would feed them with sensational words that they would want to hear. Such self-styled pastors and prophets specialise in establishing dependency instead of solving problems and are often unhelpful to marriages.

An overreliance on the opinions of pastors and religious leaders have been known to create a dependency syndrome where some people would not make an important decision, unless they have spoken to or prayed with their pastor. Also, some people have defied their own common sense and followed superstitious directions of pastors and prophets to the detriment of their marriages.

Some women have been known, at the direction of their pastors and prophets, to add special concoctions into their husbands' food in attempts to fix problems in their marriages. Some men have been known to consult spiritualists for charms to win their wives' affection. The truth is, fixing problems in a marriage takes much more than special prayers and concoctions, just as winning a

spouse's affection will take something other than tricks and charms.

Annica and I believe some religious counsel are important to some families. However, when the influence of a religious leader consistently competes with a spouse's input concerning their own marriage or when a spouse is more devoted to a religious leader than they are to their spouse, that is a problem which should not be ignored.

Closely associated with relationships that married people have with their religious leaders is their relationships with their religious institutions. That is an important relationship that needs clear boundaries. Without boundaries, the amount of time a person commits to participating in religious events or volunteering at the religious organisation could easily get out of control at the expense of their marriage.

Some couples participate in religious activities together and find that time to be an opportunity for bonding. That should be the case if both partners agree on the amount of time they choose to spend participating in such activities. Even if your spouse is at religious functions as often as you are, that does not answer the question of whether you are spending enough of your free time attending to each other. Even if you lead the religious organisation or a department in the religious organisation, devoting more time to activities there than to your spouse suggests misplaced priorities.

Religious functions can be a fun social experience, but that does not replace the quality time the two of you must spend focusing on each other. I enjoy attending bible studies and conventions with Annica, and appreciate the

fellowship we get to share with other people. However, I have reserved my right to participate in religious activities on my own terms.

Boundaries are necessary for managing your relationship with religious leaders, and with your religious organisation. Assess how much you rely on your religious leaders for counsel on decisions versus how much you involve your spouse in those same decisions. If you share personal information with your religious leader that you do not share with your spouse, that may be a sign that you trust your religious leader more than your spouse. If you trust your religious leader more than you trust your spouse, then you have some work to do to reverse that order.

By all means, relate well with your religious leaders, consult them when you deem it appropriate, attend Bible meetings and religious services, and volunteer to serve in the religious organisation, but don't forget to honour the boundaries.

d) Faithfulness and Infidelity

Some marriages may not have to confront the issue of sexual infidelity, but no marriage is immune to having one or both partners compromise their faithfulness to each other. Infidelity may be physical or emotional, but in all instances, there is a third party involved. Establishing and enforcing boundaries for mainly members of the opposite sex – at work, in your social circles, on social media, and in your heart and mind – would prove helpful in protecting your marriage from infidelity or cheating.

Physical cheating involves sexual encounters like fondling, kissing and intercourse with someone other than your spouse. Emotional infidelity happens when a spouse develops a non-sexual romantic intimacy with someone other than their spouse.

According to data from the 2016 General Social Survey from the Institute for Family Studies, 20% of married men and 13% of married women reported having sex with someone other than their spouse. That is about one out of every five married men and one out of every eight married women. According to the aggregate data compiled by the Infidelity Help Group:

- 44% of men who cheated wanted sex more often
- 40% of women who cheated wanted more emotional attention
- 40% of cheaters had their affairs with a friend, 35% with a co-worker
- 33% of cheaters had affairs to find out if they were still desirable

The eye-popping picture these numbers paint is the reason couples cannot bury their heads in the sand and pretend infidelity would never happen in their marriage. Most importantly, you should discuss with your spouse what would constitute physical or emotional infidelity and what would make them have an affair. That could be an awkward conversation but either of you may have a different definition for cheating or infidelity, and you will not know unless you ask.

When you are both on the same page as to what counts as cheating and what could make your partner have an affair, you can both proactively prevent the opportunity for an affair.

Cheating is usually a display of selfishness and immaturity. No matter how justified a person may feel about cheating, it is what people do when they pacify themselves with substitutes or sacrifice their integrity for short-term pleasures. Married people who cheat, and their cheating counterparts, often do so to satisfy a temporary need. That is why most affairs either leave one or both parties disappointed. Sadly, some cheating scenarios continue for so long that the two people consider themselves to be in a relationship.

Even the trust that two people share when one or both of them are cheating is temporary. It is only a matter of time before one of them betrays the other's trust. Like a friend of mine says: "Trusting someone you are having an affair with is like giving money to a thief to keep for you; it is only a matter of time that some of that money will go missing".

There is never a justifiable reason for the hurt one causes their partner by getting involved, sexually, with another person. Being cheated on makes you feel lost and dejected if you have invested emotionally and psychologically in a relationship. The foundation of your confidence would be shaken so severely that it may be difficult to trust another person. It is devastating.

In our basic element, human beings are animals. Most animals have no self-control or personal code of ethics. Fortunately for humans, we have evolved to a higher level

of consciousness that helps us determine right from wrong and operate with a clearer moral compass. That is why most human beings will not take something that is not theirs, even when they have an opportunity to do so without anyone knowing. That is also why most human beings do not act on every thought that occurs in their brain. With growth and maturity, most people develop the ability to sort through their thoughts, act less impulsively, and are less likely to cheat on their spouses.

As I grew up and developed a greater sense of awareness of how my private and public actions reflect who I really am, I came to understand how cheating makes me look like a fraud. I also realised how cheating does not only hurt my partner, but myself as well. Avoiding cheating in a marriage requires a high level of self-restraint to control your thoughts and actions, and also to react to other people's actions with good judgement.

Here are three things that both men and women can do to develop the necessary self-discipline to avoid cheating or infidelity:

1. **Understand your basic instincts.** The body is made up of cells and evolutionary memory. These cells remember the behaviours and emotions from our polygamous grandparents and have the basic instinct to want more than one sexual partner. Also, your emotions are controlled by your ego, which is selfish and greedy. Your body and emotions have the capacity and tendency to let you behave like an animal – a cow, a dog, a cat, a goat, a pig… any animal.

Understanding that your body and emotions will behave in their primitive ways, especially if you let them, is how you can begin doing a better job of not letting your body and emotions lead the way. Make a promise to detach from your "animal" mind.

2. **Know and retrain your mind.** Your mind operates at three levels of awareness – **a conscious level**, where you are aware of your thoughts, feelings, memories and wishes in that moment; **a subconscious level**, where it draws from its record of your habits and repeated actions; and **a superconscious level**, where it overrides actions dictated by your conscious and subconscious levels of thinking. Stated differently, your conscious mind determines your actions, your subconscious mind determines your reactions, and your superconscious mind regulates your actions and reactions to ensure they reflect your true intentions.

   If you are going to be able to override your default or evolutionary memory of your body, you must activate the superconscious aspect of your brain and act with intention and not just on impulse. You activate your superconscious mind when you repeatedly tell yourself that you will not mate with someone other than your spouse **no matter what**. Your mind is powerful enough to override your sex hormones, but you have to train it to do so.

3. **Activate your spiritual self.** You are not just a package of physical matter experiencing emotions – there is a spiritual part of you. Your spiritual self is the God part of you, and that is what makes you create good things, care about others and not want to do things deliberately to hurt another person – just like God. Activating your spiritual self involves putting your conscious knowledge into action. The more your physical self is in touch with your spiritual self through practices like prayer, meditation and affirmations, the more your actions will reflect the God in you. A person who has spiritual awareness feels the pain of others. A spiritually-aware husband knows that his body wishes to have multiple sexual partners, but he also has enough empathy to feel the pain his wife will feel when she is betrayed. Likewise, a spiritually-enlightened wife knows it is not "just" flirting or "just" enjoying a guy's attention when she is tempted to cheat emotionally or physically. Activating your spiritual self goes beyond participating in organized religion. It is an ongoing process of developing the God aspect of your being. Here is how you can do that:

   i. **Meditate.** Quiet your mind, observe your thoughts and listen for inner wisdom

   ii. **Pray:** Acknowledge God, ask for guidance and enablement, and express thanksgiving

   iii. **Practice Gratitude.** Take notice and reflect on the small and big things that are good in your life

iv. **Make Life Better for Others.** Give your attention, time, money, and ideas to help make someone's life better without expecting anything in return.

The opportunity to cheat will come, but you have a choice in your response. Every time you override your basic instinct to cheat, your cells learn and they are better equipped to deal with the next temptation. As you retrain your mind to operate at a superconscious level, you will learn to take actions that reflect your values. Activating your spiritual self helps you focus on not only what you want, but also on what will make others experience joy instead of needless pain.

Years ago, I wrote a song to affirm my commitment to my wife, who was my girlfriend at the time. I was in Nigeria as a guest of Chief Dele Momodu for an Ovation Red Carpet charity event. Later that night, 2Baba (formerly known as 2Face Idibia) invited me for the grand opening of his night club.

The driver who picked me up suggested that we should pick up a couple of young ladies to be my companions for the night. I knew enough about the way things work when an international star has companions for the night – and my body would have loved to go along.

My mind, however, recalled that Annica is the only one I was committed to having sexual relations with. Hence, I would not do anything that would hurt her even if she had no way of finding out. I remembered how gentle, thoughtful and loving she was towards me when we were on the phone

shortly before the driver picked me up. I instructed the driver to skip picking up the young ladies.

I was at the night club long enough to help open the club and interact with many of the guests. All that while, thoughts of Annica were flying through my head affirming why she was worth my faithfulness.

I returned to my hotel room that night and channelled my thoughts into *Faithful*. The song's lyrics depict the level of trust I have in Annica and how she would have handled herself if she were in my shoes. The verse said:

"She is busy waiting for somebody
She's not easy, won't give in to anybody;
She is patiently waiting for her honey
She don't want your money; our hearts are in harmony;
Ɔdɔ me nkoaa, menso me dɔ ne nkoaa (She loves only me,
I too love only her)
Mempɛ obi foforɔ bi, yɛ dɔ no yɛ papabi (I want no one
else, our love is the real kind)"

Moving Forward after Infidelity

For couples who have experienced infidelity, moving forward may feel like an uphill climb. Whether it's the husband or the wife who engaged in an extramarital affair, healing from the pain of the betrayal would take some time. Learning to trust your partner again would also take a lot of reassurance. While we do not condone infidelity, we are confident that marriages that have experienced infidelity can be restored.

Restoring a marriage after there has been infidelity will require certain actions from both partners - the **offender**

and the **offended**. The following is what we recommend both of you sincerely do to reset your relationship when a partner cheats:

If you are the offender - **the person who has cheated** - do the following:

1. Do not blame your spouse for your action.
2. Acknowledge the hurt and embarrassment your action has caused your spouse.
3. Show complete remorse and mean it.
4. Give your partner full disclosure and answer all their queries without frustration.
5. Do not lie in an attempt to cover your tracks; lying will further erode your spouse's trust and respect for you.
6. Show empathy to your partner and help their healing; it may be a while before they fully trust you.
7. Cut off any contact with the person you cheated with and remove the temptation completely; show evidence to your partner.
8. If you decide to invite a thirty party in as an arbiter or peacemaker, be careful about who you invite.
9. If you feel inclined to cheat again, talk about it with your spouse and find a sustainable way to prevent the infidelity.
10. If you deem cheating to be something you can never stop, talk to a licensed therapist.

If you are the offended - **the person who was cheated on** - do the following:

1. Do not take blame for your partner's action; know that even if you might have contributed to your spouse's decision, the affair in itself was entirely their decision.

2. Accept that it has happened; you cannot undo what has happened but you can thoughtfully respond and not just react.

3. Resist the urge to bow your head in shame from the embarrassment caused by your spouse's action.

4. Don't confront the "other person" - focus your attention on your spouse.

5. Take your time to heal; do not be pressured into giving a premature acceptance speech and don't make promises you can't keep in the heat of discussions or emotions.

6. Forgive without retaliation; hurting your partner in return will cause more hurt and delay your healing.

7. Rebuild trust one day at a time by giving your partner a chance to redeem themself.

8. Show empathy towards your partner; they may be suffering too; give your partner feedback for making consistent, positive changes.

9. Consult a licensed therapist if your anxiety persists beyond your control.

10. If you consider walking away from the relationship to be the best course of action for you, do so gracefully.

It is important to note that couples who are willing to work together to heal after an affair can enjoy a healthy post-affair relationship. Some couples have even reported

that their relationship blossomed after they took conscious steps to move forward after the affair.

Faithfulness in a marriage is possible, and some married people we know are faithful to their spouses. Faithfulness in a marriage does not happen automatically. It takes investing physically, emotionally, psychologically and spiritually in the marriage. It will also take a commitment to developing self-awareness and self-control.

Human relationships are necessary, and boundaries are necessary to let others know which behaviours are acceptable and which are not when relating with one another. As the saying goes, good boundaries make good neighbours, and good fences make better neighbours. Sometimes, it is enough to establish and communicate the boundaries. At other times, you will need to remind people about the boundaries. When necessary, you may need to put up a fence to prevent trespassing.

Make sure your marriage is managed primarily by the two of you. In a healthy or balanced relationship, as much as possible, nobody should hear a negative report about your spouse. Keep your issues between the two of you and keep out third parties. Remember that the two most important people in your marriage are you and your spouse. Everyone else is a third party, and third parties need clear boundaries.

· 18 ·

LEAVING A LEGACY

Whiledriving outside Accra for a performance several years ago, Annica and I had a long and deep conversation about our ambitions and what mark we would like to make on the world. I talked about building on my impact as a musician and obtaining a PhD, becoming a consultant to the Ministry of Education and, possibly, running for office as president of Ghana. I asked what she wanted to become or what she would like to be remembered for. She took a few minutes to reflect and responded saying, "I want to be remembered as the woman who helped Okyeame Kwame become what he wanted to become".

That was a flattering but an unexpected statement. Even though I knew Annica had always been dedicated to helping me accomplish my dreams, I was deeply moved by the fact that supporting my dreams was that much a part of what she wants to be her legacy. Her response reminded me of the tremendous sacrifices she had made to see me

blossom, and that prompted me to renew my resolve to live in such a manner that Annica never regrets choosing me as her lover and life partner.

Continuing with that conversation, we talked about what we would like to leave our generation and the generations coming after us. We reflected on our roles as parents and as public figures, and discussed the enduring messages we want our lives to convey to our children and the people who knew us. In a nutshell, we were thinking out loud about what we were passing on to future generations; we were thinking about our contribution to making the world a better place; we were talking about our legacy.

The Longman Dictionary of Contemporary English defines legacy as something that happens or exists as a result of something that happened at an earlier time. Each of us is building our legacy through contributions we are making in the world by the hour and by the day. While your legacy would likely outlive you, your legacy is not for only after you are dead.

Legacy extends beyond physical things. Of course, we want to bequeath to our children physical assets that will benefit them and their children. We also want to create musical works and build businesses that will outlive us. Much more than those, the **values** we project and the **possibilities** we inspire are important aspects of our legacy. At the end of the day, our legacy will be defined by how we used our time, talent and treasures to help make the world a better place.

Annica and I hope that our marriage and our devotion to one another will form a prominent part of our legacy. We

hope that our relationship will serve as a model of a thriving marriage, where two independent people create a romantic union, override their egos and function as rational adults. We hope to use our time, talents and treasures to bring out the best in each other. We know that in order to impact the world positively, we must first impact each other positively.

My road manager, Ernest Apau (a.k.a. Aboakesie), who has been with Annica and me from when we were dating till now, has said on many occasions that he plans on using our relationship as a model for his marriage. Being the objective and balanced individual that he is, it is always humbling to hear him make a statement like that. Of course, he sometimes says that sarcastically to imply how challenging marriage can be, while simultaneously acknowledging the tact and cooperation it takes for us to get things done.

He has been with me since a few months after Annica and I got married, lives in the same house with us and has experienced Annica and me in our adult years more than any human. It is therefore encouraging since he has seen the best and the worst of Annica and me and yet consider our example worthy of emulation.

We hope that our example portrays marriage as an opportunity to experience deep love with honesty and truth, and for two people to share a common vision without losing the essence of who they are. Years into the future, we hope that others will draw inspiration from our story to improve their lives and make their own mark in the world.

On an individual level, I wish for my life to highlight the behavioural patterns that bring out the best in me in all I do. I wish to pass on the following:

- **A Legacy of Fidelity:** I want to be able to say that I was married for 25-plus years and never cheated on my wife. That is key for me. Apart from the fact that faithfulness to my wife creates harmony at home, my fidelity affirms my personal quest to heal instead of hurt people. If my legacy of fidelity helps other married people behave themselves more responsibly, then we would together save many people from experiencing the pain of betrayal and rather experience the bliss of faithfulness.

- **A Legacy of Parenting:** I want to raise children who integrate well into their society and become better versions of their parents. Annica and I are gunning for excellence and we believe our children would do more, given the nurture and support they are receiving from us. It is my hope that they are more knowledgeable than us, more empathetic than we are, and make a bigger impact in the world than we will. It is also my hope that our children are always truthful. A child who tells the truth, especially in difficult times, should be rewarded with a treat. We are instilling in ours the confidence to tell the truth at all times.

- **A Legacy of an Honest Testimonial:** I want to live an honest life without any pretence. I am living my truth without any reservation so that after my death, people who know me can speak truthfully when asked what kind of person I was.

- **A Legacy of Being a Balanced Professional:** For the people paying attention to my career and hoping

to follow a similar path, I would like them to know that it is possible to pursue their passion successfully, have a family and command respect beyond their fame. When aspiring musicians face opposition from their sceptical parents who dwell on the negative stereotypes about musicians, I hope they can point to me and say that Okyeame Kwame made it work and they will too.

Out of the assets that we are accumulating, I hope to pass some on to our children in the future and spend the rest on us. Our assets are for Annica and me to have the means in our older years to take care of major expenses should the need arise. If, for example, we need a life-saving medical procedure, we should be able to afford it and give ourselves a chance at living our best lives. For our children, I hope to leave them with two houses, two businesses and some funds. The rest will be for international travels around the world to exotic destinations, corporate social responsibility activities, and funding innovative ideas of young people.

The most important legacy we are working on leaving our children is helping them have the right **mindset** for life. If they have their minds set right, they will not even need us or any asset we bequeath to them. If we are successful at equipping our children to make significant contributions to the world, we would have done our part. The rest will be for them to carry on and make their own mark in the world.

The part about my legacy that is my highest priority has to do with our children. Everything I have to give to them I am giving them now by investing in their education, spending time with them, and passing on what I know are helpful values. I want to pass on **a Legacy of Quiet Strength and Resilience** to help them navigate aspects of life that require them to be tough and not cave in to pressure. Whenever they feel stuck and feel like they have run out of options, I want them to be able to ask themselves, "What would mommy do in such a situation?" and then press on like they have seen me do.

I have a deep respect and reverence for God's awesome authority, which gives me absolute confidence in Him. My faith in God is a source of strength and my relationship with Him informs my confidence in His ability to provide the guidance that I need in this life. It is my hope that my children embrace **the Legacy of Faith in God** that I am passing on to them. As we teach them the way in which to go, it is my prayer that they will not depart from their faith in God.

Lying is a habit that tarnishes a person's integrity. Many parents who do not consider themselves as liars do tell white lies – untrue statements about small or unimportant things made to avoid hurting other people's feelings. Such white lies are more problematic when parents tell them around their children. Examples of white lies include telling your children to tell a guest that you are not home when, in fact, you are home; telling your child to complete a task for a reward and then failing to honour your word; and telling someone you are on your way when you have not even set

off. Your children are likely to embrace such behaviours and view lying about big and small things as normal.

On the other hand, making a conscious effort to tell the truth consistently could eliminate white lies from your statements. That would set a good example for your children that lying of any kind is not acceptable. Instead of sending your child to tell a guest that you are not home when, in fact, you are home, you should face that guest yourself and let them know why you cannot be available. Instead of telling your child to complete a task for a reward you have no plan to honour, be direct with your child about why they should complete the task. Instead of telling someone you are on your way when you have not even set off, tell them you are running late and plan ahead next time to avoid the need to disappoint or tell a lie.

Children do not only do what their parents say – they do what they see their parents do. As parents, we need to be conscious of our actions in avoiding big and small lies. Children are great imitators – give them something honest to imitate. I hope to pass on **a Legacy of Integrity**, letting our children know that all lies are lies, and that all lies can be avoided if they honour their word and only make promises they can keep. This is easy when the children are confident and do the right thing. We also try to create an environment that is conducive for our children to express themselves without the fear of persecution. That way, they don't have to lie because of their parents' inability to accept the truth.

I also want them to explore all their options, live with zero regrets and take responsibility for their actions. That is **a**

Legacy of Zero Regrets. Once they decide to do something after thoughtful consideration, they must embrace the consequences, whether positive or negative, and grow from the experience. Coupled with the legacy of parenting that Kwame and I are jointly passing on, I am confident that they will be positioned to make a bigger impact in the world.

Kwame is very gracious in recognizing the significance of my contribution to his growth and development. That recognition is enough motivation for me to build my legacy around bringing his dreams to life. I am very fine with being in the background and enabling his vision. We both win when he wins. Helping him continue to develop strength and charisma is how I am building my **Legacy of Devotion to My Husband**. Supporting him to achieve his full potential is an honour.

Protecting Our Assets

In Ghana, the most significant asset for most people is a piece of land with a house on it. Many people buy a piece of land, build their house quickly without conducting a thorough search for the appropriate ownership rights to the land. They usually do that because the land title registration process is unnecessarily long and inefficient, and they risk having their land sold to another person if they leave it undeveloped for too long. As a consequence, many people own their homes, but do not have the appropriate documentation to prove that ownership.

After you have worked hard and invested your money in acquiring a property, complete the process of documenting your ownership of that property. That is a necessary step

in protecting your ownership of that asset. In addition to securing the legal proof of ownership, get insurance on the property, which is a way to manage the risk of loss or damage to that property.

Property and casualty insurance is a type of insurance coverage you get for your house, car or other property in the event that something bad happens to the property or the people occupying that property. Accidents do happen – your home could catch fire from your negligence or that of other people; you could collide with another car or with a pedestrian; or your expensive appliances could be damaged in a flood. Each of these risks could be shared with an insurance company where you agree to pay them a non-refundable amount as premium and they, in return, replace that property for you in the event of a legitimate accident. Get insured and get peace of mind.

Our children's future education is technically not an asset, but the funding for it fits in the bucket of things that we have to protect for future use. Putting money away in an **educational fund** for each of our children has always been a priority and we practise that diligently. If Kwame or I die prematurely, there should be money to pay for their education at any top university in Ghana or around the world.

Our health is a key asset which must be protected as well. Healthcare can be huge expense, especially when you have to have a major procedure like treatment for cancer. Having the means to pay $100,000 for a procedure will be convenient but as an alternative, **health insurance** will be the best proactive way to take care of all or some of that

cost. Coverage from the National Health Insurance Scheme and supplemental private health insurance helps make sure that we can get the care we need in the event of an illness.

While we take good care of ourselves and plan to be alive for a long time, it is an inevitable fact that any of us can die before we would like to. In the event that I die prematurely, Annica and my children will still need my financial contribution to continue to maintain their standard of living. The same is true for if Annica were to die prematurely. **Life insurance**, for which you pay premiums to an insurance company for them to pay a lump sum to your beneficiaries after your death, is a way to look out for the people who depend on your income.

There are types of insurance. There is term life insurance, with which you can buy coverage for a specific length of time, and permanent life insurance, which stays in force for as long as you live. You could buy a **term life insurance** for, maybe, 20 years, which may be long enough for your young children to attain an age of independence and not need your financial support in case of your death. You can choose how much you would want to be paid to your beneficiaries. Of course, the length of the term, the amount of the death benefit, and other factors, including your health history, will determine your monthly or annual premium. **Permanent life insurance** is similar to term life insurance, with the main difference being how long the policy stays in force. An insurance broker can discuss your specific situation and provide you with policy options.

The elephant in the room, when it comes to talking about life insurance among Ghanaians, is superstition. For years,

some people have held the belief that buying a life insurance policy will accelerate their death by either someone or an evil supernatural force killing them. While that belief is demonstrably unfounded, it has been perpetuated by many people for so long that the idea of life insurance is almost a taboo for some. It is amazing how some people do not think that insuring their cars will let the car get into an accident, or insuring their house will cause it to burn down, yet they believe buying life insurance will hasten their death. It beats my understanding.

The bottom line is that every valuable asset is worth protecting. Your house or houses, your car or cars, your health, your children's future education, and your life are all worth protecting.

The Importance of a Will

My father was a very meticulous man. He had a way of living in the present, but operating in the future. For instance, he built a family house for his mother and explained that it was for his children and his extended family to continue to find a common ground to relate, both literally and figuratively, after he was dead and gone. Also, he did not want his children to be burdened by the opinions of others when they had to choose who to marry. So, he made sure that his wish was clearly documented.

It was as if he saw into the future and knew that I would be marrying Annica and I would need to overcome the opinions of people in my family. My older brother also benefitted from my father's foresight when he (my bother) had to marry his wife from the Ewe tribe. Generally, Asantes

hesitate to marry outside of our tribe for various reasons. My brother's choice of a spouse met no resistance largely because my father had clearly indicated that he wanted his children to reserve the right to choose whoever they would want to marry.

For most of his life, my father was a healthy man who was full of life. There was no visible indication that he would not live until he was very old, but that was not what happened. He was 58 when he died in a car accident. He had documented many of his wishes and taken stock of his estate, giving clear instructions on how to distribute his assets in the event of his untimely death. My father left an indelible legacy by the way he mentally prepared all of us who depended on him to be able to carry on in his absence. Since he created a will, that document spoke for him even after his death, and made many administrative tasks less complicated to execute.

Before he died, my father built a cluster of stores at Ayigya, a suburb of Kumasi. He instructed that one of the stores should be rented out perpetually and the proceeds be given to the Ayigya Children's Home. Even though my father has been dead for more than 20 years, he has been contributing to his community all these years. There are many children not related to my father who have and will continue to benefit from his foresight.

A will is a legally-binding document that establishes a person's wishes for what should happen to their assets and how decisions concerning their dependents should be handled. A will provides **clarity** on exactly what they own and who should receive which asset. A will protects

your dependents from unnecessary litigation in the event that someone shows up after your death to claim an asset that you allocated to your kin. A will also prevents your kin from mistakenly claiming other people's assets that they assumed were yours.

Annica and I have built our lives together and share in everything we own. As an Akan man, I recognize the family of my origin (my extended family) as well as the family of my creation (my wife and children). The family I have created is as important to me as the family that created me, and both should benefit from the fruits of my labour. Even though I do not expect that someone will fight over assets with my wife and children, I cannot assume that a family member of mine would not show up in the event of my death to demand that Annica turn over my assets to them. Such things happen frequently to other people, especially when there are substantial assets at stake, and it is wise to proactively prevent that from happening to your spouse and children, or your extended family.

The unexpected claims to my assets may be extended to my business partners, where their business may be disrupted because a relative of mine decides to take over the business without regard for my limited ownership interest. For instance, I may have a business arrangement with a real estate developer who pays me to use my name on a skyscraper called the Okyeame Kwame Towers. Without properly documenting the business arrangement, my extended family may think I own that skyscraper and may demand it from my business partner. Even in the event that the business is fully owned by me and Annica, someone

could show up to claim half of it and interfere with the operations of the business.

In addition to providing clarity, a will ensures **continuity**. There are business ventures that will need to continue in my absence; there are people who depend on me whose standards of living would need to be maintained; there are values and ideas I wish to pass on to my children who are too young to fully understand those topics now; and there are causes that I believe in and would like to perpetually contribute to. A will helps make all that possible.

If I die before Annica, there should be clarity and continuity. The same should be true for if she were to die before me. In the unlikely event that we die at the same time, that would be the time the clarity and continuity would be certainly needed. If neither of us are around to communicate our wishes, we would have left our children and family members to guess their way through sorting out what we owned and what we would have wished to see happen after our death.

Annica and I plan on being alive for a long time. Preparing a will does not mean we think we will die soon. Rather, it is a proactive step to prevent chaos should any of us die before we are in our 80s and 90s. You don't have to wait till you are about to die before you prepare a will. In fact, the best time to prepare a will is when you have a healthy body and mind. So, talk to your lawyer if you have not done so already. Even if you have a will already, it is helpful to update it periodically as necessary.

We have been blessed with an opportunity to live life well and impact lives. We recognize our obligation to contribute to making the world a better place for ourselves and for others. Having a national and international platform to share our ideas and values is something we do not take for granted. We would like for our impact to continue for the rest of our natural lives and beyond.

If we live our lives well, we may inspire others to live their best lives. If Annica and I love each other with honesty and care, we may encourage a couple to renew their commitment to one another and be more intentional about "handling their business" in their marriage. If we pursue our dreams without fears of regret, we may enable dreams that will change destinies.

Until it is our time to go, we are leaving our mark on the world. We are not only leaving a legacy, but also living our legacy.

• 19 •

CELEBRATING ONE ANOTHER

I am extremely proud of Okyeame Kwame, my husband, my lover and my best friend. I am proud of his dedication to personal growth and development, his devotion to me and his children, his dedication to his craft as a musician, and his commitment to being a force for good in the world. His sometimes wry sense of humour keeps me laughing often, his intellectual curiosity stirs up my admiration for him, and his drive for adventure keeps me excited. I have implicitly and explicitly made it known to him privately and publicly how proud I am of him. I have done so less publicly because I tend to lean away from public display of affection.

Kwame, on the other hand, relishes in displaying his affection in the clear view of others. He lets me know in private how proud he is of me and also trumpets it from the roof top for the whole world to hear. His other preferred method of sharing his thoughts and feeling about me on

social media with his nearly 2 million followers on Instagram sometimes feels overwhelming but I always appreciate the sincerity of it. He frequently shares pictures of me with elaborate captions in which he expresses his undying love for me. I either stumble on such posts while scrolling through my social media feed or get a notification that he has tagged me in a post. I find it heartwarming whenever Kwame turns into "Mr. Romantic" on social media.

It is not the most natural thing for me to be sentimental, which Kwame characterizes as me being "hard" and guarded. To an extent, that is true. I keep my emotions on a short leash and remain practical most of the time. However, being married to a man who cherishes expressive love has taught me to shift from my comfort zone. The smile on his face and the bounce in his step anytime I celebrate him publicly makes the effort worthwhile.

I have come to embrace the sharing of photos on social media as an effective means for celebrating each other publicly. When I celebrate him publicly, I highlight his best qualities and affirm those attributes I do not want to take for granted. After many years of a spouse regularly asking in the morning how you are doing or if there is anything you would like them to do for you, it is easy to take such gestures for granted. When a spouse is faithful and loyal, it is easy to take that for granted and forget to acknowledge their devotion to you.

Many of us make pledges to one another when we get married, often proclaiming publicly the things we will do for each other, such as "to love and to cherish" and "to have and to hold till death do us part". Those words, from the

classic marriage vow, has become an automatic recital at marriage ceremonies and many people do not consider its depth. For most people, such vows are made without any idea of the challenging times that could come. In spite of the challenging times, most couples keep their word on the promises they made. When a person does what they said they would do, they are worth celebrating - privately and publicly.

One of the reasons marriage vows are made publicly, I believe, is to celebrate each other before witnesses. The presence of witnesses adds a dimension of significance to the words you say to one another. The presence of witnesses also raises the stakes. When you know others heard you make your vows, you tend to be more mindful of your actions. Witnesses help keep you accountable by keeping you on your toes and not taking each other for granted.

Celebrating each other publicly could also inspire others, especially younger couples, who may find two people genuinely fond of each other after years of being married as an example worth emulating. I am sure it will be helpful for others to know it is possible to have a thriving and exciting marriage when you pay attention to each other.

It is worth noting that your public celebrations of each other will turn out to be inauthentic and hollow if it is not an extension of private celebrations of each other. If Kwame rarely told me privately through his words and actions how much he loved and cherished me but jumped on social media as often as he does to proclaim his love for me, I would have viewed his actions disapprovingly, and I would definitely have stopped the charade. Thankfully, the

words he shares publicly are only a slice of what he shares privately through whispers into my ears and his random text messages.

We celebrate each other's victories and accomplishments. We also celebrate each other even when our efforts don't yield the expected outcome. When Kwame is nominated for an award and he does not win, I make it a point to celebrate him just as much as I would have if he had won. Celebrating each other is certainly easier in good times than during challenging times but doing so at all times is a habit that pays off.

As the years go by, you will have many anniversaries. A marriage anniversary is an important milestone that naturally lends itself to celebrating one another and reminiscing about why, when and how you met and fell in love. It is a meaningful event that needs to be celebrated in some fashion. However, waiting all year for your anniversary before you celebrate your spouse may make the anniversary celebration more of a showy display of affection than a meaningful appreciation of them. So, celebrate your yearly anniversaries but don't neglect the monthly and daily anniversaries, and all the special moments in between.

Several years ago, Kwame started a tradition of sharing on social media to commemorate our anniversary. He would write a poem or letter to me reflecting on the good, the bad and the ugly that we experienced in the preceding year. He is honest and authentic in his writings. In one year where most of the year was challenging for our relationship, he did not gloss over the fact that our year had not been as great as he would have liked. Thankfully, most of our

years are as fulfilling as he would like them, and captures them all in his elaborate essays. He goes all out in sharing generously and candidly.

My public celebration of him on our anniversaries are mild in comparison to his. Even though I use fewer words, my warm thoughts and abundant appreciation are all concisely packed into the two-paragraph posts I share on my Instagram.

I look forward to celebrating many moments privately and publicly with Kwame, and I am sure he is looking forward to doing the same. In the spirit of affirming my love for him, here is a remix of a few words I have shared to celebrate past anniversaries. Yes, it is a remix and it is all from deep down within my heart:

"Never put marriage on autopilot. It is a constant work in progress" is something you often say to keep us both alert about making our marriage the best it could be!

We did it, and we are still doing it!! Such a beautiful, quiet, gentle, honest and transparent life we share!!! If I had to do this all over again, it will surely and most certainly be with you!!!! No matter how many times you ask, wherever u ask, whenever you ask, however you ask, the answer will always be a YESSSS!!!!!

Throwing it back to when it all started, we agreed to start #smallsmall; and years down the line, God has been #faithful, and so have you. The #Realerno is definitely all you are about and I'm sure Pappy Kojo will understand :).

Hey, I am no Shakespeare but I can definitely come up with enough words to tickle your fancy. I love you and that is how I truly feel about you every day. What better way to celebrate this day than to keep Kojo Antwi's song 'Anniversary' on replay? It's playing in my head and I hope you're hearing it in your heart. Wake up to a whole new world of love. We will turn up and mash up today... and always!

As I reflected on our amazing journey, I pieced together a few highlights of the life we share. The memories are blissful and uplifting. Thank you for leading responsibly with such strength and wisdom! How you love me is beautiful and selfless. For a decade and more, you have kept your promise to hold and to cherish, and most importantly, to stay faithful to the end. Cheers to us, and to the many more years ahead. You are my superstar!

TODAY, I reaffirm that YOU CAN ALWAYS COUNT ON ME!!! I LOVE U BEYOND LUST and that's the way it's always going to be! You and me together, always and forever! #LoveLockedDown

Anniversary Message
(Shared in January 2021)

Happy happy happy extraordinary anniversary to you my love @okyeamekwame. After 16 years of being together,

and 12 years of marriage, this union still feels like a honeymoon every single day. I am in awe, in love and in absolute lust of you as the years increase. I had no doubt we would last this long, but I'm even evermore sure that we will cover eternity with love and the happiest memories as always.

Look at what you have achieved as a human being... an extraordinary dad, a responsible environmentalist, a faithful husband, a spiritual person, an incredible musician, and a super businessman. My creative genius! Your intuition is beyond supernormal. Seriously, you are the best human anyone can be with. You don't just pay lip-service, YOU LIVE YOUR WORDS!! I can always take them to the bank and cash 'em!! Papi, You are special is an understatement I WON charley!!

As we woke up today, I looked at u closely, again, again, again and again, and I knew I had surely made the best decision to be with the most incredible human being ever!! Whenever I face any obstacle in business, life, everywhere, all I have to do is just count on you and I'm sorted!!! With eyes filled with love, heart overflowing with deep respect and all my senses filled with appreciation for you, I say THANK YOU my Kwame for letting me be myself!!
I can write a whole thesis about u, but I reserve that for when we launch our book next month! You make marriage feel like a fine breeze on a sunny afternoon.

Today de3, my vibes go dey Darko in level (inside joke). Lets ride into oblivion together. No matter where the waves take us, YOU and I are LOVE-LOCKED-DOWN forever and always.

I am moved beyond words every time Annica pours her heart out in expressing how she feels about me. I feel very strongly about her too and I will never miss an opportunity to celebrate her both privately and publicly. Without a doubt, my personal and professional life is better with Annica being a part of it. Being in the public's eye, it is important that the public knows how much Annica contributes to the person that they have come to know and celebrate.

Every anniversary is an opportunity to look back and then look ahead; look back at important moments that have defined our journey and then look ahead to the amazing future that we will create together. Those are the thoughts I convey in each of my anniversary poems and letters to Annica. Below are a few examples for your reading and for Annica to relive those moments:

Facing my Fear of Marriage
(Shared in 2015, on our sixth anniversary)

Six years ago, I was afraid of the word marriage. I was afraid of how my life was going to change if I got married.

*I was afraid that a **best friend** would become a wife who would then become an enemy. I was afraid that innocent*

children and unrelated family members would be caught up in the middle of the fierce social media display of hatred and disgust for ourselves as ex-best friends.

I was afraid that a **sexy trendy girlfriend** would become a shapeless boring wife.

I was afraid that the **perfect imperfections** of a girlfriend will become a terror stare every morning and during nights when I run out of excuses to stay late at work.

I was afraid that a humble respectful girlfriend would become my **co-equal** and develop a sharp tongue which will slice my ego in public with "tweaaa."

I was afraid that the illusion of my artistic persona will diminish – **losing fame** – as I constantly exhibit my human errors and imperfections.

I was afraid that three-times-a-day excitement – **anadwo ede** – would reduce to once-a-night placation after looooong hours of begging.

I was afraid I will lose you to **religion** and that our all nights will become your all night in the fellowship of spiritual "mmaa kuo" sisters whilst the winter in my bed drives into the summer of another woman's bed.

Six years after facing the fear of marriage:

Our **friendship** is stronger than best friends had ever experienced. The joy of raising our offspring together blooms into a beautiful unit and this makes our families (extended) love each other even more than we love ourselves.

Your **sexy trendy body** though has increased in inches is still the number one reason why I am always in a hurry to be with you. This feeling is skin deep.

Your **perfect imperfection** is a constant reminder of my perfect imperfections. Overcoming our personality differences increases my knowledge and consciousness of self and others. I love that side of you that I am yet to conquer.

As a **co-equal**, I now understand that though I'm the head of this body, you are the neck that makes it turn. Though to your advantage most of the time you make the head turn in a positive direction so your "tweaaa" comes not in public.

You have sacrificed your personal dreams and my goals are your goals. You illuminate my strengths and dim my errors. My stars hide when yours shine. My fears of **losing fame** were unfounded.

Three-times-a-day excitement did reduce to once-a-night lucky strike after long hours of begging, but that's because we chase other equally important dreams during the day

We have found an important balance of sacred and secular, and have not drowned in **religion**. You know that increment

in spirituality only makes physical beings more sensitive to other people's needs.

HAPPY SIXTH ANNI – VERSARY, ANNICA NSIAH APAU. May our next sixth anniversary have a zero after it.

Seven Reasons Why I Love My Wife
(Shared in 2016, on our seventh anniversary)

1. **Understanding:** *When we were getting married, Anni downed the cost of the ceremony by accepting a modest wedding. But the thing that struck me was that she took a red material, tied it around her neck (collar), put a belt on it and that was her dress for the ceremony. Though simple, she looked radiant. So, when I was saying I DO, knowing that she would do everything in her power to make life easy for me, I said it before I was even asked to.*

2. **Fighting:** *Everybody who knows Anni well knows she is a fighter; she fights for her rights, fights for what is hers. Agyeiwaa the Eagle protects her family with all her might. Life is war, obviously, and when you have a fighter on your team, you are already a winner. She fights everything or everyone that fights against me. And it's beautiful how she never fights me.*

3. **Sacrifices:** *Annica had always wanted to be a lawyer. After her first degree in law, she met me, put a hold on it, to pursue an MBA with a marketing option so that she could*

understand and support my music business. Her long essay was in finding alternative avenues to market music. All of this was to improve my work. Four years ago, I asked her, 'What do you wish for in life?' and she said, 'I wish to be that person who supported Okyeame Kwame to be all that he wished for.'

4. **Virtue:** When I met Anni 11 years ago, she was 22 years and still a virgin. For a beautiful, attractive, classy, curvy young woman to stay on this path even when she was young, I am rest assured that infidelity is not part of this argument. (m'ada koraa). If ever I see a text message on her phone that says, 'Last night was great' my reply will be 'you have the wrong number please.'

5. **Hard Work:** Most people who work with my wife always ask me, "Why does she send her mails at 12 midnight?" She wakes up at 4:30 am to ready up the children for school. We work together, and get home averagely at 10pm. And no matter how tired she is, she is always ready to fix me food. I have sworn an oath of monogamy which makes her life peaceful during the day and 'rigorous' at night. With little resistance, she lights up my soul almost every night. After all, all my energies are concentrated at one place.

6. **Optimism:** My first point should tell u that Anni knows how to adjust during hard times but also knows how to 'chop' and enjoy during good times. Because she understands that good times with a creative man is only possible when I have a high level of peace, whenever I am troubled or distressed, she

knows how to calm me down. With just one sentence, she can put a smile on my face. Some of her favorite sayings; "we will get through this koraa", and "a million years from now who's gonna care"....Vim 'tins' all the way!!

7.   **Home Support:** *She has given me two children who fleece my skin (pun intended). You should visit my home to see Anni and the kids on homework, the perfect balance of not sparing the rod and spoiling the child, literally. When I'm out there working, I know my back is covered. She doesn't pile up their faults and ask me to come and deliver the whipping. That's why my children love me more grin emoticon. As the bible says, he who finds a wife, finds a good thing and obtains favour with God.*

So, for the same reason people are invited to weddings to witness a confession of love, today on our seventh anniversary, I confess my seven reasons why I love my wife.

Loving Annica is an Art Form
(Shared in 2017, on our eight anniversary)

MUSIC: Your voice is melody to my ear, Harmony to my soul, Rhythm to my body. When life's pressures distort my timing, you are my syncopation. My own Amakye Dede's "Akwadaa wiseewa," Kojo Antwi's "Groovy", R2Bees' "Odo". Can you please visit the same 'Osofo' that Daddy Lumba visited on the "Wind no" song so that when observers say that you have 'jujued' me I can tell them "Menya mpo"?

MOVIE: You are a movie to watch. You are an exposure, the rise, the tension, the suspense. I admire the way you interact with the antagonist (usually me), the display of mercy during the resolution. In the morning, you are Drama. In the afternoon you are Fiction. In the night you are a thriller. As real as Stephen Spielberg directing Agya Koo. You keep my mind wondering what is to come next. Anni you move me. You are Shirley Frimpong without the "Manso". You made me Chris Attoh and you are Jackie Appiah in "Perfect Picture".

PAINTING: I have a confession. There are nights when I have returned from studio only to turn the lights on pretending to be working when all that I actually do is stare at your motionless body. Without makeup, a tight dress to accentuate your body, a pose, you look more beautiful than Mona Lisa. Picasso's handy work envies you. That's when I wish I could freeze the moment and pay billions of cedis to relive it all at times. Natural strokes of God's imagination carved in love is who you are.

POETRY: The rhythm of your love always ends in a rhyme, sacrificing your time and not requesting for a dime. Not appreciating your efforts is a crime. Metaphorically, your beauty is skin-deep. Your patience, really deep. Understanding, meekly steep. My promise is, you will never weep. Your smile can stop a war. You should be at Darfur. Ironically, you are bad. Even days that you cause me trouble, you an Oxymoron, Bitter-Sweet. I have heard a car cry after you stepped out of it, because it did not want to lose your presence. The essence of this Personification leads to my Exaggeration with the waist of a wasp and the hips of an Elephant. You have the

body of Nicki Minaj and the brain of Michelle Obama. Oooo Mama!!!

PHOTOGRAPHY: You've touched my spirit with your colour-sensitive material. Every day I take photos of you with my eye, process it in my heart, to watch it in my mind. Eight years of snaps (fights), clicks (friendship), focusing, zooming-in our positives and zooming-out our negatives. Today is a Kodak moment. Let's be trapped in this imagery of everlasting love for lack of a better word. What I feel is beyond love so let me print a million copies and share it with the world. My "Adonko" song is dedicated to you.

HAPPY ANNI-VERSARY!!! Can't wait to hold your hand when we are eighty and say, "WE MADE IT!!" Tonight, we will dance "Adonko" cos you inspired it.

Love Letter to Annica
(Shared in 2018, on our ninth anniversary)

Thirteen years ago, when I asked if you would marry me, what I actually meant was if you would mummy me. Be my friend in times of need, warm my bed and heed to my emotional greed.

When I asked you to marry me, I needed a driver to increase my speed, to nurture my seed and multiply my breed. When I said marry me, I just needed someone to shield me from my insecurities, to be blind to my impurities, understand my insanity, and legitimize my humanity. I didn't know that

'marry me' meant throwing my freedom to the dogs, and realising that the woman is the boss; accepting that the man is the horse to be ridden and whipped to stay on course.

When I asked you to marry me, I didn't know I had to be a daddy to a woman grown already, that I had to be friendly even when I'm angry, be understanding at night when you say No! Daddy!! When I asked you to marry me, I didn't know that the acceleration of our lives was going to be in my hand, I didn't know that our children will compete with the same rehearsal time with the band.

When I said marry me, I didn't know I had to constantly create your security, expect your criticism, compromise my expressionism and legitimize my own reputation through role 'modelism'.

When I said marry me, I didn't know I had to earn my freedom through self-respect, lead the family through a Democratic process, and accept feminine direction without opposition.

When I asked you to marry me, I didn't expect to find mischief in an Angel. When I said marry me, I expected a Messiah of a woman, not a human woman with flaws, weaknesses, misguided passions, temporary selfishness, an overprotective partner who is fallible just like me. Like I said, all I wanted was to make legal the friend that I had found in you, and no matter how sweet or painful, I love this friendship.

Thank you for marrying my troublesome self for nine years. Today, I ask you to pleassssse marry me for 51 years more. Pleasssse, say yes! Happy Anni-versary!!!"

11 Lessons in 11 years
(Shared in 2018, on our ninth anniversary)

1. Enjoy the period of attraction. *I remember 11 years ago all I could think of was my Annica. We said so many nice things to each other. She used to say "Kwame, you have the softest hands" and then one day I gently touched her neck and she said, "Aiii, your hands are painful!" Love can make you feel like a romance god until she hits your buttocks one day and say, "We have become like a brother and a sister." To be attractive is crucial it makes you feel good and wanted but like beauty it fades away.*

2. Enjoy the partnership. *I remember when we were ready for marriage. Nothing could separate us. Not class, nor family, nor religion, nor friends, nor personalities. In fact, nothing could separate the bond. Then the children appeared and suddenly they became the priority. I lost my nights, lost my romantic trips and lost my privacy. The sudden intrusion of children stole my wife and turned her into a mother and a protector. The more mother she displayed the less of a wife I enjoyed until I learnt to appreciate the partnership of all four of us.*

3. Learn how to fight well. *Anni and I barely fight. We have a few misunderstandings then a sorry is said and then our lives return to good old default. The few times we have fought in 11 years almost ruined the relationship. It wasn't the cause that caused the problem. It was the nasty words that we spewed when angry. The words of an angry*

soul kills love from within. As you tell her the brutal honesty that breaks her spirit. So now my advice is instead of a "Your action was foolish" I say "your action was disingenuous". Instead of "You are wicked" I say "you are inconsiderate". Fights are accepted in relationships but insults are not.

4. Communication is not the key; it is the door. *Transparency is not the same thing as communication. Communication is the honest discussion of all things. From intent to the negative thoughts of I wish I could kiss my crush just once. Honest discussions about emotions, finances, actions, inactions, whereabouts, flirtatious messages both intended and unintended and even gossips should be reported to your spouse without hesitation. Except of course when he or she has proven to misuse such sensitive info. When communication is regular and consistent people open up in relationships. Body language is also crucial. When nonverbal coms are good in a relationship you can look at the posture of your spouse during her sleep and tell the mood she is in. People will tell you to be selective with how much you tell your wife but I say if you have nothing to hide and you talk about everything, you never run out of juicy gossip. I mean tell her your password and even tell her about messages on your phone you have deleted including the reason. Communication is the door leading to everlasting peace.*

5. Say sorry even when you are right. *I learnt this the hard way in my fifth year. One time I took offense for something that I thought Anni had done wrong. And I sent her harsh messages to scold her. Then she apologized for her*

actions and then explained the reason for her action, which was to protect my interest. I felt so stupid. One, for misjudging her and two, for the leadership she had shown by apologizing for doing nothing wrong. From that day on, when I can, I apologize for every misunderstanding in my home. After all, I am the oldest in the family. The logic here is everything u do, whether good or bad must not offend your love. Plus saying sorry before a discussion has a humbling effect on anger. The other time I woke up and said "Anni, sorry." She said for what and I said for all the wrong things I will do during our sweet but tough journey.

6. Perfection is an illusion. *If you are looking for a perfect person to love, the question whether you are perfect yourself? If you want a perfect relationship before you are happy, then your intelligence is working against you. Two different people from two different homes cannot create a perfect home unless the meaning of perfect changes from lack of blemish to constantly working on lowering the effect of the blemish. The few times I feel my relationship is perfect are when we are conscious of the troubles that abound and feel we are intelligent enough to overcome them. But I am an extrovert with an introvert wife and that is the definition of imperfection in my house. However, understanding is a sure cue to solving it.*

7. Disillusion is real. *It gets to a time in a long-term relationship when the illusion of attraction and romance is 'cleared off your eyes'. At this stage u know your partner. They have done and said things to u that u thought was impossible*

in the earlier stages. This is the time to re-evaluate your relationship and acknowledge its true value. Cheating at this stage is very possible but most people who cheat focus on the pleasures that are outside than the peace that is inside. There's nothing out there which is sweeter, holistic and wholesome than a partner who just showed u their real colours. This is the time that real true love starts in the relationship because at this point you are not together because you are delusional but you are together because you are consciously aware of their flaws. But you love the fact that this 'troublesome' one is your choice.

8. **Be careful; the children are watching.** *Parents here know that children do not listen to what we say they do what we do. They are great imitators. They are able to decipher moods and hidden language. So, watch how you treat your spouse because your children may treat their spouses the same. If the idea is to make the world a better place let's start by treating our closest friend well. I asked my son what is his greatest wish: he told me his greatest fear... that one day mummy and daddy will be living in separate houses*

9. **Stay sexy.** *Eleven years ago, I had no six-pack abs. I just had a nice one pack that I used to brag about. But now my chest is a little broader, biceps and triceps are good enough for female to cry on! Today, the six packs cry "hold me" whenever I take off my shirt. But even with these exaggerations my wife still sees me as old cargo! I must still beg and push and push before 'doors open'. So, don't lose yourself! The aging relationship is bad enough for your lover Stay exciting! Be*

charming hit the gym; run a few miles on weekends. Buy a set of "dirty" lingerie. Google how to spice up an aging marriage.

10. Upgrade Yourself. *Always keep going, keep knowing, keep rising, keep learning, stay refreshing. Change is the only constant! Don't stay stale! Keep evolving! Keep shocking your spouse pleasantly! When I met my wife, I was a high school graduate and she was getting a master's degree. But now I also have a master's degree so she's no more a master of me. Even though marriage is not a challenge, exposure and experience can create ever-evolving excitement.*

11. Do unto others… *My role model for morality and deep spirituality is Yeshua bn Josef (Jesus Christ). After all he said, he summarized a three-year sermon into two sentences – "Love your God" and "Love your neighbor". The closest neighbor to you is your spouse! So, if you make her cry you have failed this simple spiritual test! My song FAITHFUL was birthed in Nigeria when I almost "picked up a chic". Then this concept hit me. Then I asked myself if someone is "picking up" my Annica how would I feel? The argument of polygamy and monogamy is laid to rest when "do unto others" (love your neighbor) is activated effectively. Thank you for reading and wishing us a happy anniversary and an exciting future.*

12 Misconceptions About Marriage
(Shared in January 2021, on our twelfth anniversary)

Marriage, they say, is the greatest teacher. It has taught me how to love and be loved. It has challenged my expectations about how my wife should act. Marriage is a gift and a curse wrapped beautifully in a box with all of its troublesome content. But with a wife like @mrsokyeame it is an exciting adventure. On our twelfth anniversary, I wish to say thank you for teaching and moulding me into a person with gentle attributes. Thank you for helping me understand.

Here are more things I have learnt in our years together:

1. *The society promises a wife but I got a friend. Through my experiences, I was somewhat promised a female companion who was going to take instructions from me the 'leader' and obey my commandments. But you taught me that marriage is sweeter when we can relate as friends and express ourselves freely around each other with respect but without fear of prejudice.*

2. *The society told me the husband is the boss but I got a co-manager. You taught me that the 'male boss' thing is only prominent in public but in private all human beings are the same. Children, women, adults and teenagers need the same levels of recognition. So when a wife is respected she doubles her love and respect for her husband. So I learnt to respect you and found greater respect for others. Thank you.*

3. *The society told me the man is more intelligent than the woman. But you taught me that knowledge is not a depository of men. It is available for all genders who love to assess it and activate its wisdom. Before I debate with you, I research well into the area and still cannot defeat you no matter how unprepared you are. Your mind is sexy as I watch how you use information in ways most men fear to dare. The respect you've earned in my house affects all women. Thank you.*

4. *The society told me marriage makes us one and no longer individuals. I was expecting my wife to suspend her personality and interests and adopt a new persona based on our shared goals. You taught me that your love is part of your individuality and without freedom of self you are constricted in the marriage. This was difficult at first, but when I learnt to love your individuality, I have become a more understanding person and a better team player. Thank you.*

5. *The society told me I can fix my partner. You taught me the only one I can fix is myself. I have the sole responsibility to unlearn my habits that disturbs our friendship and relearn ones that are accommodating. I fought with this idea till I understood that unless I am balanced, we are in serious trouble. You make adjustments sometimes but your fixing is your responsibility. I sleep better knowing you are in control of at least your love for me. Thank you.*

6. *The society told me I could still have my boys boys without danger. You didn't fight off my 'boys boys'. You became my best friend and slowly opened my eyes to the dangers of random late-night hangouts. I remember the frequent unplanned meetings for friendship purposes. You gave me more friends at home (our children), found ways of increasing my work load and became a good listener. You taught me to value my family over social life. Thank you.*

7. *The society told me to expect perfection but you taught me to see your imperfections as my perfection. You said we must become blind to the pressures associated with marriage and its expectations. You encouraged us to chart our own course and make our own mistakes. Your daring nature causes us to makes some mistakes and also causes us to frequently learn new things. You have made me a braver person. Thank you.*

8. *The society said having children will automatically improve the quality of marriage. I love my children beyond measure but the sacrifices we make for them to be happy , fulfilled and enchanted by life sometimes takes away from the fun we could have if we didn't have them. The children , fun to nurture but expensive to entertain. I now know that I should enjoy the journey and not endure it. They are watching.*

9. *The society told me a spouse will make you feel better about yourself. Be there for you when you need a listening ear, give you sex whenever you desire it and*

relegate their needs and prioritize yours. This was a total fallacy. You try to do all the above but you are more effective when you have prioritized your needs and achieved your goals. You've helped me understand that a happy wife is a happy life.

10. *The society told me that marriage shouldn't be work . Love is automatic and should fly on auto pilot. I was told that if I have to work on love then it is not love . Through our relationship, I have come to know that love in itself is work. It is a promise to help your partner grow and blossom. It is work in progress to forgive over and over again. Love how you work on my weaknesses and work on my strengths. Thank you.*

11. *The society promised me that money answereth all questions in a marriage . I thought money could bring happiness to our marriage , but the more efficient I become at making money the less attention I give to the family. It is the same energy You say. You help me find the balance, saying that beautiful cars , international travels and money in the bank is enchanting but finding the balance between spending time with the family and making money is mark of a true gentleman. Thank you.*

12. *The society said marriage will stop infidelity. The pressure we all put on married couples to be stoic and morally upright creates the delusion that spouses will not cheat once they tie the knot. I pinch myself whenever I find myself admiring other girls . I watch how you*

admire other men . The ability to withstand infidelity is tied to morality not marriage which usually becomes boring and monotonous. I have learnt that the longer the marriage the higher the propensity to cheat . Thanks for being dynamic in this marriage .

I am grateful for your friendship, attention, kindness, vigilance, intelligence, strength, grace, stubbornness, aggression, troublesomeness, quarrelsomeness, God-loving qualities and emotional strength. I do not think any other person could love me and teach me to blossom like you have.

I am sure our love story and the amazing experiences is a book that many will love to read. I cannot wait till February when we share our that book on love and relationships with the world.

Even death cannot separate the love and respect I have for you. You and I exemplify #lovelockeddown I LOVE YOU LIKE LIFE, and I want you to always remember that.

· 20 ·

CRUCIAL CONVERSATIONS: STAYING MARRIED, STAYING TOGETHER

O ne of the most consequential decisions most people will ever make in their lives will be their choice of a spouse. You will establish a home with that person and share the most intimate aspects of your life with them. You will share the best and worst years of your life with this person and this person will be the one you will count on to be there for you when you are at your lowest, as well as be there to celebrate your successes. You will hopefully create and raise new human beings together, if you so desire, enable each other's dreams, and grow older and wiser together.

When two people willingly choose to be devoted to one another and seek each other's best interest for the rest of

their lives, they forsake all others and plan to stay together in good times and in the bad. For many couples, their lives flourish in marriage as they benefit from the support of their partners and experience stability in their lives. For many successful couples, their marriages succeed because they share a common vision, strong friendship and mutual trust. **Most importantly, a marriage's success will be because each partner becomes a pleasurable experience for themselves as well as for their partner.** They learn to stay together through the changing scenes of life, with no tolerance for separation and divorce.

Not many people get married thinking that they may have to end the marriage at a point in the future, but the blunt reality is that many marriages end up in divorce or separation. Some marriages turn sour leaving the couple with regret and resentment for each other. Some couples may appear to be married, even though they would only be living together as house mates in actuality. In the Ghanaian setting, divorce comes with a stigma. As a result, some couples stay together and endure the pain of the dysfunction, even after the marriage becomes toxic and injurious to their mental as well as physical health. Those who leave their marriages sometimes remarry. Some eventually find happiness and some never recover from the negative impact of their failed marriages.

While unpleasant experiences may have tested some people's faith in marriage, the anecdotal evidence still points to marriage as the most viable route for individuals to live long, healthy and fulfilling lives. Marriage is desired by most people, but most people assume that happiness

in marriage is a given. This is a huge flaw in the minds of people on how they perceive marriages. Marital happiness requires a commitment from both parties to be less selfish every day and to give without expecting to receive anything in return. The happiness a person gets from a marriage is in equal measure to the attention they devote to it.

As important and consequential as marriage is to a person's life, it is surprising that there is no formal process that teaches people how to get married and stay married. Individuals have to figure that out on their own from observing others and sometimes through trial and error. It is true that many people learned a lot about marriage from informal sources such as their parents, religious organisation and community. It is also true that many people would benefit from formal training on how to get married and stay married.

Marriage counselling is a nice idea, but it is often a formality many people go through just to get permission from their religious organisation to get married. In situations where the counsellor does not know the couple well, marriage counselling is even less effective. Knowing a couple well means the counsellor takes the time to understand each partner's background, personality and aspirations. Could there be a more comprehensive and accountable approach to helping people learn about getting married and staying married? Certainly.

Here is an idea that may sound like a crazy one, but it is worth considering. Just as most vocations require some training and a test to measure basic proficiency before a certificate is issued, marriage certificates should require

a course and a test. Marriage 101 or Fundamentals of Marriage could be the name of the course. It could cover the topics discussed in this book and more, and a passing grade could be required of all final-year tertiary students. Even though the students may not learn everything they need to know to experience successful marriages, the course will likely dispel myths, help them become more self-aware, and increase their chances of having fruitful marriages when they decide to settle down.

Deciding to share your life with another person is an honourable step that could yield many blissful outcomes. Marriage comes with good things. Sometimes, it comes with challenges. In the worst-case scenario, things could get ugly. Therefore, before and during the marriage, it is important that each partner learns to enjoy the good, deal with the challenges, and address the ugly when it begins rearing its head.

Staying married and staying together requires a daily renewal of your commitment to care. It will require that you take the journey one day at a time and do your best each day. Just as you do with other commitments such as taking on a job or enrolling in school, your success requires that you put in work and not put your obligations on auto-pilot. Marriage will require that you go about it "small, small". Learn to crawl, and then learn to walk; learn to run, before you learn to fly. With focus, patience and perseverance, you will not only stay married, but also thrive.

Whenever you think of a phrase to describe your marriage, we hope that it is "Love Locked Down". Please use the following helpful resources to enhance your marriage.

a) Topics for Crucial Conversations: Staying Married, Staying Together

Several marital issues can be resolved through open and honest conversation. Such conversations minimise the need for assumptions and provide clarity on the couple's daily decisions. Here are some crucial conversation starters for married couples:

- What are you most proud of about our marriage?
- When was a time that you felt very loved and appreciated?
- What could I do to make you feel more loved and appreciated?
- How well are we doing in managing boundaries with our in-laws?
- How well are we doing in managing boundaries with our friends and co-workers?
- How well are we doing in managing boundaries with our religious leaders and religious organisation?
- How well am I balancing work life and the home?
- How well are we managing our use of social media?
- How well are we developing our minds?
- How can we improve upon our general wellness, including nutrition, health and fitness?
- How often should we go for routine health exams?
- What hobbies can we enjoy together?
- Where would you like to travel for our next vacation?
- How well are we managing conflict?
- What do you consider sexual infidelity?
- What do you consider emotional infidelity?
- How satisfied are you with our sex life?

- Is there any other type of infidelity that we need to guard against?
- What will make you cheat on me, and how can we prevent that from ever happening?
- How well are we doing raising our children?
- Would you like to have more children? If yes, when and how many?
- Where do you see us in a year?
- Where do you see us in five years?

b) The Intimacy Check-up

Intimacy is the feeling of closeness, trust and empathy that a couple develop as they get to know each other through the sharing of life moments and experiences.

i. Circle the rating that best describes the quality of each type of intimacy in your marriage.

PHYSICAL INTIMACY
involves all physical contact that a couple use to express their affection towards each other; these include hugging, kissing, cuddling, sexual intercourse, holding hands, and standing or sitting close

Excellent   Good   Needs to Improve

EMOTIONAL INTIMACY
is what makes partners share their feelings and emotions without fear of judgement or ridicule; this makes partners interested in each other's feelings and then respond with care and affirmation

Excellent   Good   Needs to Improve

INTELLECTUAL INTIMACY
refers to freely sharing ideas with each other, valuing each other's opinions and accepting differences in opinion; this makes partners share values and interests, and enable them to hold meaningful conversations

Excellent   Good   Needs to Improve

SPIRITUAL INTIMACY
exists when the couple can share their deep thoughts and beliefs about matters of faith and the non-physical world; this allows partners to acknowledge each other's spiritual journey and remain respectful of their differences

Excellent   Good   Needs to Improve

RECREATIONAL INTIMACY
is when the couple can play and have fun together; they have some shared interests, show interest in the things their partner enjoys, and create experiences that they could enjoy together

Excellent   Good   Needs to Improve

ii. *Discuss ratings with your spouse and cite specific examples to support your ratings.*

iii. *Identify specific actions you could take to improve or maintain each type of intimacy*

c) Asset Protection Checklist

Included below are some of the important documents that should be accessible by you and your spouse when the need arises. You may keep them locked in a safe deposit box or in another secure location within or outside your home. Some of these documents may not apply to all couples and some may have more than one of some documents.

Real Estate:
- ☐ Land Title Registration
- ☐ Mortgage Documentation
- ☐ Rental Agreement
- ☐ Home Insurance
- ☐ Receipts for Major Purchases

Cars:
- ☐ Car Ownership Documents
- ☐ Copy of Car Insurance
- ☐ Copy of Road Worthy Certificate

Estate Planning:
- ☐ Wills
- ☐ Powers of Attorney
- ☐ Life Insurance Policies

Miscellaneous:
- ☐ Health Insurance
- ☐ Educational Fund
- ☐ Bank Statements
- ☐ Marriage Certificate

d) Start-Stop-Continue Worksheet

Think about things you would like to start, stop or continue in your marriage. Start activities that could improve your relationship or have a positive impact on others. Stop activities that diminish the quality of your relationship or have a negative impact on either of you. Continue activities that have been successful in the past. Write your ideas below beginning each sentence with "Start", "Stop" or "Continue".

		What should we START doing?	What should we STOP doing?	What should we CONTINUE doing?
A.	Managing our Home			
B.	Making and Managing Money			
C.	Romance, Sex and Intimacy			
D.	Celebrating One Another			
E.	Managing Third-Parties			
F.				

Discuss the ideas, **decide** on next steps, and **commit** to a reasonable timeframe.

Final Thoughts

Fix yourself before you start dating. Fix yourself before you marry. When there are problems in your marriage, focus on fixing yourself. Do not try to fix your partner. It all starts and ends with you.

For Annica and me, the things that make our marriage work, even though we have two different personalities, are:

1. **Self Awareness:** We both know who we are and accept our differences.
2. **Selflessness:** We both put the group's best interest ahead of our individual interests.
3. **Gratitude:** Gratitude is the water that floats our boat; when a grateful person criticizes you, you know it is coming from a good place.
4. **Forgiveness:** There is no love without forgiving; we consistently forgive and do not keep any bottled-up anger.
5. **Freedom of Expression:** Each of us is free to say anything to the other; we say what we mean and mean what we say.

I have promised myself never to try to fix my Annica. We manage our relationship with love and respect, and that is how we keep our love locked down.

Whatever you do, **don't try to fix your partner**.

APPRECIATION

O ur lives have been enriched by the many people who have played important roles in our life. These have been family members, friends, colleagues, mentors, business partners, fans, and people we met only once. To all these people, we owe a debt of gratitude for the unique ways each of them have contributed to our journey.

It is really difficult to find someone to invest in your dream especially if the promises to deliver social impact and not supernormal profit. Eric Amankwah did not hesitate to financially partner with us to make the dream possible. We are grateful.

We are extremely grateful to our loving parents Jeanini Sonoh-Adjei, Florence Sonoh-Adjei, Kwasi Nsiah-Bota and Alice Nsiah Bota. Thank you for creating us and teaching us how to navigate this wild world, and for pouring your love into us. We love you too.

Our Family: Kwaku Nsiah Boateng, Kwaku Nsiah Boamah, Kwaku Nsiah Amankwah, Ama Nsiah Konadu, Kwasi Nsiah Nyantekyi Bota, Kwame Nsiah Bota, Eunice

Tetteh, Ozias Sonoh-Adjei, Onazia Lee, Onyx Sonoh-Adjei, Xonia Appiah (Santeshair), Kofi Sonoh-Adjei, Jasmine Sonoh-Adjei (Mefscuisine), Raymond Yeboah, Ernest Appau (DJ ABK), Arold Akwasi Boateng, Alex Kofi Tetteh, Jerry Michael Lee, Jemimah Sonoh-Adjei, Eric Akwasi Appiah Kannin, Millicent Sonoh-Adjei, Solange Jean Tetteh, Nolan Nana Sarpong Appiah, Vida Amponsah (Eno Vida), Oduro Frikyi, Frank Boadi, Victoria Medie Helwani, Yasmeen Helwani Nsiah, Rev. and Mrs Ampadu and the entire Amoadu family.

Our Friends: Earl Ankrah, Kwame Baah-Acheamfour, Agnes Baah-Acheamfour, Akwasi Amo (DJ Andy Dosty), Abraham Ohene-Djan, Bice Osei Kuffour (Obour), Abeiku Santana, Whitney Naa Quaye, Sam Nana Akwasi Okyere, Georgette Peprah Marfo, Lady Prempeh, Ben Andoh, Dr Appiah, Dr Kwame Boadu, Cynthia Abeka Okwan, Faustina Acquah-Mensah, Akosua Akrasi, Chris Afriyie (Samora) and Adwoa Serwah Bonsu, Fred Acquah-Mensah, Nuhela Seidu, Hon. Sam Okudzeto Ablakwa, Kwame Farkye (Swift), Adina Thembi, Inna Patty, Gladys Wiredu, Sandra Ohemeng (Sister Sandy), Papa Kow Sessah Acquaye, Nana Obokese (Kojo Sahara), Kojo and Yaa Sarkodee, and Elikem Kunyehia, Mr. and Mrs. Adisi (Bola Ray), the entire Lynx Entertainment family (Alberta Mensah, Angela Mensah, Albert Mensah, Richie Mensah), Eugene Marfo (Kuami Eugene), Dennis Dwamena (Kidi), Sarah Huang, Richard Ohene Sika, Naa Ashorkor Mensah-Doku, Deloris Frimpong-Manso (Delay), Matthew Ansah, Matthew Mensah, Linda Safoa Antwi, Kojo Akoto Boateng, the Wear Ghana Team (Awurabena, Gideon

and Angorkor), the Details By Neyomi team, Emmanuel Anderson, Mrs Owusu Kusi (Ohemaa Woyeje), Ali Zeidan, Kwasi Kyei Darkwah, Yaw Sakyi Afari, Doreen Avio, Awo Duah, Marcus Baffoe, Bettina Afari, Mr and Mrs Ecow Smith-Asante, Prince David Osei, Clemento Suarez, Nii Tete Yartey, Kofi Anthonio, Dentaa Amoateng (MBE), the Entire Roverman Team, Jerry Justice, DJ Adviser, Ebenezer Nana Yaw Donkor (NYDJ), Ebenezer Anangfio, DJ Ruben, Isaac Gede, Lydia Forson, Richla Osei-Wireko, Yaw Oppong Agyemang (Wayo), Dennis Puah, Papa Loggy, Sammy Baah Flex, George Ofori, Eric Kwakye (Oxygen), Jeffrey Anku, Bernard Ashiadey, Annabel Ashiadey, Clifford Owusu, Nana Amakye Dede, Kojo Antwi, Ransford Antwi, Appiah Dankwa (Appietus), David Kojo Kyei (Kaywa), Dr Faisal Ayembilla, Kabutey Ocansey, Caroll Esi Held, Priscilla Adjekai Quarshie, Beca Donald-Knott, Bernard Aduse-Poku and Stella Dwomoh Aduse-Poku, Chief Dele Momodu, Hon. Kennedy Agyepong and Linda Armah, Mavis Agyapong, Agbeko Lotsu, Kojo Enos Agyapong, Akumaa Mama Zimbi, Antoine Ofori Mensah, Kofi Okyere Darko (KOD) and Ophelia Crossland, Dr Kobby Mensah, Ezekiel Tetteh (Stip), Philipa Adu-Brobbey, Astus Ahiagble, William Kyei, Anita Hato, Richard Brown (Osebo The Zaraman), Mohammed Jamal, Joshua Senavoe (XO), George Quaye, Saint Christos, laud Marcus, Saint Kankam, Fiifi Banson, Kiki Banson, Nana Kwame (Nokus), Albert Wele Ali, Richard and Mary Nsenkyire, Edwin Baffour, and Adu Nti (Madras de Beatmaker), Edwin Baffour.

Couples Inspiring Others: You lead by example, inspiring the world and leading the way to show that love

is real. Thank you. Special mentions to you: Mr and Mrs Van Vicker, Mr and Mrs Adjetey Anang, Mr and Mrs Amoateng (Quophi Okyeame and Stacy), Mr and Mrs Reggie Osei (Rockstone), Mr Eugene Baah and Mrs Beverly Afaglo Baah, Mr and Mrs Majid Michel, Mr Rex and Mrs Rebecca Omar, Mr and Mrs Avle, Mr and Mrs Navarro and Shannon Moore, Mr and Mrs Kafui Dey, George and Baisiwa Dowuona-Hammond, Essie Quansah and Benedict Owusu-Brown, Kojo and Yaa Sarkodee, Mr Peters and Mrs Sharon Sharpe Peters, Mr Eric Owusu and Mrs Erica Jemima Owusu, Dr Pambo and Dr Mrs Pambo, Dr Nyame Mireku and Dr Mrs Betty Mireku, Mr Ibrahim Sezgin Koca and Mrs Neslihan Sezgin Koca, Mr Michael and Mrs Ama Pokua Agumeh, Dr and Mrs Hopeson, Mr and Mrs Kwesi Pratt, Mr Kojo Choi and Mrs Elizabeth Choi, Dr. Sonnie Badu and Anne-Marie Badu, Mr and Mrs Aboagye, Prof. Joshua and Dr Mrs Patience Weigewor Abor, Dr Nii Saban Quao and Ambassador Arikana Chihombori Quao.

Our Dream Supporters: H.E. Dr Mahamudu and H.E. Samira Bawumia, Dr Peter Arthur, Prof. Charles Marfo, Dr and Mrs Paul Sekyere-Nyantakyi, George Andah, Cynthia Lumor, Samuel Attah-Mensah (Sammens), Mark Okraku Mantey, Andrew and Ophelia Poku-Amankwaah, Clifford Poku-Amankwaah, Patricia Poku-Amankwaah, Hon. Rashid Pelpuo, Imad Gorayeb, Sylvaina Gerlich, Bobby Banson, Prof. Paolo Galizzi, Akwasi Agyemang (GTA), Hon. Ziblim iddi, Nana Appiah (Vyrus), Nana Appiah Mensah, Nana Osei Afrifa, Uncle Sam Obeng, Cynthia Osei and Kwame Nti Kwarkye, Madam Amy Frimpong, Madam Esther Cobbah, Jessica Opare Saforo, Mr Nuamah Fameych,

Hon. Dzifa Gomashie, Prof. Rita Akosua Dickson, Kwame Adinkrah, Hon. Matthew Opoku Prempeh, Hon. Yaw Osei Adutwum, Hon. Gifty Twum-Ampofo, the Ministry of Education team, Mrs. Linda Larbi, Samuel Afari Dartey, Victor and Ama Beausoleil, and the Darling Ghana team.

Our Great Team: Ernest Appau (DJ ABK), Arold Akwasi Boateng, Jacob Kwaku Gyan, Joshua Akwada, Ebenezer Boakye-Yiadom, Yaw Barima Owusu, James Kwaku Poku, Joseph Sampah Adjei, Charles Akrofi, Kwame Dadzie, Kojo Deku, Ibrahim Ben-Bako, Sarfo Boateng (Sarboat), Vincent Darko Ntow, Aboagye Mintah, Collins Monte Darteh (Monte Oz), Mr. Nii and Joan Quaye Mensah.

Our Amazing Colleagues: Fadda Dickson Narh, Kwame Sefa Kayi, Kwaku Sintim-Misah (KSM), Gloria Sarfo, Frema Adunyame, Kwabena Kwabena, Nana Kwaku O. Dua (Tic), Epixode, Abiana Eldah Dickson, Diana Hopeson, Martha Ankomah, Anita Erskine, Efya Nocturnal, Apiorkor Ashong-Abbey, Yvonne Okoro, Rebecca Donkor, Kafui Danku, Caroline Sampson, Afeafa Nfojo, Nana Adwoa Awindor, Berla Mundi, Ameyaw Debrah, Anita (Luv FM), Serwah Amihere, Moesha Boduong, Nikki Samonas, Jessica Williams, Bertha Kankam (YaaYaa), James Gardner, Too Sweet Annan, Regina Van Helvert, Elikem the Tailor, DKB, Benny Banco, Coded, Blazey, Kwesi Arthur, Mr Drew, Kofi Mole, Amerado, Fameye, Ajeezay, PY Addo Boateng, Afia Pokua (Vim Lady), Silver Lady, Jeremie Van-Garshong, Akwasi Boadi (Akrobeto), Eugene Osafo-Nkansah, Jackie Acquaye, Joshua Ampah (Keche Joshua), Andrew Cudjoe (Keche Andrew), Joana Gyan Cudjoe, Kalyjay, Nii Atakorah Mensah, Daniel Grahl and the High School Band, Kofi

Ayew, Sadik Abdulai Abu, Afriyie Wutah, Benedicta Gafah, Jesse Michael Foley, Jay foley, Mona Montrage (Hajia 4real), Giovanni Elolo Caleb, Saddiq Abdulai Abu, Frank Kwame Apeagyei (Kwame London), Charles London, Black Rasta, George Britton, Papa Bills, and Manasseh Azure.

Lydia Forson, thank you for being our third eye. To our friends in the media, thanks for your support throughout the years. OK World and OK Ladies family members who support our dreams every day with passion and zeal so we succeed, thank you. To all who have helped in diverse ways for us to share this book with the world, thank you.

Event Coordination: Miss Nana Afua Serwaa Adusei, Mrs Nana Sarfowaa Anane Bawar, and Mrs Abena Obeng

Event Planning for Book Launch: Party Hub

Costumes: Uncle Paul (Black Natal Couture) and Details By Neyomi

Makeup: @Tutu_Makeup_Gh and @allure_by_ben

Hair: @santeshair and @santeshairforkids

Photography: @sarboatphotography

Graphic Design: Vincent Sam Darko Ntow

Media Partners: Citi FM, Citi TV, and Citi Newsroom; Multimedia, UTV, and B&FT

AFTERWORD

by Eric Gyekye Amankwah
Executive Publisher

When two people build a lasting relationship based on love and mutual respect, it is one of the most refreshing human relationships to behold. Kwame and Annica have been a shining example of what a marriage can be, and I am grateful they are sharing their story and ideas to motivate others to make the most of their relationships.

Based on the reported statistics concerning the percentage of marriages that fail, it is tempting to assume that the future of marriages is bleak. That assumption is only possible when people are not aware of the many successful marriages that exist in our communities. Thankfully, Kwame and Annica have been a public example of a successful marriage.

An inside look into how they developed their relationship and how they keep it exciting is a worthwhile experience

that, hopefully, will strengthen many marriages and serve as a guide for people looking to get married. I find the candid and enlightening manner in which they share their stories to be refreshing and empowering.

I am passionate about the subject of creating lasting love relationships, which is what drew me to this project in the first place. I am honoured to know Kwame and Annica and their inspiring story, and I hope this book is of great benefit to everyone who reads it.

The book's unique approach – the fascinating stories, the thought-provoking ideas, and the intuitive worksheets – promises to be a useful resource for many individuals around the world. My immense thanks to Kwame, Annica and Kyei for committing many days and nights to this project and delivering a stellar work that will help many people now and in the future.

One of the greatest gifts from God to humanity is the gift of love. Each of us has a responsibility to do everything we can to love fully and deeply.

So, read and re-read this book, benefit from the wisdom herein, share it with the people you love, and make the most of your opportunity to experience the greatest gift of all – love.

Let each of us keep love locked down in our respective relationships. Wishing you all the best, with love.

APPENDIX

ADINKRA SYMBOLS

Featured in the design of the pages introducing each of the four parts of the book are Adinkra symbols, graphic marks and motifs created by craftsmen to express proverbs, philosophies and popular sayings in Akan culture. Widely used throughout Ghana, these symbols can be found on jewellery, clothing, furniture, artworks, decorations and in many aspects of Ghanaian life.

There are hundreds of Adinkra symbols. Below is a selection of symbols related to love and what they signify:

Symbol	Name	Significance
	Adinkrahene *(chief of adinkra symbols)*	*greatness, charisma, leadership*
	Akokɔnan *(the leg of a hen)*	*mercy, nurturing*
	Akoma *(the heart)*	*patience, tolerance*
	Akoma Ntɔso *(linked hearts)*	*understanding, agreement*
	Ananse Ntentan *(spider's web)*	*wisdom, creativity*

ADINKRA SYMBOLS

Symbol	Name	Significance
	Asase Yɛ Duru *(the Earth is heavy)*	*divinity of* *Mother Earth*
	Aya *(fern)*	*endurance,* *resourcefulness*
	Bi Nnka Bi *(no one should bite the other)*	*peace, harmony,* *democracy*
	Boa Me Na Me Mboa Wo *(help me and let me help you)*	*cooperation,* *interdependence*
	Duafe *(wooden comb)*	*beauty through* *effort*
	Dwannin Mmɛn *(ram's horns)*	*restrained* *strength*
	Ɛban *(fence)*	*safety, security,* *boundaries*

ADINKRA SYMBOLS

Symbol	Name	Significance
	Ɛpa *(handcuffs)*	*law, justice, slavery*
	Ɛse Ne Tɛkrɛma *(the teeth and the tongue)*	*co-existence*
	Funtunfunefu Denkɛmfunefu *(siamese crocodiles)*	*unity in diversity, oneness*
	Gye Nyame *(except for God)*	*supremacy of God*
	Hwemedua *(measuring stick)*	*examination, quality control*
	Hye Wonhye *(that which cannot be burnt)*	*imperishability, endurance*
	Kɛtɛ Pa *(good bed)*	*good marriage*

ADINKRA SYMBOLS

Symbol	Name	Significance
	M'ate M'asie *(what I hear, I keep)*	*wisdom,* *knowledge,* *prudence*
	Mɛ Ware Wo *(I shall marry you)*	*commitment,* *perseverance*
	Mmerɛ Dane *(time changes)*	*change, life's* *dynamics*
	Mpatapɔ *(knot of reconciliation)*	*peacemaking,* *reconciliation*
	Nea Onim No Sua A, Ohu *(he who does not know can* *know from learning)*	*knowledge, life-* *long education*
	Nea Opɛ Sɛ Odi Hene *(he who wants to be king)*	*service,* *leadership*
	Nkɔnsɔnkɔnsɔn *(chain links)*	*unity, human* *relations*

ADINKRA SYMBOLS

Symbol	Name	Significance
	Nkyemu (the crossed divisions made on adinkra cloth before printing)	*skillfulness, precision*
	Nyinkyin (twistings)	*initiative, dynamism, versatility*
	Nsoroma (star)	*guardianship*
	Nyame Bi Wɔ Soro (There is a God is in the heavens)	*hope*
	Nyame Nwu Na M'awu (God never dies, therefore I cannot die)	*life after death*
	Nyame Yɛ Ohene (God is King)	*majesty and supremacy of God*
	Nyansapɔ (wisdom knot)	*wisdom, ingenuity, intelligence and patience*

ADINKRA SYMBOLS

Symbol	Name	Significance
	Ɔdɔ Nnyira Fie Kwan (love never loses its way home)	power of love
	Onyankopɔn Adom Nti Biribiara Bɛyɛ Yie (By God's grace, all will be well)	hope, providence, faith
	Ɔsram Ne Nsoroma (the moon and the star)	love, faithfulness, harmony
	Pempam Sie (sew in readiness)	readiness, steadfastness
	Sankofa (return and get it)	learn from the past
	Sankofa (return and get it)	learn from the past
	Sesa Wo Suban (change your habit)	transformation

ADINKRA SYMBOLS

Symbol	Name	Significance
	Wawa Aba *(seed of the wawa tree)*	*hardiness,* *toughness,* *perseverance*
	Woforo Dua Pa A *(when you climb a good tree)*	*support,* *affirmation*

LIST OF INCLUDED WORKSHEETS

Part I:

a) Topics for Crucial Conversations: Finding Someone to Love

b) The Dating Goal Worksheet

c) The Dating Assessment

d) The SPISS Assessment

e) The Relationship Spectrum Questionnaire

Part II:

a) Topics for Crucial Conversations: Before You Say "I Do"

b) Getting Married Worksheet

c) Most Important Personal Values Worksheet

d) The Relationship SWOT Analysis Worksheet

e) Personality Assessments

Part III:

a) Topics for Crucial Conversations: Getting Married and Starting Out

b) The Marriage Creed

c) Family Balance Sheet

LIST OF INCLUDED WORKSHEETS

Part IV:

a) Topics for Crucial Conversations: Staying Married, Staying Together

b) The Intimacy Check-up

c) Asset Protection Checklist

d) Start-Stop-Continue Worksheet

INDEX

INDEX

INDEX

INDEX

Religion 98, 141, 145, 161, 191, 193, 194, 224, 226, 229, 302, 333, 334, 341
Religious leaders 71, 108, 123, 283, 293, 295, 296, 297, 355
Religious Organization 297
Romance 129, 256, 257, 258, 259, 260, 261, 263, 280, 341, 343

S

Sante's Hair for Kids 212
Saucing 211, 212
Serendipity 49, 50
Settling 127
Sex 33, 72, 79, 80, 97, 140, 141, 145, 146, 147, 148, 149, 150, 151, 152, 153, 154, 155, 157, 216, 229, 242, 245, 255, 256, 257, 261, 262, 263, 264, 265, 266, 267, 268, 269, 275, 276, 277, 278, 279, 280, 297, 298, 301, 355
Sexual Appeal 277
Sexual immorality 147, 148, 154
Sexual problems 268
Sexual rejection 274
Sika 233, 240
SMART 45, 46
Social media 27, 57, 58, 60, 61, 62, 81, 87, 89, 90, 162, 175, 181, 186, 187, 217, 218, 219, 246, 282, 295, 297, 326, 327, 328, 333, 355
Stakeholders 54, 196, 199, 282
STD 147, 150
Stigma 61, 265, 266, 352
Suits 217, 219, 220
Survey 65, 138, 262

T

Third parties 126, 160, 183, 271, 282, 283, 284, 307
Thomas-Kilmann Model 221
Transformational technology 209
Transparency 202, 226, 229, 230, 231, 232, 235, 236, 237, 238, 245, 291
Trust 4, 15, 112, 113, 115, 126, 150, 153, 157, 204, 229, 230, 231, 232, 236, 256, 269, 271, 290, 293, 294, 297, 299, 304, 352, 357
Twitter 60, 61

V

Valentine's Day 187, 259
Values 18, 20, 22, 35, 41, 69, 110, 113, 114, 119, 140, 145, 164, 185, 224, 240, 270, 303, 310, 314, 322, 323, 357

W

Wedding 49, 135, 191, 192, 197, 198, 244, 287, 335
Will 320
Woara 32
Worksheet 98, 160, 163, 164, 166, 360, 381, 382

Y

YouTube 214, 219

ABOUT THE BOOK

Falling in love is one of the best feelings in the world. Beyond falling in love, many people desire a meaningful relationship that makes them feel loved and fulfilled.

Okyeame Kwame and Annica share anecdotes from their compelling love story and offer their unique points of view on finding and maintaining lasting love relationships. With practical tips and relatable ideas, they bring fresh perspectives to dating, intimacy, sex, conflict, finances, communication, transparency, commitment, collaboration, security and excitement.

Whether dating, in a relationship, engaged, or married, this book offers an innovative resource to help you find clarity about the kind of relationship you seek.

Through the stories, research, concepts and worksheets, this is a uniquely pragmatic approach to finding a life partner and navigating the sometimes-elusive areas of love and family life.

ABOUT THE CONTRIBUTORS

Okyeame Kwame (Kwame Nsiah-Apau) is a man of many talents - award-winning musician, entrepreneur, creative director, developmental agent, products and brands developer, and a philosopher. His many awards and honours include the 2009 Ghana Music Awards Artist of the Year and the Key to the City of Cincinnati. He has served as a goodwill ambassador for UNICEF's 'Super Dads' initiative, which aims to drive increased understanding of how children's environments and experiences in early childhood can shape their future health, well-being, and ability to learn. He serves as the climate change ambassador for Ghana. As a 'Made in Ghana' ambassador, Okyeame Kwame promotes indigenous Ghanaian products, businesses, and culture. With nine studio albums to his credit, Kwame is the CEO of OK Communications, the custodian of the OK brand, and a high-performing professional with a master's degree in Marketing Strategy from the University Of Ghana Business School. His most cherished role is being a husband to his beautiful and intelligent wife, Annica, and father to his two lovely children.

Annica Nsiah-Apau is an entrepreneur, product developer, talent manager and brand architect by profession. A mother of two and a wife to Okyeame Kwame, she holds a degree in Law and a master's in Business Administration in Marketing (Brand Architecture) from Kwame Nkrumah University of Science and Technology. Annica is a co-opted member of CIM UK. She's the General Manager of OK Communications and the OK brand. For twelve

ABOUT THE CONTRIBUTORS

years, she has successfully managed Okyeame Kwame as an artist, a development agent and a brand ambassador for multi-nationals. She is the author of the OK brand book and a business development manager for Sante's Hair For Kids. Married since 2009, she has become the definition of a happy wife and a modern mother. Annica has received many awards and praises for the way she manages her husband and children, but her true satisfaction is in seeing her family blossom. Annica resides in Accra, Ghana with her husband and their two children.

Kyei Amoako is an author, communications practitioner and a researcher motivated by how effectively stories can connect people. His previous works include *Life In Progress: Winning Where It Matters* and *Leaders Don't Have To Yell: National Team Coach on Leading High-Performing Teams.* An eternal optimist and technology enthusiast, Kyei takes delight in solving problems and bringing ideas to life.

Eric Gyekye Amankwah is a chartered financial consultant and Chief Operating Officer of FNG Financial Services. Focused on delivering value for clients and partners, Eric uses his knowledge and passion for financial products to help individuals, families and organizations manage risk and secure their financial future. As a strategic partnerships consultant, Eric facilitates capital mobilization for emerging market opportunities and international collaborations. Eric is a member of the Real Akwapim Men Society and a Board member of the Ghana Institute for Human Development.

"Fix yourself before you start dating. Fix yourself before you marry. When there are problems in your marriage, focus on fixing yourself. Do not try to fix your partner. It all starts and ends with you."